A

Gypsy

Life

A
Gypsy
Life

Adventures of Clare and Edward Allcard

Aboard Their Yacht Johanne

CLARE ALLCARD

W · W · NORTON & COMPANY · *NEW YORK* · *LONDON*

FIRST EDITION

The text of this book is composed in Times Roman with the display set in Windsor Light Condensed. Composition and manufacturing by the Haddon Craftsmen. Book design by Marjorie J. Flock.

Library of Congress Cataloging-in-Publication Data

Allcard, Clare.
   A gypsy life / Clare Allcard
      p.   cm.
      1. Allcard, Clare. 2. Allcard, Edward. 3. Seamen—Biography.
   4. Women sailors—Biography. 5. Johanne (Yacht) I. Title.
   GV812.5.A65A3 1992
   797.1'246'092—dc20
   [B]   91-46345

ISBN 0-393-03072-5

W.W. Norton & Company, Inc., 500 Fifth Avenue, New York, N.Y. 10110
W.W. Norton & Company Ltd., 10 Coptic Street, London WC1A 1PU

1 2 3 4 5 6 7 8 9 0

*I dedicate this book
with deep love and gratitude to my parents,
Ro and Kinny Thompson*

Contents

~~~~~~~~~~

Illustrations follow page 128

MAPS

A
Gypsy
Life

1. Of Dream Ships and Fish Poison

"QUICK, CLARE! Come and see! There's the most fantastic boat on the slipway. It's our dream ship; it really is!"

He was crazy, of course, even to think of buying another boat. We had too many boats already. We seemed to collect them, haphazardly, the way other people collect stray cats. And I blamed every one of them on Edward. After all, he was the one passionately in love with ships and oceans, the one who insisted on rescuing beautiful old sailboats from the evil clutches of decay.

The most beloved of his collection was *Sea Wanderer,* a thirty-six-footer built in 1912. She had grass growing on her decks, hornets nesting in the mast, and rats everywhere when E. spotted her, lying in a mud berth near New York. He bought her for a song, rebuilt her, then sailed her single-handedly around the Horn and on across the Pacific and Indian Oceans to our native shack in the Seychelles, east of Kenya. There his compassionate eye fell upon *Black Parrot,* a fifty-four-foot local trading schooner. She had been out of work for two years. Now she lay hauled out under some palm trees awaiting his return, along with *Clarita,* a clinker-built, open fishing boat, and *Claritita,* my own diminutive sailing dinghy. And then there was the little matter of the caravel, surely the craziest scheme of all—to build a seventy-foot replica of Columbus's *Niña* on a tiny granite island in the middle of the Indian Ocean. Edward had already cleared the site and cut a stock of timber when, in a rare moment of sanity, we decided to complete one long-term project, Edward's single-handed circumnavigation, before getting totally entangled in another. Corralling our three-year-old daughter, Katy, in his arms, he gave her a big hug of farewell, kissed me goodbye, and departed. Slipping quietly away from our base in the Seychelles, he and *Sea Wanderer* sailed past the Cape of Good Hope and back to Antigua, West Indies. There they tied the knot in what must have been one of the most protracted solo circumnavigations ever.

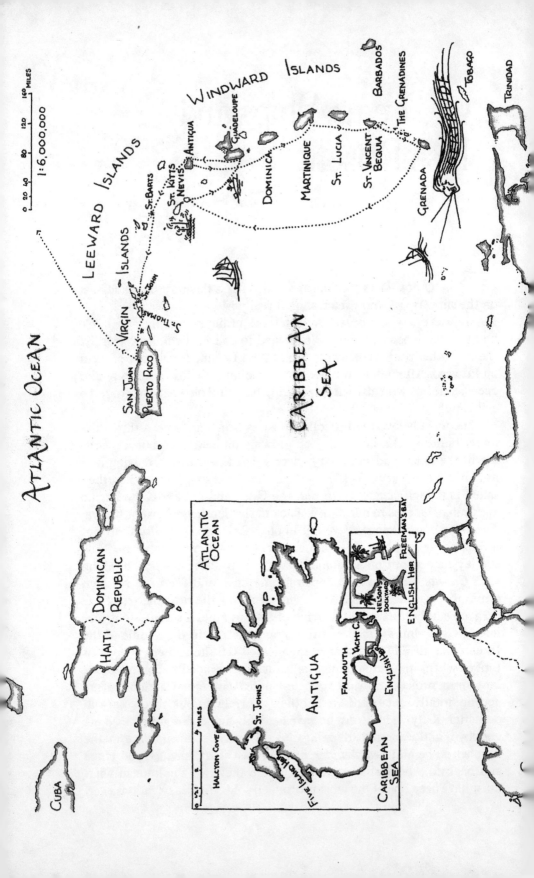

And it was there, in Antigua, that he found her.

By then we were reunited, living ashore in English Harbor, while *Sea Wanderer* had a last, rejuvenating refit before being sold. I should have been cooking Katy's supper and putting her to bed.

"Quick, Pops! Find some clothes. We're going to look at a dream ship!" Perhaps our collection of battered boats was not entirely Edward's fault after all.

That walk to the boatyard stands out vividly in my memory: the dirt track splotched with puddles from a recent shower, a bend in the road, and, suddenly, stretching out from our feet, a brilliant carpet of saffron-yellow butterflies all supping from the small pools of murky water. As we approached they took flight, a shimmering haze of gold. Rather symbolic as it turned out—all that gold fluttering away.

I first glimpsed Edward's dream ship as she stood all alone on the slipway, a black silhouette against the evening sky. Unusual among Baltic traders, her stern was tucked up, neat and heart-shaped, while her hull curved as gracefully as a newborn moon. Edward was quite right. She was superb. Climbing aboard, Edward paced out her length. He paced out her width. He muttered and multiplied and finally marveled. She was exactly the same size as the planned caravel, but with one striking difference: this boat was already built.

As tropical darkness fell, we walked home along the now-deserted track. Sleep was unthinkable. Questions whirled through my mind. What was her story? Would the owners sell? Could we afford to buy? Would they sell? Could we . . . ? I was hopeful.

Johanne Regina, for such was her name, had all the outward appearance of an Allcard "find"—in other words, she was in urgent need of care and attention. The next morning the yard manager explained why. Until recently, *Johanne* (pronounced "Yohanner") had lain abandoned and half-sunk in the Antiguan harbor of St. Johns, a writ nailed to her mast. Then, an amazing Antiguan woman bought and raised her. Mrs. Edith Mathews had absolutely no intention of selling. She had even renamed the boat *Edith M.* By trading between the islands, *Edith M.* was going to make the Mathew's family fortune, or so they hoped.

We retreated but did not despair. Edward, a naval architect by profession, looked on in silence as they fitted a propeller, far too small for heavy trading, to *Johanne*'s shaft. He watched without comment as wormholes, guilty of her original sinking, were quickly smeared with cement or paint rather than individually plugged. Above all, he took heart from her change of name, for, as every sailor knows, one is simply asking for trouble changing a boat's name. No, we did not despair.

Meanwhile, *Sea Wanderer*'s refit was taking longer than expected (refits always do). Our hotel bills mounted, our savings dwindled, and I became a trifle anxious. But help was at hand. In exchange for keeping an eye on the clubhouse, the Antigua Yacht Club generously offered us the shelter of their sail loft—a sail loft that came complete with beds, sloping pine rafters, and a dormer window that looked out, unglazed, over the emptiness of Falmouth Harbor.

From there Edward worked on *Sea Wanderer* while, twice a week, Katy and I walked the dusty road to Mrs. Bailey's shop. The sun shone as we skirted the long, slow sweep of Falmouth Bay. Shaggy goats and sheep, indistinguishable apart from their tails (goats' up, sheep's down), stood a moment to inspect us as we passed, then reverted to tearing and nibbling at the dried grass verges. Funny how the outward journey always seemed miles shorter than the homeward trudge, weighed down with two bulging baskets of supplies. Sometimes, out there in the heat, as cars whizzed by in a swirl of dust, I was tempted to question the unquestionable: the sacred tents of the "simple life" itself. What was so darned simple about it, anyway, I fumed, resting my laden baskets in the gutter. Right then even the minor complication of a wheelbarrow would have been gratefully accepted.

Happily, between the pleasant walk out and the long haul home, Cora Bailey always had time for a chat.

"There's some nice fish in the refrigerator," she called out one morning. "Caught fresh today."

I peered doubtfully at the thick white steaks.

"What is it?"

"Barracuda."

"Barracuda! Yikes! I thought people died from eating that." (The fish's poisonous reputation derived from Antigua's position slap on the divide between an area to the south, where barracuda is usually safe to eat, and an area to the north and west, where it is not.) But Cora only chuckled at my fears. "No! Don't worry! This one okay! I'm eating 'im myself for lunch."

"Right! I'll come back after lunch and, if you're still alive, I'll buy some." We laughed. I bought some anyway and, later, Edward and I dined deliciously off the succulent fish steaks. Next time Mrs. Bailey had barracuda for sale I did not hesitate but bought several portions, stacking them away in the yacht club freezer. That night, after Katy had gone to bed, I cooked us a special supper of curried barracuda.

They say the poison is accumulative, that the bigger the barracuda the more poisonous it becomes. Ours must have been a monster. It put fifteen people, including the man who caught it, in the hospital. They were the lucky ones. Antigua's yacht club lay, totally isolated, down a dirt track. We had no neighbors, no telephone, and no transport to take us to a doctor.

Kneeling in the yacht club showers, we clung to the lavatory bowls for support. Vomiting tore at our guts. Sweat, coursing down our thighs, formed foot-wide pools of liquid on the floor. Our heartbeats slumped. Consciousness came and went as, ice-cold in the tropical night, we gasped for breath like landed fish. And like landed fish, I thought we were going to die.

An hour later, bodies still shaking with shock, we crawled up the loft ladder, Edward with an empty metal bucket in tow. Heaping *Sea Wanderer*'s blankets onto the bed, we huddled underneath them in a vain attempt to get warm. There followed one of the longest nights of my life. Edward was hit the worse. Not only was he, at fifty-nine, more than twice my age but, being a good little wife, I had given him an extra-big helping of fish. All through the night I fought off sleep, listening to his every gasp, terrified lest he stop breathing altogether: my Love killed off by my own cooking.

A gray glimmer seeping under the shutters announced the dawn. I called Katy. At four years old she looked a bit small to spearhead a rescue mission. Nevertheless we sent her out in oilskins against the rain and stuffed a note in one pocket. Thus equipped, she sallied forth along a half-mile track to our nearest friends and neighbors, Desmond and Lisa Nicholson.

A famous tribe, the Antiguan Nicholsons. Commander Vernon Nicholson (Royal Navy, retired) founded his Caribbean charter business almost by accident. He originally set out from Europe in 1948 to sail, with his wife, Emmy, and their sons, Desmond and Rodney, to Australia. They reached English Harbor, Antigua, in 1949 and stayed. Desmond and Rodney both married and produced children. The Nicholson clan took root. And now, alerted by Katy, Desmond's American wife, Lisa, came flying to our rescue. Bundling us into her car, she whisked us off to stay with Emmy and Vernon, her remarkable parents-in-law. Emmy, artistic, fine-featured, and gentle, made the perfect foil to her adoring husband, Vernon, himself a gorgeous extrovert of a man bubbling over with generosity and laughter.

For twenty-four hours it was touch and go whether Edward would survive. Then the crisis passed. Frail as winter's dried leaves, we were content simply to be alive and in such extraordinary surroundings. I have never seen a house remotely like it. Imagine, if you will, a gunpowder magazine, or, if such things are unfamiliar to you, then an immensely thick-walled tunnel—and then imagine a fully draped fourposter bed standing at one end. That tunnel formed the original core of what was a most original home. The Powder Magazine had been built in 1807, in the heyday of the British naval base in Antigua. Around two sides of it Emmy and Vernon had added a spacious, low-ceilinged room with windows for walls and trees outside for shade. The views, across the inlets of English Harbor, were a constant joy. Nonetheless the greatest joy for us lay indoors, in "Emmy's bath."

In an alcove adjoining our bedroom, Emmy had re-created a sand dune. On it she had scattered seaweeds and fan coral and beach-washed conches and spider shells. Once arranged to her satisfaction, Vernon enclosed the sea garden in clear plastic with a clear plastic bathtub suspended above. Two or three times each day, Edward and I immersed ourselves in the warm waters of Emmy's bath, for warm water is the sole comfort of fish-poisoned bodies. Ciguatera is a curious poison. In attacking the central nervous system it sends all normal sensations haywire. Anything cold, a metal door handle or a drinking glass, feels scalding hot. Your skin itches and tingles frantically yet is painful to the lightest touch. The mere act of breathing hurts the lining of your nose and your eyes water in sympathy. Worst of all, everything aches abominably, especially ears and jaws and teeth. Edward was to suffer tingling "fish-poison" arms for another five years. But for the moment we had to get moving, and we set ourselves a target—as soon as we could cover the twenty yards to a certain bush at the corner of the house we would go home. And so, three weeks after we had staggered across the Nicholsons' hospitable threshold, we shuffled back to the sail loft. There, feeling about as robust as yesterday's egg custard, Edward had another trauma to face.

Sea Wanderer, her refit complete, had been launched. Now she had to be sold. Man and boat had lived together for twenty-four years; one might as well sell off a life-long friend. We wouldn't sell to just anyone, that we had definitely agreed. The plan was to advertise her at an extortionate price. Edward could then bring the price down, if and when he felt we'd found a suitable buyer. The plan did not work, mainly because our ideas of market prices were years out of date. Shortly after the advertisement first appeared, a man telephoned from Florida. What further equipment would he need to sail *Sea Wanderer* back to the States? There was not even the hint of a haggle.

Softly replacing the receiver Edward turned to me, his tired eyes dazed. "It's ghastly!" he whispered, "I think we've sold her." And we had, with most of our worldly goods still aboard. Anything we kept would have to be air-freighted halfway around the world to the Seychelles. Boatless and still listless from the fish poisoning, we began, in desultory fashion, to prepare ourselves for departure. But then, as so often happens, the Fates stepped in.

The very day after *Sea Wanderer* laid course for Florida, we were awakened by a car horn blasting beneath the loft window. Grabbing a towel, Edward threw open the shutters and glared down. Below lay an enormous, battered blue limousine. Beside it stood the fine figure of Mrs. Mathews, flanked by her two grown sons. They had come to sell us our dream ship. We dressed on the double and were soon speeding toward their home at Tin Village, a suburb of Antigua's capital, St. Johns.

In the fantasies of any self-respecting town planner, Tin Village would undoubtedly feature as a nightmare—a crowded ramshackle sprawl peopled by sturdy individualists. Mrs. Mathews's own street, hedged on either side by the carcasses of dead automobiles, soon petered out at the capital's steaming garbage dump. Even by Tin Village standards the Mathewses' residence stood out as remarkable. Mrs. Mathews, recently deciding to diversify into ship chandlery, had found their clapboard bungalow somewhat cramped for space. No problem! All that was called for was a bit of courage—and vertical thinking. Thereupon the Mathewses raised their family home ten feet into the air so that the chandlery could be housed underneath. What a woman! Big, warm, and resourceful, she was creating, single-handedly, a future for her children while their father lived far away in cold-clouded Britain. Inviting us up the outside staircase that she herself had built, Mrs. Mathews led us into her castle in the sky.

There we sat, in a brightly tinseled living room, sipping tea and tensing each time Mrs. Mathews moved, terrified in case the whole tottering edifice should collapse under us. We heard how *Johanne*'s wormholes had indeed given trouble. First the rising bilge water had ruined a cargo of cement, then a cargo of sugar. In the end *Johanne* was reduced to carrying the household effects of migrants journeying from island to island in search of work, and that didn't pay. Quite apart from the leaks, there was the problem of size. Mrs. Mathews wanted a bigger boat, a proper coastal steamer. *Johanne Regina* was for sale.

Delicately, like a verbal two-step, Edward and Mrs. Mathews maneuvered around the subject of terms and price. Eventually, after much bargaining, it was agreed that the boat was to be sold ready for sea, her inventory to include anchors, chain, compass, engine, and sails. We would buy *Johanne* if, during a twenty-mile trial sail from St. Johns to Falmouth Harbor, she proved herself seaworthy.

At our approach, the jets of water issuing from *Johanne*'s bilge pump tactfully died. But around us men continued to off-load anything and everything that could be moved; even the engine manual disappeared, while only the lack of a screwdriver saved the Sestrel compass. *Johanne* could not have been more thoroughly stripped had she sailed through a scrapyard. But no complaints, please. This was our dream ship, and her trial sail was about to begin.

A trial it most certainly proved, especially for my nerves. Out of *Johanne*'s four tanned sails only the mainsail would actually hoist, and even that was of little use. The mainsheet, a line which should have allowed the great gaff-sail to swing out at right angles to the boat, had unraveled at one end to form a four-foot "cow's tail," and was so short that the boom hung, fettered, to within two feet of amidships. As for the mizzensail, it had met with a most unfortunate accident. The main engine's exhaust pipe was an ad hoc affair poking up through the cabin top, and directly below the stowed mizzen. Just as children cut lacy patterns out of folded paper, so the hot exhaust had burned an artistic series of six-inch holes through the folded sail. But this was mere quibbling compared with *Johanne*'s magnificent lines. Edward was enraptured.

On the foredeck stood a 1929 semi-diesel donkey winch, a most beautiful specimen of industrial archaeology. It was so beautiful, in fact, that one yachtsman, a gifted painter, begged to be allowed to capture it on canvas, and others seriously urged us to donate it to an industrial museum. From my point of view its chief drawback was that the engine part of it no longer worked. The winch, which had been converted into a windlass to haul up the 350-pound anchor, operated only by hand. For the present, however, it was *Johanne*'s West Indian crew who worked the handles.

Once under way, with the General Motors (G.M.) 4-71 howling in my ears, I turned to gaze at Antigua's passing coastline. Halfway through the rainy season, the island was looking its best: fertile, green, aflourish with the rustling cockades of palm trees. Did Columbus see it like this when, in 1493, he named the island Antigua, after Santa Maria de Antigua, the miracle-working Virgin of Seville? It seems probable because, come the dry season, the island's lush grasses wither to a pale and brittle beige and balding verges reveal a litter of last year's beer cans. Even before beer cans, Columbus could not have given the island the sacred name of Antigua during the dry season.

Abruptly, grim splutterings from the engine burst in upon my thoughts. In seconds I had our whole inventory under review: no engine, no sails, no food, no lifeboat or proper radio—and the nearest downwind land a thousand miles away. Fear in full flood, I searched the skipper's face for answering panic. There was none. And, in a flash, I knew why. This happened all the time. Only practice could produce that touch of nonchalance as the man spun *Johanne*'s bows toward the shore. He had everything else judged to perfection, too. At the very moment that we dropped the anchor, the G.M. choked herself to silence.

A visit to *Johanne*'s engine room did little to reassure me. That bit of string, leading from the G.M.'s air cleaner to a rusty nail in the bulkhead, was it really enough to replace seven of the manufacturer's original eight bolts? And what of all that bilge water? Deep and black and stinking, its muffled gurglings sounded distinctly sinister. An hour of judicious fiddling and the men were ready to have another go at the starter. Instantly sparks leapt, bright as comets, across the engine room. Faulty wiring to the batteries had created a direct short. With much ado, the gallant G.M. heaved and wheezed into life—there was nothing, after all, that a little maintenance could not fix.

Half an hour later, safely anchored off the yacht club in Falmouth Harbor, I relaxed—a wee bit prematurely. It soon became clear that launching and manning *Johanne*'s fiberglass dinghy also called for some pretty singular skills. Luckily for us, Mrs. Mathews's eldest son, Teddy, had the routine well in hand, or was it in foot? First he flung the dinghy into the water, then he sprang nimbly after it, arriving just in time to thrust his big toe over the jet of water now spurting up through a large hole in the dink's bottom. Once firmly positioned, he called for a floorboard from the engine room and for his passengers from the deck. Armed with the board, his big toe still strategically plugging the hole, he solemnly paddled us ashore.

Later, I did vaguely wonder why we'd bothered with the ritual of a trial sail. What could possibly have happened to persuade us not to buy *Johanne?* To a wooden-boat addict like Edward, *Johanne*'s "faults" were the brandy butter on top of the Christmas pudding; they genuinely added to the pleasure of rescuing her. They also lowered her price. And so on the following day we gathered before lawyers in St. Johns to pay Mrs. Mathews the exact same sum of money that Edward had been paid for *Sea Wanderer.* In return, we received the ship's papers for *Johanne Regina,* built in Fåborg, Denmark, in 1929, a gaff-rigged ketch, sixty-nine feet on deck with an eighteen-foot bowsprit, eighteen-foot-six-inch

beam, and six-foot-eight-inch draft. *Johanne Regina,* ex–Baltic trader,
dear dream ship, was ours.

It took less than a day to shift all our possessions aboard our new
home. The campaign to restore *Johanne* had begun. First we had to
move her around to Freeman's Bay, the outer portion of English Harbor. There she would be in easy reach of her future life-support systems:
Antigua Slipway and the ship chandlery of Carib Marine. A pack of
friends joined us for that first short voyage and, by subsequent standards, the trip went remarkably well. Except when an abandoned fishing net grappled *Johanne*'s bow, not a thing went wrong—until, that is,
Edward rounded up into the wind to anchor. Then, without warning,
the engine lost ahead. All the gearbox oil had silently transferred itself
into the bilges. Hastily, we shoveled out the Small Anchor (a mere 275
pounds, as opposed to the Great Anchor, which weighed 350 pounds).
Surging down through the sparkling water, it was closely followed by
75 feet of rusty chain.

"That should hold her!" called Edward. What a lot we still had to
learn about our dream ship. At the very next gust of wind the Small
Anchor dragged—and all hell broke loose. Owners of half-million-dol-
lar yachts watched in horror as eighty-five tons of ancient Danish oak
glided gracefully, stern first, through the anchorage. For the second
time that day we sampled the joys of operating a 1929 donkey winch on
which all the donkeys have long since died. Link by link we raised 75
feet of five-eighth chain followed, inch by inch, by 275 pounds of anchor. Another three months passed before we discovered that the winch
had a brake—rusted solid in the "ON" position.

Once we had the anchor raised, Edward quickly spotted the fault.
At some time in its long history, the Small Anchor had been twisted 45
degrees out of true. So, rather than stick its fluky point into the bottom
of the harbor, it simply lay over on its side and slid. For the next few
weeks *Johanne* rode to the Great Anchor instead.

2. Rats, Roaches, and Other Scavengers

OUR FIRST NIGHT ABOARD *Johanne* teemed with surprises, for it wasn't until after dark that we discovered the full extent of our investment. It appeared that we were proud owners not only of sixty-nine feet of venerable vessel, but also of an exclusive holiday resort for the wealthiest, most obese cockroaches in Antigua; the really loathsome kind, with long wiggling antennae and huge chestnut wings. *Johanne*'s other houseguests, rats, were to me mere trifles in comparison.

Next day we bought two stout rat traps and rifled through rubbish bins in search of empty jam jars. Edward set the traps with fiendish cunning, though not, of course, with cheese. Oh, dear me, no! No one uses cheese in the West Indies. No one eats cheese in the West Indies, certainly not rats. No, the best West Indian rats like fish. As for the jam jars, we dropped spoonfuls of honey into them, then hid them in those secret nooks and crannies so dear to cockroach hearts.

Our second night aboard *Johanne* was not so much surprising as downright miserable. For a start, it rained. And when it rained the rain poured in. *Johanne* was clearly suffering from a lack of caulking between her deck planks, and so were we. But Edward had not rescued eighteen boats from the brink of oblivion without learning a trick or two. Now he brought out long lengths of American oilcloth to spread over our bunks. Under these we lurked.

In time we became experts at raising our knees to the precise angle at which water cascaded onto the floor and not into our bunks. At least I did. Unfortunately Edward's bunk was above and outboard of mine, so his rainwater inevitably had to pour onto me. However, that second night we were still beginners. And what with hiding from the rain, swiping at skittish cockroaches, and trying to persuade Katy that the scamper of rats was but the pitter-patter of raindrops on the hatch cover, none of us slept. Our "bag," on the other hand, was spectacular. By morning two piebald (or were they skewbald?) rats lay dead in the traps, while a good hundred resort clients seethed in dark fury inside the jam jars. The problem was how to get rid of them. Eventually we learned the trick of covering them with water followed by a drop of liquid detergent. They die instantly. For the moment we relied on a fair wind and tide to carry them away from *Johanne.*

Cowering under my oilcloth that night, I may not have slept but neither was I totally idle. I had had a nasty thought. What if some unimaginative welfare officer were to pounce on us at dawn? Would she not certify us insane and lock us up? Visions of her official report flitted through my mind:

Confidential Report on Home Visit to Family Allcard
9th May 1974

I found the family Allcard living in conditions of utmost squalor. The home has no running water, no electricity, no furniture, not even any proper sanitation. A bucket in one corner serves as a toilet. Another bucket is used for washing dishes. Mother Allcard cooks crouched on the floor beside a single kerosene burner. Around her, supplies lie stacked in cardboard boxes. Large cockroaches are in evidence in broad daylight. The Allcard home is built out of old bits of timber, some of it worm-eaten, much of it ingrained with dirt. There are no windows in the home. The only light and air enter through a hole in the roof. In bad weather this hole is covered with a piece of tattered canvas, plunging the family into total darkness. When it rains, water pours into the sleeping area and the Allcards wrap themselves in oilcloth to keep dry.

I could not help thinking that we might find it a little difficult to persuade such a welfare officer, such an unimaginative welfare officer, that this really was our greatest dream come true. Or it would be—once we got rid of our unwelcome guests.

Katy's accident the next morning did nothing to soothe my already frayed nerves. Kate was an adaptable child, she had to be. Born in New Zealand, she had already lived in Portuguese East Timor, Singapore, Kenya, England, and Seychelles—not to mention quick visits to Australia and India en route. In the last five months she had moved house five times. But she was still unused to *Johanne,* so she made her way forward to the bow clutching a precious toy in each hand. She was about to learn, once and for all, that golden rule for safety afloat: "One hand for the ship and one for yourself." It must have been a wash from a passing speedboat that threw *Johanne* into a languid roll. Katy lost her balance, could not bear to drop either toy, and fell headfirst on the broken rim of an iron ventilator.

The first I knew of the accident were loud bellows from the foredeck. In those days loud bellows, unaccompanied by tears, were a rather trying feature of our otherwise adored offspring, so my voice did not exactly light up with sympathy.

"Oh dear, what is it now? What's happened?" My small daughter stood before me, head down, clasping her face with both hands.

"Come on, then. Let's see what you've done."

One look and I, too, was yelling. "Edward! Help! Kate's had an accident." Blood was streaming from her forehead. Through the cut, a cyclops eye of polished skull glistened, and her whole face was bathed in a rich red gore.

Half in shock, my mind shifted to automatic: stop the bleeding, find some shade, have her lie down, but keep her head up.

"Quick, a clean handkerchief, got to stop the bleeding, then we'll get her to a doctor."

We returned late in the afternoon, Katy proudly sporting seven stitches and both her parents utterly exhausted. If the first three days aboard *Johanne* were anything to go by, life promised never to be dull.

By the time the roaches were routed and Kate's stitches removed, our life had settled into something of a routine. Edward worked all day, every day, on *Johanne.* His list of "Jobs to Be Done" was formidable. The worst of *Johanne*'s planks had to be replaced. To keep the sea where it belonged, on the outside, her whole hull would have to be recaulked; for the moment, the bilges filled, and we pumped them out, twice daily. The engine needed to be stripped down, all rope and wire rigging renewed. Sails had to be made or mended, a head (marine lavatory) installed, and the decks caulked. And that was just for starters. There were also the cabins and bunks to build, to say nothing of a saloon to create out of half the cargo hold. As yet I had no sink or stove, no galley, and, naturally, each day we thought of something more to add to that daunting list.

Meanwhile I divided my own time among boat refurbishing, household chores, and Katy. With *Johanne* a dangerous shambles, we enrolled Katy at a local kindergarten, which meant getting up at 6 A.M. to cook breakfast and pack a sandwich lunch before rowing her ashore to catch the seven-o'clock school bus. Personally, I was glad of that early start because, despite having lived aboard *Sea Wanderer* on and off for several years, I still knew next to nothing about sailing. Edward had always done that alone; my part of the operation was to help maintain the boat when in port. I could give any number of intimate details about scraping masts, chipping keels, and anti-fouling bottoms, but pathetically few about jibing or running by the lee. One thing I did know, however, was that aboard ship there's a right and a wrong way to do almost everything—and that, given half a chance, I'd invariably do it wrong. It had never bothered me before, but here in English Harbor, among a bunch of highly experienced, highly critical yachtsmen, such ignorance embarrassed me. I went in dread of making a fool of myself in front of Edward's friends, friends he had made when I was still in grade school.

Spurred on both by shame and by the thought that at last we'd all be going cruising together, *en famille,* I used those early morning starts to practice basic nautical skills, such as bringing a rowboat alongside a dock without crashing into it. There were also all those complicated bends and hitches to be mastered. None of your Boy Scout, rabbit-down-a-hole bowlines allowed on *Johanne.* Bowlines would be tied in proper, fisherman style or not at all. In the end I reckon I could have tied that darned knot behind my back, underwater, with my eyes closed.

The first time I rowed Katy ashore, I sent up a quick prayer that everyone else in the Dockyard would still be in bed. Concentrating hard, I brought the dinghy alongside the quay. No nasty crunch. Carefully shipping the oars, we both stepped ashore, without falling in. Hey! This wasn't so bad. I passed the dinghy painter through a mooring ring and then, with a final flourish, tied a bowline. A surreptitious check for mistakes was followed by a sigh of relief. I hadn't made a fool of myself after all. Then a gravelly drawl came to me from the luxury motor yacht alongside: "Say, you have been practicing hard, haven't you." I could have died.

Once I'd seen Katy safely off to school, I either went shopping or scrubbed clothes in Nelson's Dockyard. (From 1784 to 1787 the British fleet in English Harbor was commanded by a brilliant young naval captain, Horatio Nelson, hence the Dockyard's present name.) When the Nicholson family first sailed into English Harbor, they found the once-famous dockyard abandoned and half buried under rampant weeds. Forming a conservation group, they set about restoring the Dockyard to something like its former glory. Weeds gave way to grass. Blood-red hibiscus and fragrant frangipani bloomed. The eighteenth-century officers' quarters were refurbished to house twentieth-century charter skippers and Carib Marine's grocery and ship chandlery pitched up in the Georgian pay office. The commanding officer's house was reopened as a museum and, using 200-year-old ballast bricks, they transformed the engineer's office into the Admiral's Inn Hotel. Thanks in large part to the Friends of English Harbor, Nelson's Dockyard is today Antigua's greatest tourist attraction.

In this fever of restoration Emmy and Vernon did not forget their cruising friends. Laundry facilities, cold-water taps and washing lines, were set up in the grass-covered ruins of the cordage-and-canvas store. And that's where I went, with my buckets of dirty washing plus soap and scrubbing brush, to do the laundry in much the same fashion as Nelson's men of old: on hands and knees and with a maximum expenditure of elbow grease.

Back on board, *Johanne*'s own cleanup continued. When we first bought her, the stench from her bilges was such that most visitors beat a hasty retreat to the decks. Not only had the bilges been treated as a urinal but *Johanne*'s interior bulkheads (walls) were still encrusted from where she had lain, half sunk in stinking mud. Using soapy water laced heavily with antiseptic, I launched an all-out attack on the old girl's innards. Then, hot and exhausted, I usually followed lunch with a quick siesta. After the nap it was time to collect Katy and row her, plus her friends, to the beach. When it comes to friendship, boat children recognize few barriers of age or gender. One of Kate's first great pals was Garth. Six years old, he was a splendid, all-American kid who rowed over to introduce himself the moment his family had anchored in English Harbor. In no time the two children were eating their way through a cultural exchange. Katy offered Garth his first glass of British orange squash and he introduced her to the delights of a peanut-butter-and-jelly sandwich. At one time I counted sixteen children living on boats in English Harbor. For the most part they lived enchanted lives. Packing picnics, the older ones raced their sailing dinghies to the far side of the bay, where they swam off empty beaches, gazed into clear rock pools, and followed overgrown tracks through bush that cried out to be explored. For the little ones, Nelson's Dockyard with its ruins and replicas of historical capstans was an adventure playground in itself.

Returning from the beach at sunset, Kate ate her supper, listened to a story, had a good cuddle, and went to bed. Our next half-hour was spent scrubbing decks. By waiting till after sundown to douse the planks, we gave the salt water a chance to penetrate the wood rather than evaporate. Any residual salt would then draw in the nighttime dew and further swell the planks. If only we could induce *Johanne*'s decks to swell enough, they might stop leaking. Meanwhile we switched our sleeping quarters to the one dry place on *Johanne,* under the tatty canvas covers and loose-fitting hatches of the hold. Laying a deck in the hold had been Edward's first major job. Once down, the hold became our sitting room in the heat of the day and our dormitory at night.

Decks scrubbed, we each had one more chore to cope with. As Edward wrestled with the Briggs and Stratton bilge pump, I squatted in the hold and grappled with a fiendish pressure stove. (Impure fuel kept clogging up its jet.) The battle won, supper eaten and cleared away, we spread a mattress on the floor and went to bed. Another dream-ship day was over.

Converting and restoring old wooden trading boats calls for more skills than you might at first imagine. Carpentry and engineering, rigging and painting, all those are pretty obvious, but what about scavenging? I had received an introductory course in the art when visiting Westhaven Marina in New Zealand. My instructor was a retired naval commander who stressed that pupils should be ready to rise at dawn if they wished to harvest the full fruits of the garbage bins. I soon saw what he meant. In one bin alone, ideally situated at the end of "Gin Palace Jetty," he unearthed a spotless white mohair cardigan, a stack of 45-rpm records, a very useful assortment of stainless-steel off-cuts, and a complete set of drinking glasses, unbroken and in their original packaging. English Harbor had its own professor of scavenging, though this chap's interest lay in a different branch of the specialty: big-time recycling. Each day he would rummage through the dustbins, fishing out wealthy yachtsmen's cast-offs. These he carefully cleaned and repaired and then sold, secondhand, in the local chandlery.

Having sold most of our own worldly goods with *Sea Wanderer*, *Johanne* had to be equipped from scratch, but many of our needs were unobtainable in Antigua. So I, too, began regular visits to the garbage pens. On the whole my scavenging was very successful, though occasionally things went embarrassingly wrong—such as the time Edward and I found a boom support, or gallows, chuckled on top of a stack of rotten wood. Checking around, everyone assured us that it had been dumped there weeks before, previous owner unknown. Pleased, we rowed it out to *Johanne* and maneuvered it into place. Not perfect, but, with a little fixing, it would do. We shortened its legs with a hacksaw, welded on feet to fit, and bolted the whole to the cabin top under the mizzen boom. Then the owner returned. Understandably peeved, he had come to ask for it back.

Such setbacks apart, the recycled fitting-out of *Johanne* prospered nicely and never more so than when high drama swept the Dockyard. A yacht called *Sea Horse* had arrived. At least we thought she was called *Sea Horse*, until an indignant English knight came along to set us straight. Apparently the man who was posing as the yacht's owner was nothing of the sort. He was the yacht's skipper and a thief. Doing a moonlight flit from the Med, he'd sailed the yacht across the Atlantic, changed her color to silver, filled in the carved name board with putty, stuck a large plywood sea horse on her prow, and renamed her *Sea Horse*. As the avenging knight stalked in one end of the Dockyard, the thief sneaked out the other and took to the hills.

The Englishman had no interest in prosecutions. He wanted only to sail the yacht back to Europe as quickly as possible, but first something had to be done about her soft furnishings. Grimed with dirt and dog hair, they were enough to fill a fastidious soul with horror. The English gentleman's soul was most fastidious and his solution, radical. Burn the lot. That, anyway, was his intention until I got wind of the proposed arson. Good heavens, what was soap for? There was nothing there that a healthy soak, scrub, and dry in the hot sun would not cure. More to the point, good thick blankets were unavailable in tropical Antigua, and we would want such blankets for crossing the Atlantic. I suspect the poor knight found my enthusiasm almost as horrifying as the soft furnishings, but then he didn't have an empty home to equip on a tight budget.

3. Out of the Water, a Worm's-Eye View

THREE WEEKS after we bought her I watched, elated, as *Johanne Regina* was hauled slowly from the water at Antigua Slipway. At last we could get our hands on all those wormy planks. At last the old girl's rescue could begin. But then, as more and more of her hull rose from the water, my spirits nose-dived. That planking really did look dreadful. Rescue her? We were dotty to even think of it. But come on, now! Positive thinking, that's all that's needed. What a blessing that Mrs. Mathews changed her mind just when she did, before we flew off and left *Johanne* to her leaking fate (and speaking of leaks, we could now stop pumping, as long as *Johanne* stayed firmly on dry land), plus what a stroke of luck that Antigua Slipway had David Simmons for its manager. There was little or nothing that man did not know about restoring wooden boats.

The moment *Johanne*'s scabby beard of weed and barnacles had been scraped clear, David and Edward were clambering about her bottom debating tactics. With some difficulty they picked out her six worst planks for renewal, planks that in places were so honeycombed by teredo worm that you could break off great chunks with your bare fingers. Armed with axes and crowbars, saws, hammers, and chisels, a team of West Indian carpenters soon had chips of old planking, like hunks of holey Gruyère cheese, flying across the yard.

Unlike other ship worms, such as gribble and martesia, teredoes use the chisel-edged tips of their tails to tunnel along, rather than straight into, the planks. In *Johanne*'s case this meant that the final, inside inch of her three-inch planking was often sound. That, in turn, went some way in explaining why she was afloat at all. Teredo worms have one other redeeming feature (if anything about a ship's worm population can redeem it): they are very unenterprising types. Happy to go on boring back and forth along the same old plank, it is rare indeed to find a worm willing to venture from one plank to another. Better still, they practically never shift from planks to frames.

Planks, though essential, are easy enough to replace. Frames are not, which makes them arguably the most vital part of any wooden ship. Their life is her life. Rising up from the keel like mammoth ribs, they give the boat both her skeleton and her strength. Those ribs are one of the first things a surveyor inspects—if he can. Unfortunately, unlike yachts, wooden cargo boats have a double hull. One set of planking, on the outside of the ribs, keeps the elements at bay, and another set, on the inside of the frames, is almost as watertight. This second set of planks is the ceiling, and it keeps the cargo from tumbling into the bilge and the bilge water from messing up the cargo. Clearly with this type of construction, there are very few places where prospective buyers can check the state of those all-important frames. Even with a survey, buying an old cargo boat bears a more than passing resemblance to a game of hazard. So, as the carpenters cut away the last concealing inch of outside planking, Edward and I edged closer, hardly daring to look, in case *Johanne*'s frames proved rotten.

Imagine the relief when plank after plank was torn away to reveal frames still massively robust after forty-five years afloat, so robust that when, later, the carpenters came to drive six-inch boat nails through the drilled new planks into *Johanne*'s old, undrilled oak frames, they had to summon Peter Roach. He alone in the boatyard had enough strength for the job. The yard foreman, Peter was a classic, gentle giant of a guy, the sort of chap who would tenderly lift up a crying child yet split the sleeves of his own T-shirt each time he flexed his biceps. Now, resting the huge sledgehammer on the ground, he laughed and shook his head in disbelief and said, "Man! You sure got no need to worry about them frames. No need to worry at all."

David ordered greenheart for the new planking. A superb South American hardwood, it is used the world over for underwater jetty construction. Quite apart from being hard and strong, boat worms don't fancy it. Once into their stride, Antigua's carpenters renewed *Johanne*'s three-inch planking at the incredible rate of two fifteen-foot lengths a day. Indeed, they worked so swiftly that, in the end, they replaced twelve planks, not six, and all without scuttling our budget.

Nonetheless, on that first slipping, we undertook only one further repair: to *Johanne*'s keel shoe. An extra piece of wood stretching full length under a boat's keel, the shoe's job is to protect the keel from the depredations of both hungry boat worms and careless skippers who take misguided short cuts through uncharted coral reefs. In no time our carpenters had prepared a splendid greenheart shoe four inches thick, eleven inches wide, and a total of fifty-six feet long. With any luck it would work even better than the old one which, in its way, had done a noble job. There was virtually nothing left of it.

Edward, meanwhile, was inside *Johanne* tackling the G.M.'s fearful din. With David's help he bolted a whacking great water-trap silencer to the exhaust so that the main chamber was high above the engine, with the final outlet just above the waterline. The arrangement, though not pretty, had one clear advantage. Seawater could never drain back through the exhaust to fill and ruin the motor, something which quite often happens in brand-new yachts where, for beauty's sake, the watered exhaust runs discreetly below the floorboards—and the waterline. *Johanne*'s new silencer was a success. It cut the G.M.'s noise by some 80 percent and eliminated its stink entirely.

With her first new planks in place, we next faced a seemingly impossible task: making *Johanne*'s underwater hull watertight. While I went cross-eyed bunging hundreds of tiny wormholes with hundreds of wooden pegs, David called in the caulkers. Working with gusto, they drove the matted oakum hard into the seams between *Johanne*'s planks. Once home, the oakum had to be protected or payed. Antigua Slipway did this in time-honored fashion. First they built a fire from chips of worm-eaten planks. Over the fire they then set a pot of pitch to boil. A twist of oakum on the end of a stick served as a brush. Dipping this oakum brush into the bubbling pitch, they carefully rolled it along each seam. When cool, the pitch formed a flexible but waterproof covering to the caulking.

The caulking completed, all of *Johanne*'s new wood had to be treated, first with preservatives and then with a waterproof, anti-fouling undercoat. Next the whole underwater hull was painted with red anti-fouling, a poisonous concoction used to dampen the ardor of itinerant worms and clinging weed. With a final coat of dark-blue gloss to her topsides, JOHANNE at last looked loved—and not just around her hull either.

Foraging through David's store and Desmond's ship chandlery, we had found a 140-pound CQR anchor to dangle from the port bow and a fiberglass dinghy to tie up astern. Two heads (marine lavatories) had been installed below, while on deck we had replaced *Johanne*'s rotten sisal sheets and halyards with good Dacron line designed to last for years. But of all our aquisitions my favorite arrived right out of the blue or, more accurately, out of the oggin. We discovered it floating at the very foot of the slipway, nuzzling as close to *Johanne*'s hull as it could get—a beautiful ensign staff. Not only was it the correct height for

Johanne but it was topped by a wooden ball already drilled to take a flag halyard and big enough to support a stern light, too. In a mad moment of gratitude to Father Neptune we painted the ball gold. And what's more, nobody came to claim it back.

Antigua acts as a rallying point for cruising people worldwide. When we were there, during the single month of December, over fifty men, women, and children sailed small boats across the Atlantic to English Harbor. None stayed long. Around a central core of lofty charter yachts, Antigua's international fleet of small boats mills about in a constant state of flux, heading north to the eastern seaboard of the United States, east to Europe, or south through the islands en route for Panama and the Pacific.

Only a few sea-rovers remain, their vagrant spirits drowsing like lizards in the Caribbean sun. Then Antigua Race Week, the biggest regatta in the whole Caribbean, gets under way and even they are galvanized to action. Yachts flock from across the globe to compete for trophies. Yet, for me, the climax comes on the very last day of the week when the starter's gun unleashes what must surely be the most hilarious spectator sport ever devised on water.

The rules for the Non-mariners Race are strict but simple. First, no vessel may cost more than BWI $50 to build. Second, no vessel may touch the water or be tested for seaworthiness before the starting gun is fired. Then, with one accord, all craft are hurled from the top of the Dockyard wharf into the water, swiftly followed by their would-be crew. Sirens wail, kids shout, sea and air swirl in a riot of balloons and flags and bits of bunting. An optimistically seagoing park bench, purloined for the occasion and buoyed up by empty oil drums, collides with a wine barrel rigged with Heath Robinson paddle power. A large raft, half submerged under its crew of twenty, sails off in the wrong direction while several vessels sink outright, leaving their crews splashing about in the harbor, shrieking with laughter and hellbent on mayhem.

Suddenly it's all over, and the crowds disperse. Cruising folk return aboard to wash and rest and change their clothes, for the last day of Race Week stretches well into the next day's dawn. On that one night, English Harbor's yachtswomen cast off their T-shirts and their paint-stained shorts and dress up in their most glamorous gowns. Stepping gingerly into their dinghies, they speed away for a night at the Admiral's Inn and its brilliant Admiral's Ball.

Race Week over, we thanked the yard for their excellent work and then slid *Johanne* quietly back into the water. Bequia, 240 miles to the south, was to be our next port of call, our trip there to set a pattern that shaped *Johanne*'s cruising for twelve years to come. (When one man later accused us of not cruising at all, but merely sailing from one boatyard to another in search of the best timber and craftsmen we could afford, I felt he had a point. Not that I was complaining. By then that search had sailed us halfway around the world.) Bequia (pronounced "Beckwi") is famous throughout the Caribbean for its boat builders, its sailmakers, and its caulkers. So to Bequia we would go. There, caulkers could seal *Johanne*'s topsides (the hull above the water) and her abominably leaky decks. Sailmakers would be commissioned to conjure up some sails. We might even have time to work on *Johanne*'s interior where, for a start, a door to the heads would be nice.

Before we could set out, one further, indispensable piece of equipment was needed: a powerful bilge pump. New planks and caulking below the waterline notwithstanding, there was still a chance that, once we got to sea, the old girl might leak. So Edward flew off to Puerto Rico to consult the G.M. agent, not only about a bilge pump that would run off their engine but about spares for the engine itself, which still had to be stripped down. During his stay, Edward also ordered 500 feet of three-quarter-inch-diameter galvanized rigging wire. *Johanne*'s rusty shrouds could not hold up her masts much longer.

Edward returned with the pump in his hand luggage and quickly had it installed and working. From then on the old Briggs and Stratton "miracle worker" went into retirement, a standby for when miracles were called for. Both pumps, according to their manufacturers, could shift 2,500 gallons an hour. However, having a built-in suspicion of all motors, Edward rounded off his shopping spree with a Whale "Gusher 25" hand pump. After that even I felt secure.

Though concentrating most effort on being able to bail salt water out of *Johanne,* we did not entirely ignore the need to bring fresh drinking water into her. We bought a 300-gallon household cistern to add to the 130-gallon iron tank already carried on *Johanne*'s deck. Of some historic interest, that iron tank—it had been salvaged, along with *Johanne*'s steering gear, from a ninety-year-old Thames barge. Whatever bugs proliferated inside it, we reckoned they must have reached a pretty fine maturity by 1974. Distributing our freshwater supply between the two tanks, we lowered the antique tank into the aft end of the hold where, one day, a saloon and galley would take shape. Already Edward had augmented the hold's new deck with a handsome pine bulkhead running vertically across it, dividing it in two. With the aft ten feet reserved for living quarters, the twelve forward feet were to remain as hold—storage space for paint, line, spare wood, and, slap in the middle, the new 300-gallon freshwater cistern.

Well watered, we made final preparations for the great voyage south. Evan, a young Canadian, volunteered to crew for us down to Bequia. A self-sufficient character, he'd once built himself a log cabin twenty miles from nowhere in the middle of the Canadian wilderness. When we met him he was earning his living aboard Caribbean charter yachts, though he came with us purely for the adventure. He was not disappointed, and we had our first crew.

Crew have always been a bit of a problem among yacht owners (just as owners are a problem among crew). One does not have to be a genius to understand why. Just take a look at the number of couples ashore who split up, unable to live together a moment longer. Then imagine the difficulties faced by people who may not know one another from Adam and yet find themselves tossed together, sometimes for weeks on end, in an area not much bigger than a prison cell. Before we bought *Johanne* several friends had urged us strongly against it, solely because of the vexing question of crew. If *Johanne* was to be a happy ship then it was a question we would have to solve. Looking around we noticed that, apart from the odd case of instant antipathy and the inescapable lack of space, there were two further areas that commonly caused tension: money and status.

Most people who volunteer to crew aboard yachts love sailing, travel, and adventure but for one reason or another have no boat of their own. So, in exchange for the fun of sailing, they offer to share the expenses and work of the voyage. This can cause friction. Crew may feel that they are asked to contribute too much or that their contribution is being squandered. Owners, on the other hand, sometimes feel that they are being used as a bargain-basement charter by a bunch of idle boat bums. The second problem, that of status, is caused by owners who, heedless of the fact that their crew are first rate, manage to kid themselves that their helpers belong to some lower caste system. As most crew are highly independent and enterprising people, their indignation grows and tempers flare. Personality clashes are the most frequent cause for long-term cruises to be abandoned.

Surely, though, it shouldn't be too difficult to avoid such pitfalls. Why not welcome crew aboard as part of the family, as the friends and partners they undoubtedly are when sailing small ships across large oceans? As to the question of finance, we decided that the best solution was for no one to pay anyone anything. That way people young and old, rich and poor would have the opportunity to ship aboard a traditional, gaff-rigged sailing boat—an opportunity nowadays reserved mainly for wealthy charterers or well-sponsored Tall Ship candidates. In exchange, we expected our crew to work their passage, helping us as best they could with *Johanne*'s restoration. Having come to these conclusions, I quickly developed an almost missionary zeal toward our crew, and a fierce determination that *Johanne Regina* would be a happy ship.

4. Pumping Our Way to Bequia

THE SKY ABOVE was strangely overcast as *Johanne* cleared the narrow exit from Freeman's Bay. Turning south, Edward laid a course for Guadeloupe, the next vertebra in the long, curving tail of islands that leads to Bequia. With a handsome new mainsheet rove through her blocks, *Johanne* was free to stretch her mainsail to the breeze. Then the wind shifted and gathered strength. Now she plunged on, close-hauled into a rising head sea. Theoretically everything should have been fine. *Johanne*'s bottom had just been recaulked and all but one of her loose hatch covers were battened down, held in place by horizontal bars tightly wedged over two protective layers of canvas. Nevertheless, it wasn't long before my familiar demon, worry, had me prizing up the only free hatch to steal a peek below.

For one shocked moment my brain went completely blank. It simply refused to accept what my eyes insisted they saw—our embryonic saloon transformed into seething, churning chaos. *Johanne* rolled. A solid wall of water poured in through the yard-long inspection holes of the inside planking and hurtled clear across the saloon to thunder in fury against the other side. Seconds later *Johanne* lurched back, and the whole horrible cycle was reversed.

"Edward!" I fluted, trying in vain to sound like the calm and seasoned sailor I was not. "I think perhaps you should come and look at this."

The rising wind only mocked me as it whisked my words away.

"Edward!" I called a little louder this time. "Do come! I think we're sinking."

That, of course, was fatal. Fear, once voiced, turned instantly to panic while that proud emblem of my heritage, the British stiff upper lip, started to quiver like a rabbit's whiskers.

"Edward!" I bellowed, "Come! It's like a ruddy washing machine down here!"

Edward came.

Seconds later the main engine, the power drive for the new and mighty bilge pump, roared into life. And nothing happened. The pump that had worked so consistently in port refused to work at all. Dashing below, Evan rammed a makeshift chimney onto the Briggs and Stratton's exhaust. Then, holding the machine down with one hand, he wound the cord, lawn-mower fashion, around the flywheel and pulled. The old miracle worker spluttered into life. On deck, above the pump's staccato broadside and the G.M.'s lusty thrum, a beautiful gushing could be heard as torrents of bilge water poured into the sea . . . for a while. The trouble was that all those previously un-get-at-able bits of hull between the inner and outer planking were now receiving the spring cleaning of their lives. The bilge water positively bristled with wood shavings old and new. Any one of them could block the bilge pumps. Any number of them did.

Between them, Evan and Edward eventually coaxed the new pump into action. Yet even then, both pumps demanded constant clearing to ensure that at least one was always working. *Johanne* was taking in hundreds of gallons an hour. Her leak was barely under control. Antigua, though receding in the haze astern, was nonetheless a lot closer than Guadeloupe. More to the point, we could reach the shelter of the island's lee on a downwind run. Very reluctantly, Edward turned back, and at once, with the waves and wind now following us, *Johanne*'s leaks lessened. A couple of hours later she was safely anchored in Five Island Harbor.

Because *Johanne*'s bottom was freshly caulked, the finger of blame switched automatically to her topsides. Inspected from the dinghy, her plight was soon revealed. Ideally, the plank seams should have been closed tight, but on *Johanne* there were places near the waterline where I could stick my whole hand between her planking—never a good sign. Add to that all the recent plunging into head seas and you could understand why long hanks of old oakum had been swept clean away and why water had flooded in. Leaving Evan, Katy, and me to hang on in the dinghy, Edward nipped into the hold only to reappear with eyes mischievously asparkle and hands filled with lengths of one-inch-diameter rope. He'd just chopped up *Johanne*'s old mainsheet. At any moment I expected him to burst into song as he pounded the rope pieces into *Johanne*'s ludicrously wide seams. It was exactly the kind of absurd situation that Edward adores.

His remedy worked pretty well, too. When we again hoisted sail for Bequia, the men were still kept busy clearing and priming the pumps but the main internal waterfalls were under control. Katy, meanwhile, was demonstrating beyond doubt that she had retained her all-embracing propensity for motion sickness. She had first been sick in a swing at age five months. Since then she had succumbed in ox carts and yachts, private cars and public buses. We had had to take her out of kindergarten in Antigua because the journey left her ashen. Over the years her seasickness was to be one of the chief things that weighed against our vagrant way of living. I tried everything to cure her: pills, fresh air and songs, mind-distracting games, even sheets of newspaper tucked up the front of her T-shirt. Nothing worked. She was amazingly stoical, never cried or complained, simply puked. And boy, did I feel guilty! They said she would grow out of it. They said her stomach would settle down after a couple of days at sea. During that first long trip to Bequia I prayed that they were right. They weren't.

What with the leak and Kate's sickness, we pressed on as fast as we could, past the high volcanoes of Guadeloupe and on to the French island of Martinique where we paused, overnight, but only to let the pump-tenders catch up on their sleep and Katy catch up on her food. With dawn we were off again on the last leg of the voyage, the ninety miles to Kingstown, St. Vincent, port of entry for Bequia.

St. Vincent is a typical Caribbean island, its history storm-tossed and dramatic. Today, when the vast majority of West Indians are black, it is easy to forget that this was not always so. Sometime after the birth of Christ, there was a major social upheavel in South America. A highly organized and aggressive tribe, the Caribs, rose up against their peace-loving rulers, the Arawaks, and drove them right off the South American continent. The Arawaks fled to the West Indies, the Caribs chased after them, and the Caribbean was born.

By the time Columbus "discovered" the island in 1498, its history was already old and the warlike Caribs had once again ousted the peaceful Arawaks. It was to take the warlike Europeans another 200 years of bilateral massacre before they in turn ousted the Caribs. Meanwhile, sugar became king. Plantation owners, in search of cheap labor, shipped out poor whites from Europe under the infamous system of indenture. They were too weak, ill-fed, and ill-treated to survive, and many died. As their numbers dwindled so the despicable slave trade from Africa grew. Today, most whites on the island are tourists. St. Vincent and the Grenadines (which include Bequia) are a single, independent nation ruled by free and independent people of African descent. Of the original inhabitants, the Amerindians, there is scarcely a trace.

A strong offshore wind had Edward struggling to bring *Johanne* alongside Kingstown's busy wharf. Evan stood in the bow, a stout mooring line coiled ready in his hands. As *Johanne* edged closer, he hurled the warp with all his might to windward. Ashore, a fisherman grabbed its snaking end and made it fast. Not a moment too soon. Edward, with the helm hard over, gave the engine a last blip astern. Almost simultaneously our helper pointed toward *Johanne*'s rudder. The propeller had fallen out! Or, to be more precise, the propeller plus shaft had parted company with the engine. If the rudder had not been there, blocking their further progress, the whole kerboosh would have plunged to the bottom promptly followed by the rest of us.

We knew that *Johanne*'s previous, two-cylinder, Volund engine had itself come to a sticky end when, by a laughable mischance, a so-called mechanic had poured solder instead of white metal into its bearings. Could it be that the same bright spark had been employed to install the reconditioned G.M.? Weeks before, Edward had been somewhat startled to discover that *Johanne*'s shaft did not belong to her shaft coupling. Now, he was even more fascinated to find that the two parts had, in fact, been held together by nothing more than friction—and the very purest of faith.

I frankly revel in Edward's genius for fixing things. He had that shaft coupling off in a trice. Taking it ashore, he persuaded a mechanic to drill it with an off-center hole. Then he spent until the following dawn crouched in the bilge, patiently dragging a round metal file back and forth, back and forth across the stainless-steel shaft to carve out a groove. Finally, tapping a bolt through both the off-center hole and the groove, he joined coupling and shaft together. That creative bit of handiwork lasted till we changed the shaft itself, five years later.

Kingstown is a port bustling with activity. At one end of the scale, gaily painted sailing schooners load people and produce for trips up and down the string of tiny islands that make up the Grenadines. At the other end, hulking great fruit carriers call in to pick up bananas for shipment to Europe.

Bananas thrive on St. Vincent. Bizarre-looking plants, they consist almost entirely of immense, arching leaves whose fringed edges droop down like a horse's mane. Thrusting out from the heart of each tree comes a single, pendulous stalk tipped by a phallic bud. As it ripens, the bud opens to reveal rows of little flowers. The bottom ones produce pollen; the middle ones drop off leaving only the top ones to grow into fruit. Though the stalk itself hangs down, the bananas grow upward like a hundred fingers held out for counting. A mature stalk can weigh as much as seventy-five pounds. Picked green, the bananas are sold to

Europe where their large size is greatly admired, much to the amusement of West Indians, who wisely keep for themselves the smaller, more succulent varieties. Abundant banana crop notwithstanding, St. Vincent's most lucrative agribusiness is arrowroot, the island being the world's largest producer. They ship arrowroot to the States, Canada, and Britain, where it is used for coating computer paper.

This great fertility was recognized as far back as 1765, when, from amongst all their Caribbean possessions, the British singled out St. Vincent for the establishment of a botanical garden. That garden is, today, the oldest of its kind in the Western Hemisphere, with its place in West Indian history assured by none other than Captain Bligh himself. Some thirty years after the garden's founding, Bligh sailed into Kingstown Harbor with a cargo of strange seedlings aboard—seedlings he personally had nurtured all the way from Tahiti. His faith in the garden was to prove well founded. Breadfruit from his original plants have become one of the West Indies' most important staples.

Our own destination, Bequia, lay no more than nine miles south of St. Vincent, so, with holey sails hoisted, we let *Johanne* drift lazily across the channel to drop anchor in Admiral's Bay, one of the finest harbors in the Caribbean. The Caribs named Bequia the Island of Clouds, though I cannot for the life of me think why. In my memory it remains an island bathed in sunshine. On the beach at the head of Admiral's Bay stands a group of venerable almond trees. In their shade a cargo schooner lies hauled out for repairs. Walk a little farther from the shore and you will reach Mr. Simmons's sail loft, where he and his assistants make and mend sails. It was to this establishment that we first turned for help.

When, some months before, Captain Bruno Brown had ordered a new suit of sails for the iron schooner *Freelance,* he had passed on her cast-off main to *Johanne*. Even after twenty years of tropical sunshine, that canvas had only one corner which could truly be classed as rotten. Our sail area being much smaller than *Freelance*'s, the hope was that Mr. Simmons, after a judicious bit of juggling, could convert the rest of the canvas into a temporary main for *Johanne*. Mr. Simmons proved himself to be a past master of juggling. Not only did he alter the *Freelance* main to fit *Johanne*, but he then took *Johanne*'s old main and, avoiding its own choice areas of rot, re-cut it to fit her mizzen. The old mizzen, that sail with the artistic necklace of burn holes, was then unbent and stowed in the hold, and was later handed on to Mrs. Mathews's son Sonny to be cut into a jib for his fishing boat. All in all, a most satisfying exercise in recycling.

Evan, when not helping on *Johanne*, had taken on a key part of Katy's education. Blessed with a fine baritone, he sat on deck in the evenings strumming his guitar and teaching her such elevating ditties as "Rye Whiskey"—"So she can sing it to her grandma," he told me sweetly. In more active moods, he got Katy swimming long distance. Never one to submit willingly to parental instruction. Katy would do anything for Evan. In no time he had our bronzed sprite diving off *Johanne* and swimming across the harbor to the beach. But sitting at anchor on a boat under repair is no life for a young chap thirsting for adventure. When a job as charter skipper came up, Evan took it and so our first crew drifted out of our lives, taking with him warm thanks and good wishes for happy sailing.

We had also come to Bequia in search of caulkers and one morning, soon after our arrival, two brigandly looking fellows hailed us from the shore. Recommended as the best on the island, we had had to lure them out of retirement to work for us. The two clambered aboard heaving behind them bails of deliciously aromatic oakum. (Good oakum is lightly impregnated with tarry oils to lengthen its life.) Pulling off a fistful of the coarse brown stuff, the caulkers teased it out into hairlike tresses. Then, with a swift to-and-fro motion across the knees, they rolled the fibers into tight-knit strands, the thickness of each depending on the width of deck seam to be caulked. Raking the old oakum out of the seams, they drove in the new strands using caulking iron and mallet (never "hammer"). Caulking irons are wonderfully elegant tools. Flat and triangular-shaped, they have the working edge at the base with the apex elongated into a circular shaft crowned by a flat disk on which the caulkers hammered, different irons being chosen for different jobs. Starting out with fastidious, fine-edged "setting irons," the men looped the oakum deftly into the seams. Then stouter "making irons" took over to harden the oakum home.

The cylindrical-headed mallets were no less works of art. Made from hardwood, each had a special saw cut that ran right through the head to within an inch of either end. That slot, found on all such mallets, serves two purposes: one practical, one aesthetic. Practically speaking, the slot cuts down the jarring as, hour after hour, the caulker pounds oakum into seams. Aesthetically, the slot is a music maker, each mallet having its own distinctive tone. In the old days, teams of caulkers went out of their way to have each mallet tuned to a different note. Thus they made music while they worked.

Our own caulkers, though not particularly musical, were doing a first-class job. They finished *Johanne*'s entire decks in less than a week—and that despite the need to keep a calculating eye on the weather. Each stretch of new oakum had to be protected, or payed, with boiling pitch before a shower could come and wet it. Once all was payed up we could blithely snap our fingers at the rain. Even so, the deck job was pretty straightforward when compared with caulking *Johanne*'s gaping topsides. There the men first drove long wooden battens, or splines, tightly into the open seams; then they caulked along the upper edge of the splines in the normal way. Those seams stayed watertight until we replaced the planks themselves ten years later in Singapore, half a world away.

So slowly but surely *Johanne*'s convalescence progressed. If only my own boat-wifely chores could have gone half as smoothly. For those responsible for the island people's health, that is to say, for housewives and boatwives, market day on Bequia was the most important day of the week. That was the day the boat arrived from St. Vincent carrying fresh supplies of food. Wooden stalls quickly sprouted near the flowering almond trees and there the market women lovingly displayed their wares, either on the stalls themselves or on spotless strips of cloth spread on the ground nearby.

What a feast was there. Pyramids of scarlet peppers stood side by side with mounds of spring-green cabbages. Tomatoes nestled in the hands of bananas which, in turn, were besieged on all sides by lucious mangoes and pink-fleshed papaw, every piece scrubbed and polished and in its prime.

Although I'd had considerable experience of open-air markets, my first visit to Bequia's was a fiasco. Choosing a line at random, I stood, melting in the sun, for what seemed like eternity but was probably no more than an hour. Eventually my turn came. By then the artistic displays of produce had been severely undermined but there was still plenty to spare. Yet as I asked for one kind of vegetable after another, the stallholder's response was always the same—a sullen shake of the head. Inexplicably every scrap of fruit and vegetable on display had been pre-sold to other, invisible customers. Or so she said. What she meant was that she refused to serve me because I was white.

I stared at her, utterly dismayed. The shock came because the stallholder was a woman. Till then, in all my wanderings, I had instinctively looked to women for passing friendship, laughter, and protection. Until then I had neatly rationalized racial aggression—as opposed to passive prejudice—as an all-male phenomenon (in itself a glaring piece of prejudice for which I apologize). I had concluded that racist attacks were made either in protection of territory, like wolves peeing around their home boundaries, or as a modern version of those bizarre initiation ceremonies so beloved of men throughout the ages. (Until very recently the elders of European tribes regularly required their young men to fight each other to the death, to prove their manhood.) In today's materialistic societies, so I reasoned, fortunate youths brandish jobs and possessions, not guns, as emblems of their maturity. A few of the less fortunate resort instead to gang warfare, football hooliganism, or ethnic violence to establish their position in the male pack. Almost without exception, my own assailants have been young men, moving in gangs, their aggression put on as much to impress their peers as to frighten and humiliate me. In all the years we've lived with other races, in Africa, Sri Lanka, East Asia, and Seychelles, I've only been made forcibly self-conscious of my color in the West Indies. It was a salutary lesson.

I returned from the market empty-handed. However, life is nothing if not for learning and that woman did teach me shopping habits which have stood me in good stead ever since. Now if I plan to shop frequently at a market, I first "case the joint." I study the assembled stallholders, and normally head for the one with the kindest face, though that is not invariably wise. In particular, beware of those dear little parchment-faced old ladies with the twinkly eyes. More often than not they are past mistresses at palming strangers off with rotten vegetables. The twinkle merely reflects the size of their most recent triumph. Once chosen, I stick by my greengrocer and, generally speaking, he or she sells me good-quality vegetables in return. Occasionally a real friendship develops, giving me a closer glimpse into another country's culture and customs. In Bequia much of that task fell to Ben.

Ben was an abandoned lad, in more ways than one. His parents had died a couple of years before, and he lived on the streets of Bequia, slept there too, and, like street kids everywhere, kept himself alive by pilfering. From his well-rounded figure I guessed he was pretty good at it despite being in frequent conflict with the police. We took Ben on—he was about thirteen then—to help us paint *Johanne,* but he never really fancied the work, and who could blame him. Up till then he had spent most of each day playing on the beach and swimming in the sea. And what, after all, were wages to a lad who for years had had everything he wanted for the taking? I think Ben stayed on with us because he hoped to hitch a lift to England—that is, until the day he and I got to talking about the world. Sitting together side by side, slapping white paint onto the underside of the hatch covers, Ben suddenly asked, "You got any police in England?"

Not thinking, I laughed, "More police than all the people in Bequia put together."

Poor Ben. His eyes, already big and brown, stretched wider still with the sheer horror of it. Soon after that he rejoined his mates, diving off the jetty and racing over the sands. He still called chirpily to us as he passed but he had no further wish to visit England.

We were not alone for long. A few days later Edward's attention was caught by an apparition walking slowly through the water toward us. Ken's long fair hair was held back with a bandanna, his beard curled golden to his naked chest, and his face was thin, aesthetic, Christ-like.

"Do ya need any crew?"

"Maybe."

"Where're you going?"

"We've got work to finish here, then we're heading down-islands to Grenada."

"Gee! That's where we want to go."

"Come aboard."

So began one of our most successful partnerships. Ken, once a drama teacher, had cut loose from the rat race and was working his way down through the Caribbean, playing his guitar in various tourist bars along the way. Lucky tourists—Ken was a most gifted musician. His girlfriend was an artist. Petite, with brown curly hair and fine, open features, Gail lived her life with a certain quiet intensity. When they joined us, Ken was mad about three things: boats, music, and Gail. Gail was mad about Ken. Edward and I became extremely fond of them both.

5. Careening and Crooks and the Concord Falls

THE FIRST CHORE we tackled with Ken and Gail was ballasting ship. Cargo boats sail best when carrying one-third of their normal load so, when converting a cargo boat to a pleasure craft, one weighs her down with that same one-third load, only this time it is in ballast, not merchandise. Cheap ballast is not easy to come by and *Johanne* would need sixteen tons of the stuff. But once again fortune blessed us: *Diligence* sailed into Bequia.

We first met John and his extremely leaky Brixham trawler, *Diligence,* in Antigua where we momentarily mistook her for the local fire ship, so ample were the jet of water issuing from her bilge pumps. By all accounts his trip down the islands had been even more diverting than ours. For a start, his crew were not your everyday, run-of-the-mill types: the *Sea Horse* thief and his moll had begged a passage south. John, after checking that they were not wanted by the police, and being one of the most compassionate of men, agreed to give them a break. He needed someone to man those bilge pumps.

In preparation for the voyage, John laid in several sacks of quick-setting cement. Moments before leaving Antigua he shoveled enough cement into *Diligence*'s holes to cut the leaks to something like manageable proportions. Then they dashed out to sea. As the quick-setting cement gradually washed away, so the thief and his girlfriend pumped harder and harder until, eventually, they reached the next island. There they anchored, slept, poured more cement, and plunged on.

Safely arrived in Bequia, the girlfriend declared herself pregnant. Furthermore, due to some rare kidney disease, such a pregnancy might, she claimed, prove fatal. Ever generous, John "lent" her the money for a one-way ticket to the States, sincerely hoping she would not come back. A week later she returned. In Antigua rumors about the thief had been rife. Some said that he was the man who, for a fee, had run the *Torrey Canyon* aground on the Isles of Scilly. Others had it that he had led the raid on Marseilles which freed Israeli landing craft after the French government banned their export. Some even went so far as to allege both stories were true. In the end even I was hard put not to feel a sneaking admiration for the weasely-faced little man.

Not long after her return to Bequia both girlfriend and thief disappeared. They repaid John's generosity by taking with them his passport, checkbook, and savings. In reality they were exactly what they appeared to be—scum.

Undaunted, John proposed to forge ahead with the little repair job he had planned for his seventy-foot *Diligence*. He would pop on an outside ballast keel, single-handedly. The fact that there was no slipway in Bequia did not phase him one bit. After all, as he so rightly pointed out, there was no need to have the whole boat out of the water, only the bottom of it. He would careen her; that is, lay her down on her side in the bay so that half the decks were under water but the keel was clear. Nelson had done it often enough, so why shouldn't he? First, though, he had to get rid of *Diligence's* ballast. Afterward he planned to restore the boat to her original use as a cargo vessel and so would not need the ballast again, which was where our good fortune came in. The ballast consisted of rusty lengths of ship's anchor chain, each link some ten inches long and each length weighing a hundred pounds. Dragging the unwieldy chunks out of *Diligence's* hold, Edward and Ken manhandled them onto a barge and from there lowered them into *Johanne*.

With *Diligence* emptied of ballast, John was ready to tackle the serious part of the job. Leading lines from the hounds high up on *Diligence's* mainmast to the barge floating on the water nearby, he heaved down until the mast lay horizontal across the barge's deck. The trawler's own buoyancy then lifted her keel clear of the water. *Diligence* was careened. From scraps of wood picked up off the beach, John built up a mold, a five-sided extension, like a giant, lidless coffin nailed onto the original, worm-eaten wood keel. Lengths of chain were laid out inside the "coffin" to give the new keel added weight, then John poured in cement. *Diligence* had a ballast keel.

Ken, meanwhile, had built a wooden casing at the aft end of the shortened hold to take *Johanne's* new ballast (with her relatively shallow draft there was no room to stow it in the usual place, under the floorboards). Ballast secured, we motored back to the center of Admiral's Bay and anchored.

Two nights later a considerate yachtsman rowed over to check that we had heard there was a hurricane warning out. We had not. In minutes the peace of that tropical evening was shattered by the caterwauling of a bunch of over-excited yachtsmen. Engines revved, husbands shouted, wives shouted back as second anchors splashed through inky waters and extra chain rattled out through hawse pipes and fairleads. Those that relished the buzz of adrenaline in their veins were having a ball. Many of us were not. Torches flashed and searchlights scanned the shore for distance off. Then, with everything battened down, silence tiptoed back across the bay. This time, though, it was a taut and anxious silence. Invisible in the darkness, everyone waited—for about twelve hours.

It was around mid-morning that the wind finally raised its voice and howled. Nipping up the saloon ladder to take a look outside, I was rewarded with a most remarkable sight. Our eleven-foot, double-skinned, fiberglass dinghy had changed its mode of propulsion. That banshee wind had lifted it bodily into the air above *Johanne*'s bulwarks. The dinghy was flying at the end of its stout painter, four feet above the sea. Across the bay driving rain lashed the water to a frenzy, bouncing circlets of spray surrounded each yacht, and a white mist hung over everything like an impressionist painting of *Storm at Sea*. Ashore the damage was minor. Some roofs had blown off and a good number of trees had blown down but, we were assured, we had seen only the outer edge of the hurricane. I promptly hoped I'd never see one's center.

Sea wanderers seldom stay put for long and, with a hurricane just passed, it seemed a good moment to thank the Bequians for all their hard work and move on. We had a lot to be grateful for. Experts had caulked *Johanne*'s topsides and stitched her three trim sails. A new, waterproof cover protected the cargo hatches and *Johanne* herself was safely ballasted down for the trip south through the Grenadines to Grenada—and another slipping.

Yes. Well. You see, the trouble was that all the good caulking done to the topsides in Bequia had disturbed the caulking done to the bottom in Antigua. *Johanne* was leaking again. Not that that bothered us much as we got under way. An offshore breeze dictated the order of action. First remove the restraining gaskets from *Johanne*'s three sails, leaving them ready for instant hoisting. Next, haul up the anchor. Last, working from bow to stern, raise all sail.

Within seconds of the anchor breaking free, Ken had the triangular staysail up and sheeted over to starboard. The breeze caught the sail. *Johanne*'s bow paid off and we were away, heading for the harbor entrance. "Up main" was never quite such a painless operation as "up staysail." *Johanne* has no newfangled winches. We don't want newfangled winches—they wouldn't be in keeping with her history. Instead we rely on the multiplying power of her traditional wooden pulleys. The two double blocks on the throat halyard not only hoist the mast end of the sail's wooden gaff but also quadruple our pulling power, as do the four single blocks on the peak halyard, which hauls up the gaff's outer end. Edward and I, alone, are quite capable of raising the 750 square feet of heavy canvas—if we have to. But now it was Ken who manned the peak halyard while Gail and I womanned the throat. Conscious of Edward's eye upon us, we took care to keep the gaff horizontal as we hauled the spar and canvas skyward. Once raised, it took all three of us—me tailing, Ken and Gail heaving—to swig up the gaff's peak and so pull the mainsail's clothes taut. After that, setting the 300 square feet of Dacron mizzen was simple. Work done, we sat back and admired it. For the first time since we bought her, *Johanne* had three sails set. They might look a bit odd, two tan sails either end with an aging white canvas one in the middle, but they were full and drawing. *Johanne Regina* was truly under sail.

Edward has always ranked the Grenadines among his favorite cruising grounds. A straggle of some thirty-two, mainly uninhabited little islands, tourism had had scant impact on them. Even that coral wonderland, Tobago Cays, was all but deserted when we dropped anchor off its outer rim. Moments later towels, picnic, crew, and swim things piled into the dinghy. We were off, powered by yet another new toy, a 6-hp outboard. By shaving as close to the shore as he dared, Edward evaded the worst of the current, boiling out between the atolls, and set course for a distant cay.

Lolling about on beaches can be incredibly tedious, but, what with exploring the atolls, building sandcastles, and sharing in Katy's wonder as we snorkled over a fantasia of gleaming fish and feathery coral, the hours sped by. It seemed no time at all before we were tumbling back into the dinghy and heading home. Tropical nights fall fast, and no one wanted to be caught on the reefs after dark. "Hey! Come on! We've got a fair wind, let's sail!" cried Edward. "Up towels!" and up they went. Held by eager hands top and bottom, three towels spread like Technicolored squaresails to the wind. With an oar rigged in the stern for steering and with nothing but towel power and current to drive us, we rollicked home, singing and laughing as we skimmed past two islands to come right alongside *Johanne*. "Down towels!" was met with a split-second response: our arms couldn't hold them up an instant longer.

Over the past few months *Johanne*'s bilges had grown a great deal sweeter, which wasn't altogether surprising. They must have filtered most of the Caribbean through them by then. After giving one last scrub to *Johanne*'s interior, Gail and I spruced everything up with a fresh coat of white paint. Switching our attention to the deck, we made a splendid discovery: a cluster of barnacles, witness to *Johanne*'s days as a wreck, was still clinging firmly to her wooden stanchions. Those, we decreed, must be preserved for posterity.

While Gail and I wielded soapsuds and paint, Ken and Edward worked on the set of *Johanne*'s misshapen old jib. First they re-cut its cloth and then, with sailmaker's palm and beeswaxed thread, they re-stitched it by hand. *Johanne* could once again boast a full suit of working canvas. Her forecabin, too, was progressing nicely. Along with three full-length bunks, its own heads and washbowl, it now had a white-painted bulkhead to divide it from the hold. The hold itself remained totally chaotic and in the saloon, Edward and I still slept on a mattress on the floor while Katy bedded down on top of a wooden cargo pallet. The aft cabin, eventually destined to be our sleeping quarters, served as a temporary ship's galley. When at sea, Gail and I put the primus stove in a galvanized bucket and suspended it from the deckhead on a rope. The theory was that the bucket, plus stove and saucepan, would then swing as the ship rolled. In practice all that happened was that the stove went out, so we took turns crouching on the cabin sole, clutching the saucepan and stove together, waiting impatiently for dinner to cook.

What rare good fortune sent us Ken and Gail as crew? Who else would have coped so cheerfully with such discomfort? Without doubt they were among the easiest, dearest people we have ever lived with. If one had to nitpick and find fault then one could, I suppose, point to food as our only slight cause of conflict. We had agreed early on that I would cook lunch and Gail supper. (That way I had plenty of time for cuddles and stories with Katy before popping her to bed.) Aha! you say, such sexist cooking arrangements must inevitably lead to friction. Not a bit. The way I see it, there are jobs on boats that no one particularly enjoys: fixing engines and cleaning bilges, cooking meals and scrubbing clothes. Such jobs should be allocated according to one's ability to do them. Neither Gail nor I could fix engines. Neither Gail nor I wanted to learn how to fix engines, either. And anyway, our problem arose not from the cooking itself but from what was cooked. I have nothing against vegetarians, be they macrobiotic, vegan, or anything else, but catering to both herbivores and carnivores at one and the same time does complicate the "simple life," especially on a boat where life is *so* simple that there's only one kerosene burner on which to whip up three-course meals for five people. In the end I learned to cook all the vegetables first, serve up Ken and Gail's, and then add our meat or fish.

Supper cooked and eaten, the best part of our days with Ken and

Gail began. We scattered mattresses on the cargo hatch, slung a hurricane lamp under the boom, and then lazed back, relaxing in its warm yellow glow waiting for Ken to begin. As we murmured to each other of this and that, Ken would pick up his guitar and, softly, dreamily, send his music winging out across the night-black water to the distant stars. Those were some of the happiest days of my life.

St. George's, capital of Grenada, is arguably the prettiest town in the Caribbean. Set on a hillside, its red-roofed, whitewashed houses peek from behind lush green vegetation at the volcanic blue waters of St. George's Bay. Standing at its northern end, the Carenage, or waterfront, fairly whirs with life. Trading schooners, their paintwork bright as bathtub toys, unload at the town quay; shops and warehouses, in whites and greens, line the waterfront; and fishing boats pull in and out all day long.

Three-quarters of a mile away, on the south side of St. George's Bay, lies a lagoon, its entrance dredged to take yachts. Here Grenada Yacht Services has its pontoons and slipway and there Edward went, all eagerness, to ask about slipping. Half an hour later he returned, his usual enthusiasm sadly dashed. Certainly the G.Y.S. slipway could take *Johanne;* it could take boats weighing as much as 200 tons. The drawback was that their charges had been designed along equally hefty lines, and, on top of that, the slipway's management showed not the slightest interest in *Johanne* or her restoration. Edward determined, leak or no leak, to take her right back to Antigua. At least there she could be sure of expert workmen and a constructive welcome.

Grenada had been meant to mark the parting of the ways for us. Originally, Ken and Gail had shipped aboard *Johanne* only because she was traveling south. Though their long-term plans lay rooted in a tour of Latin America, it did seem stupid to say goodbye when we were all having such a good time together. So we didn't say goodbye; instead those two free spirits offered to sail all the way back to Antigua with us.

Before we could move at all, however, there was (as always!) work to be done. Day in and day out we labored. The term "workaholic" was tailor-made for Ken and Edward. For weeks those two men cunningly avoided taking even one day off work to tour the island. In the end Gail and I mutinied. If the men could not bear to tear themselves away from *Johanne* for one single day, we women would go alone. Grenada was just then at a difficult stage in her development. After months of fighting between pro- and anti-independence factions Giery and independence had won, but not before the tourists, mainstay of the island's

economy, had taken fright and fled. We ourselves were strongly advised
to give Grenada a miss, but, once there, we couldn't have felt more
welcome.

After hitching a lift into town, we headed for the open-air market
and bus terminal. We could barely move, the square was so tightly
packed with stalls and people. Women in cheerful cotton frocks were
selling everything from passion fruit, oranges, and avocados to tumeric
and ginger, cinnamon, cloves, and allspice. One sniff was all you needed
to know why Grenada is called the spice basket of the Caribbean.

Strictly speaking, most of the vehicles drawn up at the bus stand
were not buses at all. They were open-sided lorries converted into passenger carriers by the simple addition of rows of wooden benches, and
each bus was gaily painted in its own individual style. Many bore deco-
rative signs, ringed with flowers and inscribed with whimsical slogans
such as "High Hopes," "Why Worry," and "Just Passin' Thru."

By the time we tracked it down, the truck going past the Concord
Falls was full. We stood back, resigning ourselves to a long wait. But
then a Grenadian man climbed down and absolutely insisted that we
take his place. After much laughter and shifting of backsides, the rest of
the passengers managed to inch up enough to fit us all aboard. There
followed a hair-raising trip up narrow mountainous roads, bordered by
unguarded precipices which fell clear away to give glimpses of the blue
Caribbean far below.

The bus driver pulled to the side of the road and called out for us to
get off—this was the stop for Concord Falls. From nowhere a small boy
materialized and appointed himself our guide and guardian. Paul was a
beautiful lad, proud and eager to show us his country's plants. Here
were nutmeg trees rising eighty feet into the sky. Growing wild in Grenada's humid highlands, each one could produce 5,000 nutmegs a year.
The fruits first look like small apricots dangling at the end of long,
slender twigs. Then they burst open, horse-chestnut fashion, to expose a
hard, mottled-brown nutmeg within. Clinging around each nut a second spice lies hidden: the crimson, flat-veined latticework of mace. It
takes over thirty nutmegs to produce one single ounce of mace.

Presenting each of us with a nutmeg, Paul led on along the winding
path in search of cocoa trees. Much smaller than the nutmeg, the tropical cocoa tree is perversely allergic to sunshine and so will prosper only
in taller trees' shade. Equally peculiar is the way it grows its pods—not
on branches or twigs like any normal, self-respecting tree, but straight
out of its trunk. About seven inches long, the pods look like small,
wizened cantaloupe melons and come in a variety of yellows, pinks, and
purples. Inside each pod beautiful, shiny brown cocoa beans nestle in

soft white pith. Katy and I took some beans home, full of loving intentions to make a cup of hot chocolate for Edward. I should have known better. All my educational experiments were doomed to failure and this was no exception. The resulting liquid looked like dirty drain water and, if anything, tasted worse. Only later did we discover that cocoa beans, like their parent trees, are mightily fastidious. They demand days of attention, drying and fermenting, before you can hope to cajole them into producing a cup of hot cocoa.

We must have climbed for an hour or more before we reached the clearing around Concord Falls. Today I would go ten times the distance to touch again the mystery of that place. A strange, green, underwater magic it was, as if we stood on the floor of a vast, dimly lit cavern hidden deep inside the earth. All around us towered the rain forest while, far above, the outside world lived on, glimpsed only through a tiny window of sunlight and blue sky. Here and there below, amid the dark battleground of shadowed plants and strangling linea vines, thin shafts of sunlight shot through the forest leaves to lance the gloom with slender rods of gold. Ahead the famous waters of the Falls dropped fifty feet before they vanished, swallowed by a deep and misty rock pool.

A swim in the icy pool, a picnic with Paul on the sunbaked rocks, and it was time to leave. Our day of mutiny was over but its memory is locked up, safe forever.

6. Hurricane Gertrude

THERE'S A jolly little ditty bandied around the West Indies that goes

June too soon
July stand by
August if you must
September remember!
October all over.

It refers to hurricanes.

You might say we were asking for trouble, flouting that ditty, but I reckoned two miserable little days couldn't make that much difference. I also reckoned that if we set sail from Grenada on September 28th we'd take only three days to reach Antigua. On both counts I was wrong.

Our troubles began with the G.M. In the time since Mrs. Mathews had installed the reconditioned engine it had received some pretty harsh treatment. Once back in Antigua Edward planned to strip the whole thing right down. But we weren't in Antigua. We were twelve hours out from Grenada when the G.M., working at that moment in one of its most important modes, pumping out the bilges, gave off a muffled explosion, instantly followed by a nasty swooshing sound, and then stopped dead. A dash below revealed an appalling mess. Tracing back along the line of disaster, Edward diagnosed the cause. At some time the carbon seal for the engine's freshwater cooling system had begun to disintegrate. Ever efficient, G.M.s provide a special outlet pipe for just such an eventuality and, like a child waving its hand in class, the dripping pipe is supposed to catch the engineer's eye, warning him to change the seal. Unfortunately a previous crew member, noticing those strange drips of water, misread the signal. He shoved a large plug of cement right up the hole. No doubt the results seemed satisfactory to him—the water stopped dripping. But behind the cement the carbon water seal gradually collapsed. The cooling water worked its way out of the cooling system and into the engine. At dawn on September 29th, the G.M. came to a boil and blew off its oil-filler cap. The ensuing geyser of watery oil, or oily water, was impressive. And we were without an engine.

Around noon that day the wind picked up. Nice, you might think, just what a heavy sailing boat minus a motor needs. Not *Johanne*. For a start, the top quarter of her mizzenmast was rotten; too much strain and it might fall right off. We lowered the gaff-mizzensail, hoisting instead a small triangle of cloth, sufficient to ease *Johanne*'s steering. And what about her rusty main shrouds? That wind was really blowing now and we couldn't lower them. Almost before I'd thought the thought, the three hard-pressed windward shrouds started to snap like dried spaghetti. Well, okay, perhaps not quite. Only one snapped right in two. The others stayed linked together, but only by a couple of naked strands of wire. To take the strain off the broken windward shrouds, Edward wore ship (with no proper mizzen we could not possibly tack). *Johanne* then pointed south, 180 degrees off course, while Ken attempted a repair.

After many years of cruising in remote places, Edward is an inveterate horder of "Things that May Be Useful Sometime." With *Johanne*'s empty hold at his disposal, his compulsion had been given free rein. Among the goodies he had already squirreled below was a large quantity of old rigging wire handed down to us by a thoughtful yachtsman. No need to wait for "sometime," that wire was going to come in mighty handy right away. Wielding a cold chisel, Ken cut off six-foot lengths of spare rigging wire to make "splints" for the broken shrouds. As *Johanne* wallowed in mounting seas, he stood, precariously balanced on the bulwark capping, and clamped old and "new" wires together with bulldog clips. That done, he reinforced the shrouds on the other side before they too could part.

By the time the job was finished, *Johanne* had sagged far to the south, out of sight of land. Idly, someone tuned in to the local radio station. At once the rising wind and seas were explained: Hurricane Gertrude was on her way. West Indian hurricanes are pretty predictable creatures. Once they hit the islands they nearly always curve north. Knowing this, Edward continued to sail south, biding his time until Gertrude had cleared the area. But he hadn't reckoned with Gertrude. Apart from everything else, the capricious lady created a deafening static on the six-inch transistor that had, for the past fifteen years, served Edward as his only shipboard radio. Kneeling around it as if it were some powerful oracle, we concentrated all our powers on disentangling Gertrude's position and projected path from the incessant hisses and crackles. And each of us disentangled something different. So, at the next forecast, we made individual notes, and Edward acted on the majority interpretation. This was all frightfully democratic, but possibly not the most scientific way to dodge hurricanes. According to the latest vote Gertrude was stationary, which meant that we might in fact be traveling toward her. At the next news flash she was heading west—straight toward us.

Edward turned north.

I must confess that, although I'm a firm believer in the purity, nay the aesthetic perfection, of sail, I did wish at that moment that I could hear the old G.M. screaming round. Though we had labored hard over the past six months, *Johanne* was not yet ready for a voyage under sail alone, and certainly not one through a hurricane. Quite apart from her main shrouds snapping and that the top of her mizzenmast was likely to fall off, she then had only one headsail where today she carries three. Severely low on sails, she was also severely leaking.

The G.M. and its bilge pump were *hors de combat.* Gasoline to run the Briggs and Stratton was at a premium (dangerously flammable, Edward kept the supply of gas on *Johanne* to a minimum). This left us with the Whale Gusher hand pump, and even that had its drawbacks. It had come supplied with the short, foot-long handle. Wanting the pump mobile, Edward mounted it on a baseboard and kept it on the engine room sole (floor). Pumping out by hand was at the best of times hilarious, and at the worst, backbreaking. These were not the best of times. Bent almost double, clasping the short pump handle between hands and knees, one had, with weird and wonderful gyrations of buttocks and thighs, to build up a pumping rhythm. It soon turned into a competition—who could pump the most strokes before collapsing from exhaustion, backache, blisters, or all three. I seem to remember that Gail was the overall winner with a total, in one single session, of somewhere above the 2,000 mark. Yes, *Johanne* was suffering: a nasty recurrence of rising damp and at a most inconvenient time.

By now a touch of anxiety had infiltrated the female ranks of *Johanne*'s crew. Gail and I took a crash course in carpentry. The companionway down to the aft cabin had no outer door. There was one into the cabin itself, but that would not stop heavy seas from pouring over the stern and cascading down the steps and into the bilge. *Johanne* had enough water down there already. Keeping one eye on the already rising swell, we sawed and we hammered. We chopped two long strips off an old cargo pallet and nailed them on either side of the entrance to form vertical slots. Next came a set of fashionboards to slide down into the slots. We hoped that these, when dropped in place, would act like a wall to keep the water out.

And then it was "October all over." Right on cue, capricious Gertrude took herself off to the north where she should have gone in the first place, leaving *Johanne* pitching about in the middle of the Caribbean Sea and me digesting yet another important lesson: however short the intended voyage, always take along plenty of food. We had gallons of spare drinking water, but little to eat. By the sixth day at sea our culinary imaginations were stretched to the limit. There really is only so much you can do with a combination of rice, dried peas, dried milk, and flour. We did it three times a day.

Katy, meanwhile, had proved conclusively that not even the traditional three days at sea were going to sprout in her a sturdy pair of sea legs. Plying her with sips of water, it was a constant struggle to replace her body fluids. Severe dehydration is a real danger in small, seasick children. If I'd known about it at the time, I would have mixed Katy a cocktail: to each two pints of water add four teaspoons of sugar, one teaspoon of salt, and one teaspoon of bicarbonate of soda. Used worldwide, this simple rehydration therapy has saved the lives of countless dehydration and diahrrea victims.

What a relief it is to know that nothing lasts forever. First Gertrude's swells dropped and then the fluffy trade-wind clouds flocked back to browse on the horizon and we knew for certain all was well.

"Hey! Look at this! Killer whales!" In seconds *Johanne*'s crew members were hanging, breath held, over her bulwarks. Gail was right. Two of the impressive beasts were pacing effortlessly beside us. Some twenty-five feet long, they rolled on their sides, staring up at us with what seemed like little gourmets' eyes. We stared back in sheer wonder at their markings. The pure white of their underbellies flowed from chin to tail before curling up, like crested waves, to break the shiny blackness of their backs. Voracious carnivores, killer whales hunt in packs like wolves and attack not only seals, dolphins, and penguins but also baleen whales twice their size. One observer claimed to have found the remains of thirteen porpoises and fourteen seals in the stomach of a single killer whale. As they swam beside us, our two shrilled to each other in high-pitched voices. Maybe they were checking us out as a possible dessert. If so, they must have found us wanting, for after a short time they swam gracefully off.

We were ten days out from Grenada (and Kate was still sick) when a faint, dark haze of land showed up ahead. The fact that it was Nevis and not Antigua mattered not a jot—by then any old island would have done. Fluky headwinds, whispering under the island's lee, meant that *Johanne* took an hour to make up the coast to Charlestown. There, before a setting sun, we let go the anchor in water so clear that we could see the hook dig into the sand forty feet below. As the chain rattled out, all our tension ebbed away. We relaxed. We were safe.

Six hours later an earthquake shocked the Caribbean. In Antigua buildings split apart. Off Nevis, *Johanne*'s hull shook from stem to stern. Streaking from our bunks we watched in awe as, all around us, the black seas bubbled like a witches' cauldron. Next morning we treated ourselves to one long lie-in. We needed it.

Shortly before noon, Ken rowed us all ashore to comb the town for food: fresh, succulent food. We had vowed never again to live on rice and dried peas and dried milk. Our stores bought and a slap-up lunch eaten, Katy and I went off to the beach to play, to twist and twirl, giggle and squeal as we chased each other helter-skelter across the empty sands that rimmed the bay. To feel the rough grains tickling the bare soles of our feet and squishing up, cold and damp, between our toes was wonderful. Already, at least to a mother's over-anxious eye, Kate's wasted, seasick body was rejuvenating.

Having failed to make Antigua on the way north it now lay thirty-five miles to the east, directly to windward. So we would first sail southeast to Guadeloupe, then turn north, when, close-hauled, we might with luck make English Harbor in one tack.

Dawn found Gail and me poised on the foredeck, winch handles at the ready. Womanpower was about to swing into action. The men insisted it was good for our figures, all that stooping and straightening as we turned the heavy handles and watched the rusty chain come in, two miserly links to each reluctant turn of the handle (reluctant because, at that stage, we still hadn't discovered that the brake was on). Thank goodness the new CQR anchor was half the weight of the old Fisherman. With Ken's help, we catted (or stowed) it and then turned to hoist the sails. And lo, misfortune struck again, this time in the form of a thunderbolt straight from heaven. As I hauled mightily on the main peak halyard, an eye bolt parted at the top of the mast and a large wooden block sizzled down the freed line—slap into my face. Not only did it hurt like hell, but I lost a contact lens. We never did find the lens but we did turn back to Charlestown. *Johanna*'s block had to be replaced.

By then I'd had enough. Of adventure, travel, freedom, the simple life. You name it, I'd had it—at least until the next fair wind blew. You see, I was never cut out to be an adventurer. By the time I was twenty-one, I'd already failed to be an actress and a nurse and was, instead, fully occupied with being a wreck—both mental and physical. (The former due to an overdeveloped sense of inadequacy, the latter to the

unvarying monotony of pain given off by a kinked-up nerve.) I had
concluded that the whole business of living was a dead loss.

For more than a year I never so much as glanced at a newspaper.
But one day something, call it fate—it certainly wasn't interest—drove
me to pick up a discarded copy of the *Sunday Express.* I remember
flicking through the pages, reading nothing, and wondering why the
heck I was looking at it at all, when out from the newsprint leaped a
headline:

"Home Is a Lone Boat for Edward Allcard." Underneath ran the
story of a man who, sailing the world all alone, was daring to live out his
dreams. "Of course," said the man, "the ideal would be to [meet] a girl
with the same idea." A half-joking remark—I'm quite sure Edward had
not the slightest intention of taking anyone with him. He prized his
solitude far too much. But to me it was no joke. I sat down to write the
first fan letter of my life. I told the man that I, too, could think of
nothing more fabulous than to sail away into the pale blue yonder, but
that there was this one slight snag. I happened to be locked up in a
loony bin. Would he mind waiting a couple of months until they set me
free? Honesty further compelled me to point out that I couldn't actually
sail or cook and wasn't much to look at either.

Why the good man did not flee in terror I'll never know. Mainly, I
suppose, because he was a good man, but perhaps, too, I had unintentionally piqued his curiosity. After all, it wasn't exactly your garden-
variety fan letter. Not the sort one receives every day of the week. When
Edward invited me out for a picnic on England's rolling Downs he was
searching neither for crew nor for romance, but simply hoping that a
picnic might cheer the poor girl up. And so we met, and ate our picnic,
and walked, and talked, and some weeks later fell in love. And later still
we sailed away together into the pale blue yonder. If I was a sea gypsy,
then for sure I had no one to blame but myself—and fate.

Jury-rigging the "thunderbolt" peak block on a chain around the
masthead, we rehoisted the mainsail and reached the lee of France's
Guadeloupe Island without further incident. Indeed, to be honest, I'll
admit that we had a truly glorious sail. Wafted onward by the gracious
trade winds, *Johanne* skimmed across the sea under cloudless blue
skies. The past was forgotten. Katy wasn't sick and I was back on cloud
nine.

That night we hovered off the south end of Guadeloupe, drifting
along before the scented land breezes of a place that the Caribs had
called Karukera, or Island of Beautiful Waters. When Columbus, an
indefatigable claimer and namer of islands, came along, he naturally

changed all that, or at any rate he thought he did. He renamed the island Santa Maria de Guadeloupe de Estremadura—after one of his favorite Spanish monastries, you understand. (For fairly obvious reasons the name was later shortened to Guadeloupe.) But that word "Guadeloupe" has an interesting origin of its own. It is thought to come from a Moorish Arabic word, *Oued-el-Houb,* which means River of Love—not so far removed from the Caribs' Beautiful Waters after all.

At dawn the wind hardened, pushing us north, close-hauled, for Antigua. We must have sighted them first at around 8 A.M. In truth we could hardly miss them as they howled around *Johanne* with great shouts and whoops before hurtling northward with another roar of macho power: two young Frenchmen and a brand new speedboat.

"I suspect they may reach Deshaies Bay before us," said Edward, referring to the bay at the north end of Guadeloupe where Club Med had its home. "Still, you never know. Let's not forget the tortoise and the hare," and a whimsical, half-hopeful smile touched his lips.

Late that afternoon Gail saw a red speck toward the western horizon. Edward pulled out the binoculars and looked again. Sure enough, a man was standing up in a speedboat violently signaling to us with a red shirt. Already the boat was four miles off shore and with the trade winds blowing them steadily west, they would have another thousand miles to go before they reached land. Edward altered course and, in a neat maneuver, brought *Johanne* close enough to the boat for us to heave-to and throw them a line. But tow line made fast, he did not immediately pull them alongside. There was still the affair of the morning to be settled. After a short pause Edward turned to them and said, *"Navigation à la voile, c'est plus lente—mais c'est plus sûr!"* (Navigation under sail is slower—but surer.) Having allowed this chastening homily to sink in, he invited them aboard and we crowded around to hear their tale. It started off as one of hunger—the two lads hadn't eaten for twenty hours—so I made soup. Worse was to follow. When their outboard broke its brand-new crankshaft, no fewer than four local fishing boats refused, point-blank, to rescue them. On board they had neither spare engine nor engine spares. They had no oars, no drinking water, nothing. Realizing their danger, the owner wanted to swim for help but his older cousin (in his mid-twenties) wisely stopped him. Being mountainous, Guadeloupe looked far closer to the speedboat than it really was.

Later the Frenchmen wrote in *Johanne*'s visitors' book "Nous pouvrons continuer à vivre grace à vous. Dieu se chargera des remerciements" (We continue to live thanks to you. God will reward you), an entry that made me pause and think. The timing had certainly been remarkable. If just one of our mishaps and delays had not occurred, we would not have been there to rescue them. The short tropical dusk was close at hand, there was no other boat in sight, and by dawn they would have drifted over the horizon. Maybe that block in my face really had been heaven-sent—at least for them.

As *Johanne* closed in on Deshaies Bay, Ken volunteered to tow the Frenchmen, plus their speedboat, ashore. Too far off the coast to anchor, and lacking the sailpower to beat up wind into the bay, we hove-to outside. Launching our own dinghy we loaded it with outboard and fuel and then, rather ostentatiously I thought, with enough fresh water to last Ken about twenty days at sea. (Oars were already in the dinghy, kept permanently lashed there for when the outboard failed or we wanted to use it as a lifeboat.)

The Frenchmen delivered and Ken and our dinghy safely back on board, Edward picked up our old course, north toward Antigua, and let all sails draw. Daybreak revealed a thin, dark line stretched right across our bows. Antigua. The wind strengthened, before long blowing at Force 5 to 6, and, with my heart pounding at my ribs, we hurtled through the rock-rimmed entrance to Freeman's Bay. Shooting between two moored yachts, Edward searched out a space big enough to take us, brought *Johanne* up into the wind, and, dropping the mainsail's peak, slowed up even more. Moments later the anchor chain chattered out from *Johanne*'s bow. She'd made it.

As we bustled around the deck making everything shipshape, Gail suddenly turned to me, her small, delicate hands held out for inspection. "Look!" she cried. "Are these the hands of an artist?" I looked, at hers and then at mine, larger but in the same interesting rugged state and ingrained with dirt. "And are these the hands of a nurse?" I wailed back, at which we promptly collapsed on the cabin top, overcome with helpless laughter.

Revitalized and somewhat chastened by our wanderings, Edward and I threw ourselves with even greater enthusiasm into *Johanne*'s restoration. All around us work cried out to be done: the engine had to be stripped, rusty rigging replaced, and *Johanne* slipped so as to cure that "weep" in her stern. Delight at getting our teeth into such positive work was tempered by the sadness of bidding goodbye to Ken and Gail. Parting, especially from those who become close friends, is for me one of the greatest drawbacks to a nomad's life, though in Ken and Gail's case letters were to keep us in touch for more than a decade.

During the weeks that followed, *Johanne* established herself as a temporary haven for impecunious young men. Travelers all, they wanted no more than food and a few nights' sleep before they moved on. John was different. When we first met him, he was in a fix. Stuck on a small boat with an impossible owner, John had no money, visa, or onward ticket. His tale, too, was cautionary.

Hungry for adventure, he had answered an advertisement in an English newspaper placed by a self-styled "admiral" who wanted crew to help sail his small yacht across the Atlantic. Three young men signed on, chipping in considerable sums of their own money to pay for supplies. At their first port of call all but John jumped ship. John was too decent; he wouldn't abandon an elderly man to cross the Atlantic alone, however impossible he might be. During the crossing, due entirely to the Admiral's incompetence, they ran out of cooking gas: no hot drinks, rice, or cooked vegetables. Fresh water, too, had to be rationed to one mug a day—for John, that is, not for the Admiral. Each morning while John stood by, dry-mouthed in the tropical heat, the Admiral drew fresh water for his shave.

Once aboard *Johanne* John quickly recovered his equilibrium, except for one odd quirk. On several occasions he begged me never to call him crew. "But John, what's wrong with being crew? Edward's crew. I'm crew. I'm even rather proud of being crew." It took some time for the preposterous truth to dawn. During all the weeks that those two men had struggled together to bring the small craft safely across the Atlantic, that petty little "admiral" had never once called John by his name. Instead, when he wished to speak to him, he had barked out the single epithet "Crew!"

From the moment we arrived back in Antigua, Edward concentrated all his energies on the G.M. From Holland came a flexible coupling for the propeller shaft, and from Miami a top overhaul kit, a freshwater pump, a drive shaft and coupling for the gearbox, and a 60-amp, 24-volt alternator for charging the new, 24-volt batteries. The trickiest part of the overhaul was to dismantle the reduction gear and fit it with new parts. That done, fixing the gearbox's oil leak was child's play. Edward simply cut an old chart into the shape required for a new gearbox gasket and pressed it into place. The gearbox never leaked again and, once the new water pump was installed and the top overhaul completed, the engine was leak-free too.

My chief amusement throughout this transformation came from hearing Edward's croaks of delight as, squatting froglike in the engine room, he got to know his G.M. What had once been reviled as an acursed and noisy monster was now revealed as a miracle of engineering design. Was it Mr. Gray Marine himself who dispensed with gaskets and incorporated the fuel pump into the injectors? Whoever was responsible, Edward was converted into an ardent G.M.-o-phile, though, to my mind, the engine's real miracle lay in the fact that the thing had run at all—what with a dynamo linked up back to front and replacement oil seals installed the wrong way around, not to mention handfuls of nuts and bolts, plus the dipstick, completely missing.

While Edward dwelt, a grease-black troglodyte, in *Johanne*'s bilges, John led an assault on the accommodations. (Along with other excellent qualities, John had recently qualified as a ship's carpenter.) Under his guiding hands the after end of the old cargo hold was transformed into a saloon and galley, with one corner partitioned off for "Katy's Little Cabin." Here, crowded tight around her four-foot bunk, were high-sided shelves overflowing with cars and Lego and cuddly toys. In the wooden partition to the saloon, a large rectangular hole served both as a "window" for light and air and as a miniature proscenium for finger-puppet shows. Every remaining inch was reserved for books—so many books that one visitor likened Kate's cabin to a space capsule for a small bookworm.

Opposite Kate's cabin John created the galley. There he mounted my precious new two-burner gas stove on swinging gimbles. Beside it a bar, with two handsome two-inch-thick planks for work tops, made the framework for pot and pan storage. We still lacked sinks and a dining table, but we could now sit guests on two temporary settees, one fore and aft and one athwartships.

All that concentrated effort called for the occasional day off, so one Sunday afternoon we motored out to Freeman's Bay and anchored. Half snoozing in the sun, I watched as a smart fiberglass yacht rounded the corner of Fort Barclay and made straight for *Johanne.* All aboard had clearly enjoyed a jolly good outing. One man had even taken to dancing on the foredeck, a sort of water ballet. He had a red light clasped in each hand and was languidly painting arcs across the sky. His rhythmic grace was enchanting to behold—until my sun-soaked brain came to with a start. Maybe those weren't psychedelic paintings after all. I looked again.

"Edward! That guy's not dancing, he's sinking! Look at the freeboard."

"Good God, so he is!"

Precious seconds were lost as we sifted alternatives. Should we offer them a tow, or perhaps load the Briggs and Stratton into the dinghy and row after them? They seemed to have no pump of their own. But no! The vital thing was to get the yacht on the slipway before she sank. For that we had to have David Simmons and, thank goodness, I'd spotted him earlier, picnicking on a nearby beach.

Edward, rowing like fury, went to warn him; David then leaped into his own dinghy and raced up the harbor after the stricken vessel. With barely an inch to spare, he hauled the yacht onto the cradle and pulled her partway up the slip, leaving several tons of bilge water to drain slowly away.

Not until the tension had eased did we wonder again at the outfit's singular lack of bailing. Even if the pump on the engine had quit, surely, with all those people on board, bailing by bucket would have helped. It turned out that the owners had been faced with a predicament far more awesome than a mere sinking. They had charterers aboard. And they weren't ordinary charterers either, but a group of international travel agents who had flown in especially to sample for themselves the delights of a carefree Caribbean cruise. Unwilling to hand such guests buckets, the owners had plied them with stiff whiskeys instead.

7. Re-rigging Ready for the Crossing

Rejuvenated, the G.M.'s next requirement was a sea trial, so we motored the twenty-five miles around to St. Johns where Edward hoped to cajole a friendly cargo captain into plucking out *Johanne*'s mizzenmast. Until the rot was cut off, no new shrouds could be fitted and "standing rigging" had, at long last, reached the top of the list of "Jobs to Be Done."

The engine ran like a dream, albeit still quite a noisy one and, soon after we arrived in St. Johns, Edward contacted the owner of a 140-foot coaster. As a Norwegian, Torstein Christiansen was only too happy to help an ex–Baltic trader in distress. Mooring alongside his smart *Maruka,* we watched, a mite apprehensively, as he gingerly lifted out *Johanne*'s old mizzen and laid it, still in one piece, along the side deck. John and Edward had to saw ten feet of rot off the top of the mast before they reached sound wood. Then, to kill off any remaining spores, they doused the next few feet in Solignum. By the time all the fittings had been repositioned farther down the mast another coastal craft had come in. Her West Indian skipper, Alfred Furlonge, manipulated his crane with marvelous precision as he lowered the mizzen back through its small deck hole and on down till the mast-foot rested firmly in its mast-step, six feet below.

Poor *Johanne;* that partially amputated mizzen made her look positively deformed. Poor Edward, too. Each time he rowed away from his beloved boat, he would rest a moment on his oars, his eyes softening as they caressed her shapely curves. Then, invariably, he would glance up at her masts and heave a sigh: "Pity about the mizzen."

If it had only been the rot from her mizzenmast that *Johanne* lost in St. Johns we'd have been well pleased. But one night thieves crept aboard and pinched the outboard too. Its loss was a constant irritation. Rowing ashore for spares and food wasted time, and wasted time was something we could not afford, any more than we could afford another outboard.

Rushed though we were, we did manage one celebration: we invited the Mathews family out for a last dish of tea on board the boat they had rescued from the harbor bottom. Mrs. Mathews arrived looking truly magnificent, probably the best-dressed visitor *Johanne* has ever entertained. A wide-brimmed hat of turquoise chiffon set off her warm, dark skin, while a matching chiffon frock enhanced an already regal bearing. Like a queen, too, she rallied our flagging spirits with glowing praise for the changes wrought upon *Johanne.* Mrs. Mathews was another person I would miss.

Not long after we returned to St. Johns, a local trading sloop sailed into Freeman's Bay. We stopped work to watch in admiration as the skipper neatly lowered first one sail and then the other before bringing his craft to a silent halt alongside *Johanne.* Our rigging wire had arrived, shipped in by sail from Puerto Rico. Galvanized and semi-flexible, it was 2¾ inches in circumference and came in a coil so heavy that we had to use *Johanne*'s cargo hoist to lift it on board. For protection, the manufacturers had dipped their wire in gallons of gunky crude oil, so, before we could lay a finger on it, we had to cover *Johanne*'s decks with lengths of old canvas. Edward, on the other hand, had to be stripped near naked so that, at the end of the day, he too could more easily be hosed down.

For the re-rigging itself, we invoked another ancient incantation:

> Worm and parcel with the lay
> Serve it up the other way

Thank goodness the grooves in *Johanne*'s wire were too small to worm, or fill up, with tarred marline (a sort of thick, tarry string), for that's a squint-eyed job if ever there was one. Instead, Edward launched right away into step two: parceling. This entailed wrapping narrow strips of cloth around every inch of *Johanne*'s 400 feet of shrouds, remembering all the while the old ditty's instruction to follow the lay, or directional twist, of the strands. Tedious? To my mind it was nothing when compared with serving. For that, one winds tarred marline around and around the outside of the parceled wire so that not one millimeter of the parceling can be seen, thus forming yet another protective layer between vulnerable wire and corrosive salt air.

Armed with a serving mallet (a cunning device which Edward had fashioned out of greenheart), plus a sack full of marline, Edward sat on the hatch cover and twirled and twirled his marline-loaded mallet around the parceled wire. At each turn the marline was pulled tight—and crude oil oozed out. The mess was quite awful yet Edward, ever a perfectionist, drew quiet satisfaction from doing the job well. In the end he had used three and a half miles of marline which, at 2¾ inches per turn, works out to 80,640 turns of the mallet. Edward reaped his reward when an aquaintance, Paul, a rigger by trade, congratulated him on being the first amateur he had ever seen parcel and serve shrouds correctly. With a yearly coat of waterproof Stockholm tar, *Johanne*'s galvanized shrouds remain like new. Galvanized rigging wire is half the price of stainless steel and, in many cases, more reliable. Being semi-flexible itself, it can withstand the constant flexing of mast and hull, which causes the more popular stainless-steel rigging wire to suffer invisible metal fatigue, with sometimes disastrous consequences.

Paul's presence in Antigua was a godsend. Parceling and serving are one thing, doing a good eye splice (a loop at the end of each shroud) in heavy rigging wire is quite another. In preparation, Edward clamped a plank from bulwark to bulwark across *Johanne*'s foredeck and then bolted Paul's mighty rigger's vise on top. The stage was set. Paul, the professional, stepped forward to take the lead, while other friends joined the cast as amateurs, partly from the kindness of their hearts and partly, I'm sure, from curiosity.

Splicing, a way of integrating one piece of line or wire into another, can be awkward enough when done with ordinary, three-strand rope; with wire it becomes ten times more difficult, especially when the wire has seven, not three, strands. In our case each strand was so tough that, after clamping the wire securely in the vise, a king-size marline spike and two men were required to pry the reluctant strands far enough apart to thread another strand between them.

And what filth! Crude oil got everywhere. When darkness fell, our blackened team of riggers merged into the night with only the occasional roll of a tired eyeball to show they were still there. That group of stalwarts worked on nonstop, except for refreshments, until three the next morning. By then all the shrouds' top eye splices were complete, ready to be hooked over the mastheads and slid securely down onto the hounds forty feet above the deck. One day we might have the money or skill to splice the bottom ends of the shrouds, too. For the moment we made do—bending the lower end of each shroud around the thimble of its rigging screw and then back on itself, Edward gripped the wire together with ubiquitous bulldog clips.

To preserve the forty-five-year-old rigging screws, I stuffed them full of thick, dark grease and then, after the rigging was set up (tightened to hold the masts firm and vertical between the shrouds), I sewed

canvas gaiters over the remaining, exposed threads so that they too
were protected from salt spray and corrosion. In a concluding gesture I
painted the gaiters glossy white to contrast with the black rigging
screws. Provided one ignored those terrible bulldog clips, the rigging
looked pretty good. *Johanne* was almost ready to face the Atlantic.

That realization brought us hard up against a question that had
been gnawing at the back of my mind ever since our trip north from
Grenada. What to do with Katy? Dared we take her with us? What if
the sea was rough all the way? Might she not die of seasickness and
dehydration before we reached England? Miserably, I concluded that
we couldn't risk it. Once that decision was made, my parents, as always,
came to our rescue. They would join *Johanne* for a Caribbean cruise
during which Katy would get to know them again. Later, all three
would fly back to England and I would stick with *Johanne*. If I didn't,
then she, like *Sea Wanderer* before her, would become nothing more
than "Edward's boat," a place Katy and I visited between his voyages.
She would never be the family home I longed for and that Katy and I
both lacked.

Work on *Johanne* reached fever pitch. Not only must the old girl be
sound enough to cross the Atlantic, she now had to be habitable as well.
Investing in a secondhand, and idiosyncratic, treadle sewing machine—
it skipped whole batches of stitches at whim—I plunged into my first
venture in soft furnishings. Unable to resist, I came home from St.
Johns weighed down with yards of a flamboyant plaid in bright orange,
gray, and yellow—colors fit to lighten any saloon and a perfect match
for the rich, homey pine of *Johanne*'s bar and bulkhead. (As it turned
out, I wasn't the only one who fancied that material. Next time I went
to town I found all the shop assistants in the supermarket neatly uni-
formed in my plaid cushion covers.)

In honor of our distinguished visitors, *Johanne*'s aft cabin was to be
converted from temporary, grungy galley to luxurious master cabin—in
about three days flat. Once, in the Seychelles, I had been deeply impressed by the interior of a millionaire's yacht for there, right in the
middle of his palatial cabin, stood a king-sized four-poster bed.
Granted, there was no way one could call our cabin "palatial," but I
was determined nonetheless to have at least a whiff of that remembered
luxury. And Edward, dear chap, did his best to oblige. Lacking the
space for a four-poster he offered me a one-and-a-half-poster instead.
(The half post backs onto a bulkhead.) Well satisfied—after all, who
else do you know with a one-and-a-half-poster bed?—I whipped up a
valance in maroon-and-gold Regency stripe and strung it high between
the posts above the matching Regency-stripe bedspread. But even these

touches could not disguise the fact that, also due to lack of space, our one-and-a-half-poster bunk was really only wide enough for one and a half people. But then, we'd done our best and, as John hammered the last bunk board in place, we summoned a taxi and rushed off to the airport for a grand reunion.

We must have been about halfway there when I was overwhelmed by a fit of panic. How would my parents cope? Maybe my letters home had rather overdone the *"Johanne Regina,* Dream Come True" bit. Had I remembered, for instance, to mention the bugs? The cockroaches in particular were an embarrassment. During our stay in St. Johns they had flown back in force, to take up residence around the old galley, aft, where the new cabin now was, the cabin which, in honor of my parents, we had euphemistically christened the Great Cabin Aft. Try as I might, I had singularly failed to persuade those bugs to move forward to the saloon. As usual, I shouldn't have worried. My mother, game to the end, took a pragmatic view of both the narrow bunk and the roaches. (Her loathing for bugs is even greater than mine.) In the middle of her first night aboard her daughter's sixty-nine-foot luxury yacht, she took up her bed (or anyway her mattress) and walked on deck where she slept alfresco and bug-free for the rest of their stay.

Pa was happy as a sandboy. Not only had he always loved boats and the sea, but he was researching a book about a remarkable seafaring ancestor of his, Joe King. Joe, a Portuguese, had served for many years as Horatio Nelson's bos'n. And as Nelson, and therefore Joe, had spent four years in and around Antigua, Pa anticipated a bonanza.

He hadn't been on the island twenty-four hours before he had us all out on a family expedition to Shirley Heights where, in 1787, the British garrison first built defensive positions overlooking English Harbor. Nearby lay a military graveyard littered with desecrated tombs including one belonging to a British gunner. This called for action (my father was himself a gunner). In no time, with his infectious zest for life, he had dragooned the dockyard supervisor into finding a Land Rover, cement, trowels, and jerricans of water. Then the two of them headed into the hills where they spent a happy afternoon repairing the tombs of soldiers who had died two hundred years before—not from bullets received in battle but from the terrible fevers of the day. Of some 10,000 British servicemen shipped out to the West Indies in 1793, only some 500 returned alive. Though a few did die in action, the vast majority were carried off by the scurges of malaria, yellow fever, and dysentery. Not till 1897 did doctors realize that malaria was spread by mosquitoes. For the previous hundred years malaria was thought to be caused by the bad air (or *mal air,* as the French called it) of the shore. By 1808,

British navy regulations required all seamen to drink "2 drachms of bark in half a gill of sound wine" both before and after a trip ashore. The bark was quinine.

After two shore expeditions of our own, it was time for *Johanne* to show her paces. Not only would my parents be able to see her at her most bewitching but we might also solve the delicate question of the leak. *Johanne* was slowly sinking. Naturally we didn't want to bother our loved ones with such mundane details, especially as they knew she'd shortly be carrying us across the Atlantic. If we could just start the main engine, then there was a chance the bilge pump would pick up without being primed and they would be none the wiser. We were in luck. As we motored slowly out through the crowded anchorage I heard, over the G.M.'s familiar call, that sudden, telltale swoosh of bilge water hitting Caribbean Sea. With the bilges dry, we invited my father to take the helm and John, Edward, and I went forward to haul proudly on the main halyards. Now *Johanne* would really prove herself. The results were unexpected. Mum gave a suppressed shriek and pointed.

"Look! Look! A mouse!" Alas, there was no denying it. He had scuttled along the side deck right past her feet. Unknown to us, the little fellow had taken up residence inside the stowed mainsail. From then on, each time we hoisted the sail, out he shot. First he scrambled, panic-stricken, up the sail, then, turning tail, went scampering helter-skelter down the mast to the deck and away. An attractive little chap with fawn fur, he must have sneaked aboard when *Johanne* was alongside the dock. The mystery was, where did he go when the main was hoisted?

The lack of outboard was a curse. With six people to ferry about, it prevented us from fully exploring the creeks and inlets that abound along Antigua's indented coast. We did manage to get to Made Island where we lunched on raw sea urchins gathered off the island's dead coral. Later we sailed to Halcyon Cove and anchored off the Halcyon Hotel. There, as a treat for Katy and her close buddy Lee, we hired a pedalo, and suffered our one and only threat of blackmail. A yachting friend spied us as, blown up like a family of lobsters in bright-orange life jackets, we waited to embark on our perilous voyage. Surmising that this was the first time Edward had donned a life jacket in his life, she came tearing across the beach, camera in air, yelling "Blackmail! Blackmail! What will you pay me not to publish?" Rina was one of English Harbor's favorite characters—and that in a place well known for its eccentrics. People like the charming American who had ordered a suit of multicolored sails from a hang-gliding firm and planned to paint a dragon on his anti-fouling so that, as his yacht rose and fell in the waves, the dragon would look like a sea monster on the move. All this cost money and when the kitty got low, which was quite often, he used to row over to us to sell another pig or two of his lead ballast. Then there was an amazing man who, in middle age and without any fanfare, had rowed single-handedly across the Atlantic. He arrived, exhausted, in English Harbor and pulled into the nearest jetty. "Sorry sir. This is a hotel jetty, you can't tie up here." "Not even for a short time? I'm rather tired. I've rowed quite a long way." "Where have you come from?" "Falmouth." It was just his bad luck that Falmouth was the name of the next bay to English Harbor. Once he made it clear that he meant Falmouth, England, the hotel gave him a right royal welcome but, a week later, he left for the States; still rowing.

Single-handers were almost two a penny in the Dockyard. There was the Communist single-hander who had a Maoist calendar depicting "the happy masses" hanging in his saloon and the mathematician single-hander who, seeing the calendar, quietly remarked, "What a shame. All those people and not one of them allowed a yacht." And there was Don Riddler with his brave twenty-six-foot yacht, *Eric the Red,* a boat which had cost him £165 to build, mainly from old railway sleepers and rectory floorboards. Families, too, abounded. One lot had, out of love, kidnapped their own junkie daughter and then sailed with her across the Atlantic. Drug-free, the girl was mapping out her university career. Another family tried to make ends meet by trading from port to port as they circled the globe.

As we ourselves circled Antigua, swimming in shimmering clear water and barbecuing on sandy beaches, Katy quickly reestablished a loving relationship with her grandparents. Then, all too soon, it was time for them to fly away. Slowly, I packed her suitcase and stuffed her miniature rucksack with supplies for the trip: coloring books and crayons and a whole family of small bears. In her arms she clutched her greatest love of all, her blue-and-pink elephant. Dumbo. At the airport we had swift hugs all around, a final wave, and then all three were swallowed up in the crowd. I climbed silently back into the taxi, torn apart by doubts and fears and guilt.

Thank goodness for *Johanne.* What with hauling her out and then taking several days, and a good deal of cunning, to trace her leak, there was little time to be miserable. The source of *Johanne*'s trouble was her deadwood aft. Part of the massive hunks of internal timber attached to both stern post and keel had turned a trifle "soft." ("Soft" is a term used by doting owners to describe any small areas of rot on their otherwise peerless craft.) In no time, carpenters were digging out the rot, mainly with their fingers it was so sludgy. Once all was sound, more inches were trimmed away for safety before the men marinated what remained in Solignum. When dry, they poured cement into the hole, solidly nailed and caulked the outside plank, and the leak was cured. A careful check of all the remaining caulking, a couple of good strong coats of anti-fouling, and *Johanne* was re-launched. David Simmons had done all he could to see us safely across the Atlantic.

Edward had chosen Puerto Rico, with its G.M. agent, as our ultimate point of departure. But Puerto Rico poses certain bureaucratic obstacles in the way of cruising yachtsmen. Normally they sail into any foreign country, drop anchor, and hoist the yellow "Q," or quarantine, flag to show that they want clearnance to land. Once the "Q" flag is up, either one waits for the customs and immigration officials to come out or, more often, the skipper is expected to go ashore alone with ship's papers, three neat crew lists, and all the passports ready for stamping. Entering the United States was altogether different. Before ever reaching those sacred shores we had first to get a visa stamped into our passports—and that only entitled us to apply for an entry permit when we eventually arrived in U.S. waters. It goes without saying that these visas were not available in Antigua. So we upped sails and set off on a 400-mile round-trip to the U.S. consulate on the French island of Martinique.

Looking on the bright side of it, the trip would give our new crewman an excellent opportunity to settle in. A delivery skipper, Dave had recently brought a yacht across the Atlantic to Antigua. Now he wanted a ride back to his base in Europe. And we wanted an experienced crewman. Dave was some ten years older than John and me. Tall and lean, he combined Marlboro good looks with common sense and an easy, retiring nature.

The trip to Martinique was, for *Johanne,* remarkably uneventful. Once there, Edward spent an hour clearing us through immigration, then lowered the "Q" flag and we all traipsed ashore to search for the U.S. consulate. But before John had even tied the dinghy to the jetty, we were accosted by a blond and beefy young man. Behind him, on the dock, slouched a well-traveled kitbag.

"Is that your boat out there?" he asked in a strong South African accent. Edward nodded curtly. We were in a hurry.

"She's a real beauty!" No owner could resist that. Edward paused.

"I've just sailed one like her in the Cape-to-Rio race. Where're you bound?"

"England."

"Suppose you're not looking for crew?"

Edward looked at him again. "Right now we're off to the U.S. consulate. After that we sail to Puerto Rico and then on to Europe. If you want to come, bring your passport."

And so we were five—or five and a bit if you include the mouse.

I've always loathed Customs and Immigration. Even when I was a small child, traveling in the wake of two shiningly honest parents, I felt threatened. What would they find as they rummaged through my bags? Had I inadvertently put in something that should not be there? Had someone else? So, it was with no anticipation of pleasure that I entered the consulate's large and airy waiting room. We didn't wait long. Almost at once a slightly rotund, slightly balding man appeared at the swing gate that divided the riffraff from officialdom. His bright eyes swiftly scanned the waiting petitioners.

"I think today I'll start with my yachting friends," and he beamed straight at us. How the heck did he know? Seating us in his inner sanctum, he filled in all the forms for us, chatting away all the while and no doubt eliciting far more information than we realized. Then he gave us each a full-page stamp in our passports and, with a friendly handshake, sent us on our way. In a few short minutes, that man had persuaded me that, despite all the bureaucracy and red tape, despite the 400-mile round-trip to see him, the United States really was a great country, its citizens among the most charming in the world. I hope he was made an ambassador. He should have been.

As we walked back along the jetty another young man approached, this time asking for a lift up the islands. We were already five, more than enough for the trip. Still, it seemed a bit mean to turn him down.

"How much sailing have you done?"

"Just sailed down from Canada. Lots of night passages. Bee sailing on lakes back home all m'life." People often ask us how we find crew. The answer is that 90 percent of the time we don't; they find us. Sometimes it works out, sometimes it doesn't. This time we took the stranger in. And almost lost *Johanne.*

A forest ranger by trade, our newest crew member steered a competent trick at the helm. That night, as Edward handed over to him again, he repeated his usual instructions:

"If you see any lights at all, wake me. I'm right here," and he pointed to our bunk, a couple of feet away. He then left the ranger alone under a brilliant sky of stars.

An hour later a terrified shout slashed through my dreams. I beat Edward awake with my fists.

"Quick Edward! On deck! Something's wrong!"

Edward charged out. The coaster was only seconds away, racing straight for us. Flinging the ranger from the wheel, Edward hauled the helm hard over. Jerking the mizzensheet from its cleat, he let the line fly free. *Johanne* bore away just as the coaster rushed past, searchlights blazing and with barely twenty feet between us. Fate had been unusually kind. That very morning, Edward had replaced the mizzensheet. The old one, frayed and swollen, would never have raced out, untangled, through blocks. The sail, pinned in, would have slowed *Johanne*'s turn. We would have been run down.

We never did discover what had happened to the ranger, why he hadn't seen the ship's lights half an hour before. Was he asleep? High on drugs? Or away in some dream world of his own? The man remains in my memory as the only crew Edward has ever dismissed from the helm. His negligence had very nearly cost us our lives.

Illegal drugs on board yachts are a perennial problem. If caught with hashish in a house, the hashish is confiscated, the owner of the hashish may go to jail, but the house itself is left untouched. If hashish is found on a boat, the boat is impounded and often destroyed. That would mean the end of our home. We warn new crew that no illicit drugs whatsoever are allowed on board, but, without a strip search, one can never verify that the rule is followed. We can only trust people and keep our fingers crossed.

The rest of the trip north ran smoothly. *Johanne* surged forward under full sail where, between the islands, the vibrant trade winds blew. The flat spots, created by an island's wind shadow, she attacked with bursts of engine power. In Antigua the ranger left and *Johanne* had an efficient crew once more. But, at times, I did wonder how John and Don would get along. John, stricken with T.B. as a child, had fallen far behind with his lessons. He ensured the respect of his schoolmates by building himself into something of a muscleman. As ill luck would have it, Don, ignoring his university degree, also based much of his self-image on macho strength. Their consequent rivalry did not bode well for a long passage. One could almost see the hackles rise and the hind legs stiffen as the two circled each other, their whole bodies bristling with nonverbal antagonism. Hand over hand they raced each other up the forestays or tried to out-row each other across the bay. Undoubtedly both would be outstanding at pulling in the mainsheet in a Force 8 gale—provided, that is, they hadn't had a punch-up first.

While the men sorted out their pecking order, I set out on a marathon of list making: deciding what stores to buy and where. This was my first major effort at catering and, after the gastronomic disaster of the Grenada trip, I was taking it all most seriously. Laboring late into the night, I concocted a ten-day menu. Estimates of proteins and vitamins were drawn up (thank God no one bothered about minerals then), and confused efforts were made to offset the goodness of fresh potatoes against the extra fuel needed to cook them. Balanced menu complete, I spent further hours in the intricate calculation of just how many cans of meat, vegetables, and fruit, how many pounds of rice, pasta, potatoes, and flour would be required to feed my ten-day menu to five people for fifty days. Averaging a bit over 100 miles per day, we expected the trip to take some thirty days. To that I added two-thirds as much again to allow for mishaps; then I bought extra rice, dried milk, sugar, tea, and coffee—just in case. A little overcautious you think? Downright neurotic would be nearer the mark, but then we didn't run out of food either. Leaving the purchase of fresh food till Puerto Rico and fancy canned goods till St. Thomas, I bought most basic stores in Antigua and dumped them all into *Johanne*'s hold. They could be sorted later. For, after eighteen months in the West Indies, we were going to throw a farewell party.

Ian Spencer, the Dockyard's epicurean guru, was called in as adviser. Obligingly, he gave me two recipes for rum punch: one mild, one strong. From the start I plumped for the strong one but then, as I added bits of this and bits of that, my mind became a trifle fuddled and I inadvertently added an extra bottle of rum as well. The icebox made a handy cauldron and, with its little dispensing spiggot near the base, ensured that rum punch flowed free as lemonade; which was how most people treated it. As the evening wore on, more and more dinghies trailed astern of *Johanne* at the same time that, aboard, more and more of their owners made themselves at home. On the poop I overheard a talented artist solemnly lecture Edward on the merits of cannabis.

"Quite harmless you know, Edward. Really. My aunt's a missionary. Grows it in her window box in Amsterdam." I wondered whether Edward understood what the chap was talking about.

Behind *Johanne,* a buoyant moon floated upward, past the black silhouettes of mangroves and century trees. Moonlight flickered and darted on the water as a slight breeze ruffled the bay. It was a glorious night. So glorious that it seized David Simmons with the desire to sail. Rousing a couple of friends, he rowed off to where his lovely *Baccho* lay moored. Across the harbor came the creak of blocks and the soft flop-flop of slack canvas as they hoisted sail. Moments later the little yacht ghosted past *Johanne* and then silently tacked out to sea. Later still, a New Zealand couple, gliding homeward over the moon-washed water, sang us a parting lament, a Maori song of farewell. The breeze had dropped. Their voices, pure and plaintive, filled the night with flawless harmony. If only one could reach out and hold that harmony forever.

Two days later we upped anchor and sailed westward, giving English Harbor a last, sailors', farewell on the foghorn. *Johanne* knew something was afoot. She positively chortled as, with the clean Caribbean rushing past her hull, she headed westward toward the islands of St. Barts, St. John, St. Thomas, and Puerto Rico. In Grenada we'd picked up an early edition of a well-known cruising guide to the islands. So far we'd found it pretty inaccurate, but we fished it out all the same, hoping it would do better with St. Barts. Here the author mentioned two neighboring bays, one dominated by a shore generator, the other delightfully quiet. Anchoring in the quiet bay, Edward stopped the G.M.—only to be greeted by the noise of a generator ashore. Moments later another yacht sailed in and, as they passed close by, I heard the skipper shout to his wife, "My God! He's got it wrong again!" We reckoned they must be using the same pilot.

Our introduction to the U.S. island of St. John was none too peaceful either. Arriving in Caneel Bay at dusk, we dropped anchor just clear of a cluster of buoys; residents' yacht moorings we presumed. The wise never presume. The next morning the silence of breakfast was shattered by a mind-mashing roar delivered from a few feet above our heads. Those buoys marked the end of the flying boat's runway.

Ashore, we quickly found the immigration office and had fourteen-day entry permits stamped in all our passports. It was as we left the office that Edward caught sight of our old friend *Diligence*. She had seen some major changes since last we met in Bequia. For a start, John's whole family had moved aboard, by car. Literally. Others might hesitate before garaging two limousines on a seventy-five-footer, but not John. He simply cut a gate in the bulwarks and drove the two cars onto *Diligence*'s main deck. Mother's plants had posed even fewer problems. They could go over there, by the wheel. In fact the whole area aft looked like a miniature rain forest. There were plants everywhere: in tubs around the deck, hung up in buckets, strung between the rigging, and one particularly ambitious individual was at that very moment twining its way up the mizzenmast. I longed to know what happened when they put to sea but feared it would be nitpicking to ask.

If the plants had taken over *Diligence*'s stern, belowdecks kittens reigned supreme, tripping up unwary visitors in all the darkest corners of the hold. The latest litter brought the ship's feline population to thirteen. I never got around to counting the dogs. Their owner, John, chuckled happily at our horror. He knew we loved him.

"Eh, zat is nozing. Com. I show you somsing else." Meekly we followed our latter-day Pied Piper back on deck. Daylight was vanishing fast. Quite undeterred, John had us on all fours in a trice, scrabbling around the deck in an utterly lunatic search, made more lunatic by John himself who, intent on preserving our final surprise, adamantly refused to tell us what we were looking for.

"I know he iz here somvere," our host kept muttering as he peered first under one car, then the other.

"Aha! Zere you are you little b—!" And out from under the second car shot a large white rabbit.

John was one of the most inventive, brilliant, entertaining, impossible, warmhearted spirits I have ever met but we were meant to be sailing to the Seychelles, not chasing white rabbits around floating garages in the dark. The next morning we set sail regretfully for St. Thomas.

Lying only three miles west of St. John, St. Thomas soon justified its reputation as a Mecca for canned goods. It was as I returned from the supermarket, attempting with two hands to control three severely overladen and bloody-minded carts, that I almost collided with a grease-blackened figure—a figure that looked oddly familiar. It was. Beneath the grease lurked John Campbell. We'd first met in English Harbor shortly after he'd sailed the Atlantic single-handedly. Then he had come bounding up to Edward, a twinkle in his eye, and blithely announced, "I think I'm a sort of relative of yours." Fuddy old Debretts might not have recognized the connection. We most certainly did. After all, was not John's ex-wife also Edward's third cousin's goddaughter? Meeting in St. Thomas, we were both in a mad rush, so we parted after a hasty exchange of addresses (he gave me his parents' address and I gave him mine), and a promise to keep in touch. Eighteen months later we went one step better. John moved on board *Johanne.*

Fearful that our precious U.S. permits would run out before we were ready to leave, we hurried westward, this time bound for Puerto Rico. During the forty-mile trip, the lads and I sorted through our canned goods. Traditionally, at this point, yachtsmen are supposed to laboriously strip off the labels from the tins, mark the contents on the lids, and then lather the lot with varnish or Vaseline—all precautions against rust, and part of a pernickety ritual in which Edward, for one, had never taken part. And if he hadn't, I saw no reason why I should. So, ignoring all rites, we divided the cans into five separate piles, each containing the tins required for one ten-day menu. John and Don then shoveled four of the piles into four separate sacks and heaved them into a spacious locker at the foot of our bunk. I arranged the fifth pile along a shelf behind the galley water tank. For the first ten days of the trip I'd be able to reach all necessary supplies without once fumbling in dark

lockers to find them. Delicacies such as smoked ham, cream and aspar-
agus. I buried in a particularly inaccessible locker, to be unearthed only
on days of celebration. In the most easily get-at-able locker of all, I
stacked a collection of easy-to-cook, easy-to-digest, rough-weather
foods. By the time we reached Puerto Rico, first island of the Greater
Antilles, we had all our canned goods neatly stowed.

   Unlike Antigua or Grenada, Puerto Rico is no "Caribbean jewel set
in a sparkling sea." It is a serious land mass. Granted, at something over
3,400 square miles, it's smaller than the Lebanon, but it is three and a
half times the size of the Grand Duchy of Luxembourg and eight times
the size of Hong Kong. The last stop in our Caribbean rovings, Puerto
Rico would have been no more than a hasty business trip if it had not
been for Luis. I first noticed him as we rowed across the canal toward
town. Sitting on the bank, he stared at us so intently that, for a moment,
I thought one of us must have forgotten to dress. But no, it was *Johanne*
who'd caught at his youthful heart strings. The minute we stepped
ashore he was beside us, putting himself and his car at our disposal.
   Over the next two days, Luis ferried us to G.M. merchants and ship
chandlers, coffee sellers and rope makers. He invited us to a fabulous
pub in Old San Juan where guests at the bar swung peacefully to and fro
on swings hung from the ceiling. And all the time Luis talked about
boats. The scion of an old Puerto Rican family, Luis was a true Creole,
speaking Spanish not English at home, for his mother spoke nothing
else. (That word "Creole" can cause a lot of confusion. It comes from
the Portuguese *crioulo*, meaning "produced by" or "reared at home."
Centuries ago, Portugal-born Portuguese used *crioulo* to refer to other
Portuguese who had been born in—produced by—one of their tropical
colonies. Nowadays "Creole" has many nuances of meaning, hence the
confusion, but it still retains that connotation of being a local product of
a warm country. Thus you have Creole, or regional, cooking in Louisi-
ana and the West Indies, and, in the Seychelles, the Seychellois speak
Creole, a distinct local patois derived from French but "produced in"
the islands.)
   When, eventually, Luis made a tour of *Johanne*, he was fired into
such orbits of enthusiasm that he earnestly begged to sail with us to
Europe. I hated to turn him down but our crew was already complete.
Undaunted, Luis countered our rejection with an invitation to dine at
his family home. Sitting outside in a shaded arbor, surrounded by a
garden full of hummingbirds and bougainvillea, we supped out of a
paella, or dish, two feet in diameter. (The food gets its name from the
container.) Laid out on a bed of rice, superb mussels, still half hidden in

their shells, contrasted with juicy rose-pink prawns and white, shoelace coils of squid. In the midst of his family Luis fell almost silent, happy to listen as his father regaled us with tales of past battles fought against giant fish. One such marathon had left the old man bedridden for a fortnight. Was that the same fish that Luis later showed us, gigantic, stuffed and mounted, hanging in pride of place above the entrance to his father's fishing club? I no longer remember.

I do remember, vividly, the Puerto Rican policeman. Alone on board, I was standing guard over *Johanne* when he came to call. Before I met Luis's mother it had never occurred to me that there might be people in Puerto Rico who spoke no English. Yet here I was, face-to-face with another, a charming guy with whom I chatted most amicably for fifteen minutes or more. At any rate, I think it was amicably, I'd never spoken Spanish before in my life. But now, in my desire to communicate with an attractive man, combined with my determination to keep that same man from prying through my boat, all the Spanish I'd ever heard, mostly in films *mis amigos,* came galloping to my rescue. Every time the poor guy made noises about *"el barco"* I either failed hopelessly to understand or said my husband would be back soon. In the end he left, in search no doubt of a cool, dark bar and a long, stiff drink. He never did get to look on board *Johanne.*

I was up early on D-day, off to buy enough fresh food to keep us all bulging with vitamins for several weeks to come. My informants at the Club Nautico knew of no open-air markets but directed me instead to the nearest supermarket. And what a store it was. I felt like a real yokel as I stood there, gaping at acres upon acres of fruit and vegetables, stretching in uneven hillocks to the distant walls. Never had I seen such vegetables; all so spotless, so sanitized. Surely nothing so crude as earth had ever touched those pristine forms? But most of all I marveled at their incredible size: grapefruit as big as melons, tomatoes the size of Seville oranges. In the past few years I'd become pretty adept at keeping vegetables fresh in the tropics. (Unlike most yachts, we've never had a fridge. Apart from their electrical parts, which are allergic to salt air, many of them demand an hour of engine every day to keep them cold.) Refrigerator-free, I quickly learned that potatoes, onions, pumpkins, and cabbages last longest and that, among fruits, oranges and apples were the most reliable. So it was these foods that made up the bulk of my shopping list as I wandered, all innocence, into that Hall of Illusions. There my list was forgotten forever as, reverently, I picked up one huge tomato and then another. I rubbed my thumb over their taut and glossy skins, and swiftly stifled past warnings about the rottenness of supermarket food. After all, everyone else was buying the stuff. True.

But, unknown to me, everyone else then rushed home and shoved it all straight into a refrigerator. I lovingly deposited each wondrous purchase in the special, airy baskets I'd slung ready for them under *Johanne*'s beams.

Ah! What moral tale hung in those baskets! What joy my vegetables would have brought to some pulpit-thumping preacher seeking a subject for his Sunday sermon—a tale of the mighty falling and the meek inheriting the earth. For it is quite astonishing how quickly blown-out self-importance collapses into flatulence and rot, even in a vegetable. Within a day, half my prized, "fresh" stores were putrid: oranges turned into sponges, green peppers reduced, overnight, to dark tendrils of slime slowly dripping through the open weave of their baskets. In forty-eight hours the only fresh food left on *Johanne* were potatoes and onions, plus one solitary cabbage. But by then we were in the Atlantic and could not turn back.

As soon as I returned from my ill-fated spree, Edward went off to get clearance from the harbor and immigration offices. Once granted, one has twenty-four hours to leave the country. Our plan was to grab a full night's sleep and then start out at dawn. But as he filled in the clearance forms Edward suddenly realized the date—Thursday the 12th. Tomorrow would be Friday the 13th. No sailor worth his salt sets out to sea on Friday the 13th. For the rest of Thursday *Johanne* was in ferment as we hustled to get everything stowed: spare wood and paint pots secured in the hold, dinghy lashed firmly to its stern davits, books battened into bookshelves, and personal possessions shut tight inside their lockers. Edward topped up the water in the G.M.'s cooling system, checked the oil level, and made sure the fuel filters were clean. Then, clutching a sheet of very fine wet-and-dry sandpaper, he dived over the side and gave a last polish to the propeller.

At 11:10 P.M. on Thursday the 12th of June, we cast off from the banks of the canal, warped *Johanne* around till she was pointing out to sea, and, using the G.M. to clear the waterway, set off for England, 4,000 miles away on the other side of the Atlantic.

8. The Atlantic

As an initiation to transatlantic sailing, one couldn't ask for better. The weather behaved impeccably, producing trade winds where there should be trade winds and brave westerlies where the brave westerlies should blow. We were becalmed in the horse latitudes and buffeted by gales off the Azores, all strictly according to the book. But wait, I go too fast. On our very first day out of Puerto Rico the wind sprang up from somewhere south of east and sent *Johanne* scudding off at a good 5 knots—to somewhere north of north-northeast. And let no one scoff at *Johanne*'s inability to sail closer than 70 degrees to the wind. Unlike a racing yacht in similar conditions, the old lady stayed almost upright, bearing us over the water in considerable comfort.

Sun and sea; steer and sleep; stars and sea; sleep and eat. The ocean's rhythm, like a hypnotic mantra, pulsed through our senses, flushing out the stresses of the shore, leaving only the simple tensions of balancing sails with wind and waves, and course desired with course made good. Finally I could understand Edward's love of ocean cruising—not that my own contribution to that, my first ocean passage, quite lived up to my secret visions of "Woman the Intrepid Traveler." With four men aboard I fell, without thinking, into the far less heroic role of the "little woman." I took charge of the galley and the cooking; I scrubbed sheets and washed dishes while the others did all the manly bits like heaving on lines, greasing blocks, and steering *Johanne* through the lone watches of the night. So much so that, if it hadn't been for another tradition, and Edward's manipulation of it, I might well have remained entombed in the galley forever, as many boatwives do. On second thought, though, "entombed" was hardly the appropriate word on *Johanne.* As her galley remained without a sink, I spent a good deal of my time sitting on deck, the dirty dishes in a bucket clasped between my knees. But to return to that tradition: dating back to windjammer days, it ruled that the ship's cook not only prepared the food but also took responsibility for the jibs. *Johanne*'s jib being large, I was assigned to the staysail. And there, on the foredeck, as my confidence grew, so too did my enjoyment of the actual mechanics of sailing. I even volunteered to steer while the experts chatted over their afternoon tea.

A great institution, afternoon tea, particularly on long sea voyages when, by four or five o'clock, everyone has caught up on last night's sleep, or lack of it, and is ready for a good game around the wheel.

Tea was over and the sun almost set when, on our second day out, a yell from the helmsman triggered a stampede to the fishing line. Without a reel, Don warily hauled in the plastic line, foot by foot, so it fell in neat green coils on the deck. *Whumph!* The fish depth charged, and Don let go. The fish resurfaced. The line slackened. And so began that age-old struggle between man and fish. Haul in and play out, haul in and play out. This time it was man who won. A fine kingfish lay dead on deck. Half an hour later the lads fisted aboard a three-foot wahoo. Fresh fish for supper, and breakfast—and lunch the next day.

As *Johanne* approached the horse latitudes her daily runs plummeted from an exhilarating 134 miles noon to noon to less than 30. Till then I'd always imagined that it was squalls and gales that wrecked a sailing ship's gear. Not a bit. It's the calms that follow storms that cause most damage. High winds can vanish in seconds but the swells they create linger on for many hours, sometimes days. With no wind to fill her sails, *Johanne* floundered about, at the mercy of every passing wave. Rolling to windward, her massive booms and blocks would dip, hover amidships, then hurtle back to leeward with a terrifying crash. Wanting to tame the main boom's gyrations, we heaved down more firmly on its rope preventer. But we dared not heave too hard for, high above the deck, *Johanne*'s great wooden gaff was cutting swathes across the sky, trying, it seemed, to tear the tired old sail from head to clue. Yet we could not lower the sails for they acted as our only stabilizers. Remove them and the boat would wallow even worse. "Slopping! Banging! Wrenching! Rolling!" Edward's log entry reflected his deep hatred for such cruel boat abuse.

Finally the transition was over and the water, once so deeply furrowed, now glistened, smooth as black marble. Somewhere out there, in that motionless sea, were the ghosts of horses that gave the place its name. It was here, becalmed in the horse latitudes, in the middle of the Sargasso Sea, that the Spanish conquistadors are said to have watched, helpless, as their drinking water ran low; here that they levered their dying horses over the side in a vain attempt to save water for their dying men. Later convoys found only the horses' blown-up carcasses, entangled in sargasso weed, to bear mute witness to their masters' fates.

Sargasso weed—how those words echo with the romance of something read about but never seen. I had imagined it as long, floppy ribbons, twining octopus-like around the horses' legs. In reality, Sargasso weed is a mass of short, brittle twigs, each one stiff and yellow and yet endowed with such a jumble of arthritic joints that it cannot help but tangle with its neighbors to form matted islands in the sea. Boat hook in hand, I dipped swiftly into a passing clump, then dropped my catch into a glass jug filled with seawater. We gazed in wonder as a whole ecosystem of minute creatures, many almost transparent, crawled and wriggled about their yellow pasture. Then someone gasped and pointed. There, motionless and camouflaged among the weeds, hung a tiny sea horse. Barely one inch long, he floated upright, staring back at us as haughtily as any potbellied lawyer about to intimidate the accused. Guilty as charged, we hastily lowered the little fellow back into the ocean and wished him bon voyage.

Becalmed, at least we could finish some of the jobs abandoned in our superstitious flight from Puerto Rico. A few sharp coughs followed by prolonged stuttering and the portable Honda generator swung into action, rousing a flock of terns to indignant protest. It took John and Edward, plus power tools, one morning to construct the wooden frame to support my galley sinks. Away, galvanized buckets full of greasy dishes! Their place was taken by two stainless-steel tubs and a proper draining board. (Twin sinks are ideal at sea: one for the actual washing-up, the other for holding the clean dishes until you've a hand free to dry them.)

No sooner was the galley complete but the battle of *Johanne*'s main began. No sail, not even a canvas one, can be expected to last indefinitely. After twenty-one years' use, and aggravated by the recent calm, *Johanne*'s main was falling apart at the seams. Kitted out with sailmaker's palms, beeswaxed thread, and three-inch-long sail needles, Don and Dave settled, cross-legged, on deck to restitch the damaged sail. An hour later it was rehoisted, only to be lowered the following day for more repairs. And so it continued, up and down, up and down, all the way to England.

On June 28th Edward wrote in the log: "Passed a bubble!"—a noteworthy moment for sure. That day we'd made precisely twenty-four miles in twenty-four hours and a good half of that was due to a fair current. Before setting out I'd wondered whether perhaps I'd get horribly bored stuck so long at sea. As it happened, there simply wasn't time for boredom. When not steering, cooking, eating, or sleeping there was always the boat to maintain plus innumerable hobbies to pursue. Don and John ransacked the ship's library and unearthed Hervey Garrett Smith's *The Marlinspike Sailor*. From then on they filled every free moment reproducing his fancy knots and ropework. Yes, that's right: Don and John. Heaven only knows what turned the tide in their relationship, but within a fortnight of leaving land the two were firm buddies and had started a veritable cottage industry in the fo'c'sle. Raiding *Johanne*'s hold for bits of rope and canvas, Don created intricate ropework belts and John stitched himself a handsome canvas rucksack, complete with a woven carrying cord that ended in a complicated Turk's-head knot.

Edward's and Dave's pursuits were more philosophical. As far as I know, neither penned poetry but both enjoyed solitude and silence and the wild beauty of the sea. For myself, when I wasn't gazing at the stars and the birds and the sky, I either curled up with a book or indulged my passion for scribbling on the blank pages of clean notebooks. There was one other activity ideally suited to those days of flat calms and clear skies: Edward inaugurated a *Johanne Regina* School of Navigation. It was to be the first of many.

There are several different systems of celestial navigation, each one defended, tables and azimuth, by its followers. Thus Dave came aboard carrying his trusted H0249 in several large volumes, while "Professor" Edward entered our first navigation class waving aloft his own, much loved, H211. Little known and usually out of print, H211 comes in a single slim volume hardly thicker than a pamphlet, yet it covers the whole earth and will last until the end of it. Dave watched as John and I struggled with navigation's basic principles. (Edward is a firm believer in Basic Principles. I, on the other hand, will happily grab at any neat rule of thumb provided it's handed to me on a plate.) Naturally, Dave preferred his own tried-and-tested system. Good heavens, with H211 you have to do an extra subtraction. Yet he could not deny the convenience of that slim volume, especially for a delivery skipper. By the time we reached England a closet conversion had taken place, and Dave borrowed H211 to have it photocopied.

On board *Johanne* a seafaring routine had emerged. Edward, on call twenty-four hours a day, rose every couple of hours during the night to check that all was well. Once darkness fell the others took turns at the helm, their four-hour watches followed by up to eight hours of sleep. Day and night Edward made all major decisions, including when to tack or lower sail. *Johanne,* too, played her part. She reduced her leaks to a minimum, though backbreaking hours bent over the short-handled Gusher had become a thing of the past anyway. Before leaving Puerto Rico, Edward had incorporated a four-inch Whale deck pump into *Johanne*'s already extensive pump repertoire. It came complete with a four-foot-high handle and, at every stroke, shifted an impressive half-gallon of water.

We had been at sea for a fortnight when Don pointed east and said he could see an object bobbing about. The rest of us, screwing our eyes into slits, saw nothing at all. Fearing it might be a lifeboat, Edward swung *Johanne*'s bowsprit in line with Don's pointing finger and started the motor. As we drew closer it did look like a lifeboat, and then more like a hull torn from a trimaran. No doubt about it, someone would have to swim over and investigate. The someone was, of course, John the Willing. Only when he was standing astride it, à la conquering hero, did a nasty thought cross his mind. 'You will come back and pick me up, won't you?" Dear John, you could see his point. A hundred feet from *Johanne,* perched all alone atop the hull, he looked the epitome of a cartoonist's castaway.

The fifteen-foot hull must once have sported a ballast keel to keep it upright and a mast and antennae to hold a night-light and transmitter for, on closer inspection, it turned out to be a scientific drift buoy. Keel gone, the whole thing lay on its side, stricken and useless. As a matter of fact, worse than useless. A fiberglass yacht colliding with that hulking float would have sunk in seconds. We discussed lifting it aboard but, in the end, our British upbringing prevailing. After a lifetime of obedience to such commands as "Keep Off the Grass," "Queue Here," and "Stick No Bills," we were hardly likely to rebel against an order which, written in capital letters and two different languages, commanded "DO NOT TOUCH."

According to the buoy's owners, its reason for fouling up the Atlantic sea lanes was serious scientific research—barnacle research. They even made a moving appeal, in both Spanish and English, for finders not to disturb the barnacles. To *Johanne*'s crew, still high on the relief of finding crustaceans and not corpses, the request seemed idiotic. Who would want to disturb them, apart from the survivors of any yacht unlucky enough to be sunk by the fiendish thing. We used an empty wine bottle to contain our message. It conveyed the glad tidings that, due to a lunch which had included substantial helpings of baked beans, their precious barnacles had, in the nick of time, been preserved from our ravenous clutches. Tying the bottle onto the base of the float's bent mast, we cast the buoy adrift, complete, no doubt, with thousands of dollars' worth of transmitting equipment.

At the beginning of our voyage we basked in the calms. By June 29th we were heartily sick of them. And, right on cue, a moderate southerly sprang up to set *Johanne* free. In moments she had her wings spread wide, flying through the water toward our goal. Twice the following day the words "Absolutely perfect" appeared in the log. Two days after that the wind grew gusty. After all our grumbles about the calms we now had to quell equally vigorous complaints about the wind. But then a noon-to-noon run of 146 miles blew all our moans away. The following day the wind shifted to *Johanne*'s quarter and we were over the moon. The old girl had clocked up a magnificent personal record of 184 miles noon to noon. The log entries reflected our euphoria. Below Edward's "Drivin', drivin' before the brave westerlies" was Dave's "Giant squid leapt aboard (2 inches long)"—and was it Don or John who wrote "Skipper! The moon's rising!"?

Spirits were still running high when, most unusually in mid-ocean, a ship, *American Ranger,* passed close across our stern. Edward called out, "Come on! Let's try and call her up." When we bought *Johanne,* she came complete with a defunct ship-to-shore radio. At any rate, Teddy Mathews said it was defunct and, looking at it, we saw no reason to doubt him. But now we gathered round as Edward flipped switches and twiddled knobs on the antiquated, double-sideband set. Turning the receiver knob to full volume, he spoke into the mike: *"AMERICAN RANGER, AMERICAN RANGER, JOHANNE REGINA."* Their reply practically blasted us out of the cabin. Mind you, they were so close we could almost have heard them if they'd simply shouted from the bridge. Still, it was fun to know the old radio had some life in it. We'd never had a ship-to-shore radio before. It was good, too, to hear the captain say, "Gee! You look kind a nice sailing along out here."

The next day the strong winds moderated but already, over the past four days, *Johanne* had averaged a smacking 161 miles noon to noon. With the calmer weather came more marine life—or maybe it was just easier to see. A turtle swam past, its head held imperiously high as it cast a baleful look in our direction. A school of dolphin, accompanied by a single whale, appeared to port, but without the call of the G.M. to excite them, or the vibration of a fast-moving hull to draw them close, the creatures took no interest in *Johanne* and passed smoothly on their way. Near midnight, over an almost motionless ocean, came the individual sighs of dolphins breathing. John recorded in the log: "More dolphin to port, just taking their time like us." A gentle chap was John.

At around 2 P.M. on July 7th, a couple of days after being blasted by *Ranger*'s radio, a very different noise pierced our carefree isolation. A strange humming sound, it came as if from a great distance and then crept closer and closer. Almost upon us, it stopped. Just like that— *phut!* A plane, perhaps? That's certainly what we thought. We scanned the sky, but the sky was a sheet of purest blue with not enough cloud to give cover to a fly. So then we scanned the sea; if not above, then that hum must be below us—maybe a Russian submarine poised to surface and attack. If we'd heard the noise only once we could have dismissed it out of hand. But it came again and again, each time stopping right by *Johanne*'s stern. And then it quit as suddenly as it had begun—until the following afternoon, when the whole eerie performance started again, except that now the hum was coming at regular ten-minute intervals. We christened it UHO, (Unidentified Humming Object), and carefully recorded each visit in the log.

The final entry appeared at 5:55 P.M.: "U.H.O. heard . . . noise stopped dead astern." Ten minutes later U.H.O. was no more. A triumphant "I.H.O.! Aircraft spotted flying west!" had us all laughing with relief—though really we'd known it was a plane all along, hadn't we? The plane was flying many thousands of feet above us, invisible except when its gnatlike wings caught, for a fleeting moment, the slanting rays of the evening sun. The explanation was simple. As the plane, presumably on high-altitude reconnaissance, approached from windward, its engines hummed louder and louder. The moment it passed overhead and to leeward, the wind carried all sound of it away and the hum stopped dead. What was less easy to explain was why the episode had been so disturbing. Was it because everything in our modern world has to have a good, scientific explanation? To hear and not to see or understand is, we discovered, peculiarly unnerving.

As the breezes shifted, blowing first from one direction and then another, so Edward had us shifting sails to take the best advantage of each puff. A light wind on the beam brought out a jury-rigged mizzen staysail. Then the wind went dead aft. A nifty bit of sail handling and we had the mizzen jibed over and guyed out on the opposite side to the main. Sailing wing and wing like that is a favorite game of yachtsmen. The trick is to keep the wind dead astern. The slightest shift and you must instantly alter course or risk one of the sails crashing over in an accidental jibe. In any sea, *Johanne*'s swinging gaffs make the whole game even more riveting. But, apart from honing one's skills and raising one's adrenaline level, sailing wing and wing in mid-ocean is pretty pointless. Most sailboats, including *Johanne,* make their best passages with the wind on the quarter, not dead aft. When there is so much space available, it's more sensible to plump for the most advantageous quarter rather than the perfect course. The wind is bound to shift before you've run too far off your route.

Our own playtime was brought to an abrupt end by the black underbelly of an evening line squall rising menacingly toward us. We had that mizzen jibed back before you could say "spit." The temperature shot down. The wind swept onward, a dark shadow on the sea, and the rain, chasing after, beat the water into dancing whiteness. The squall hit with an 80-degree shift of wind, but Dave had already anticipated it. As *Johanne* heeled to the sudden blow, he had the helm hard over and never once allowed her sails to flog. In twenty minutes the squall had passed, but for the next three hours an overcast sky unleashed a steady drizzle of rain—the first real, English rain I'd seen in two whole years. It was beautiful, sad, misty rain, the sort that dilutes the light and color of the day, and so different from West Indian rain, which falls in hefty gouts from blackest squall clouds and then, in half an hour, gives way to radiant skies. I'd missed my English rain. I'd missed the complexity of England's seasons: the thrill as naked woods put out their first green haze of spring, the companionship and comfort of thick sweaters and warm fur boots in winter—joys that Kate will never sense within her bones. A child of the sun, she says those leaden English skies press down upon her skull. Maybe our stowaway felt the same.

Certainly it was shortly after that initial bout of rain that our West Indian mouse bolted for the warmth of the saloon. Not that we saw him. What we saw were ominous signs of nestmaking among the charts. The challenge was on. We put out mousetraps and, for a whole week, fought each other for supremacy. The mouse won paws down. Though we were ever so crafty he managed, seven nights in a row, to extract the bait without tripping the trap. After that we called a truce, to save face more than anything else. If he stopped chewing important landmarks from the charts, we would stop laying traps. He honored the truce to the letter (probably his nest was complete by then). Obviously a gentleman, it was still to be some months before we went further and gave the chap a name. And, to be honest, that was only done in the vain hope that, by naming him, Katy would be less alarmed by his nightly habit of grinding down his teeth on the wood at the head of her bunk.

One hundred miles northwest of the Azores *Johanne*'s barometer slipped below 30 inches of mercury. Swells rolled in from the southwest, warning of wind to come. The wind picked up and shifted: south-southwest 4–5, southwest 6. *Johanna*'s captain toured her decks, inspecting every lashing, ordering the dinghy more securely tied, checking that the hatch-cover wedges were all hard home. There was no need for a weather forecast—the falling barometer, mounting swell, and shifting wind all foreshadowed an Azores gale.

Between midnight and the following midday, the wind gathered strength. At noon, the mizzensail, always the first to come off in a blow, was lowered to relieve *Johanne*'s steering. By mid-afternoon she was riding the edge of a southwesterly gale. Astern, waves, rearing to twenty feet, curled back their white-tipped lips in cold disdain and then shot toward us. Each time I thought for sure we must be pooped. Each time *Johanne* would lift her neat-turned stern and force the venomous wave to hiss by beneath her.

At 5:30, with nightfall near, Edward took the helm and sent us forward in lashing rain to lower the hard-pressed main. On *Johanne* you can't just let the halyards fly and grab the falling sail—there's that damned gaff to cope with. Dave, our most experienced hand, took over its command. Freeing the downhaul line, he led it aft and, for extra control, threaded it through the center of a double bollard on the windward deck. I didn't envy him. The other end of that thin line was attached to the outer end of the gaff. As we lowered the sail his job was to restrain the flailing spar.

What a battle! At a signal from Edward, John and I lowered away on the halyards. And all hell broke loose. Sixty feet above the deck the gaff whipped itself into a frenzy. Below it, 750 square feet of flogging canvas thrashed and cracked and dragged it to within six feet of the deck. Horizontal rain stung our eyes and coursed in chilly rivulets down our necks. John and I made fast our halyards and then slithered aft along the windward deck. Dave clung to the downhaul like grim death yet still the gaff swung loose. *Swoosh!* We ducked, then pounced, and trapped the swinging gaff and lashed it with the downhaul to the boom. With the gaff safely fettered we were free at last to join Don in his wrestling match with the sail. Flinging ourselves in unison on the canvas, we tamed it bit by bit, till all was securely tied. Scary? No—quite amazingly exhilarating. Sitting passively in the stern, watching *Johanne* buffeted by waves, wondering how long it would be before she shed her caulking like old men shed their hair, wondering when one of the thousand remaining wormholes would finally break through and sink us— that was the time my insides were a hollow cavern full of fear. But out there on the hatch covers—toiling side by side to lash the sail, hearing the lovelorn wind howl in the rigging—there really was no time for fear. Instead, I thrilled to the excitement of the struggle, trembled before the wind's fury and the waves' contempt, and grinned in triumph when finally we had that canvas trussed and tamed. Never in my life had I felt so alive, so free.

After that, lowering the staysail on a pitching foredeck was a cinch. *Johanne,* with nothing but jib and bare masts to drive her onward, ran off northeast before the wind and waves. As darkness closed around us, the barometer fell to 29.85 inches and the wind shifted to the west and dropped to a moderate breeze. We held our breath and waited. Later, when the depression moved on, that moderate wind would circle, counterclockwise, around the compass, veering and gathering up its power ready to blast us yet again, this time from the northwest. There was nothing to do but wait and stare into the darkness, trying to pick out the cresting waves as they reared above our stern. Fear and cold crept back into my bones.

Plied with hot soup and black coffee, Edward had been at *Johanne*'s helm for hours, tirelessly piloting her down the free-fall slopes of the waves, fighting to prevent her from swiveling sideways and broaching out of control. It was fear of being rolled upside down that kept me on deck. One's first gale at sea sure gingers up the imagination, though I did have a precedence to dwell on. It was here, just north of the Azores, that Edward, all alone, had been rolled over in his old yacht *Temptress.* He suffered cracked ribs and broken toes, and *Temptress* lost her mizzenmast and broke her main boom.

Whoosh! A monstrous wave crashed on top of my head, plunged inside my oilies, and soaked me to the skin. Time for a trip below in search of dry clothes and hot soup. If I'd learned one thing it was that in rough weather one eats small amounts of food and often. That way, no one can get in a flap and confuse the pangs of hunger with the first twinges of seasickness. In fact, not one of us was sick the whole trip, but how I thanked God Katy wasn't there.

In those days, when all *Johanne*'s hatches were battened down, no light or fresh air penetrated to the galley. In the shadowy world of weak electric light, I dived into my emergency locker, seized two cans of tomato soup and one of processed peas, chucked their contents into a saucepan, and put them to heat on the stove. So far the catering had gone surprisingly well. With people waking at different times after their night watches, I'd given up serving breakfast and simply left out the ingredients for everyone to help themselves: oats, dried fruit, and nuts ready to make Meusli, Néscafé and tea standing by to chase sweet sleep away. At midday we ate a light meal, maybe soup with cheese and biscuits or a salad followed by pudding. Supper was the main meal of the day. Hearty helpings of meat and vegetables were eased down by canned fruit. At night, a couple of thermos flasks near the aft hatch provided the helmsman with hot liquids. Liquids. All at once I became aware of the sound of water on either side of me, large quantities of water chasing up and down between the frames. Before long someone would have to man the deck pumps. But first the refreshments. A bucket may not be as classy as a tray for serving food, but on a boat pitching about in a gale it's a lot more practical.

Westerly gale notwithstanding, we hoisted the staysail at dawn.

Then, as the wind abated, the main and the mizzen went up too. *Johanne* was racing flat-out, on course for England. At 2 P.M. the barometer began its rise. The second half of the gale was on its way:

> First rise after low
> Foretells stronger blow

Abruptly the wind veered to the north-northwest bringing with it more rain. Running *Johanne* off before the wind, we lowered the jib and the mizzen and then braced her up again to continue on her course. During that third night of foul weather the wind shifted again, this time to the north, piling up confused seas which leapt at us from all angles, occasionally lopping right over *Johanne*'s high bulwarks. For the first time people complained out loud about the cold. But all complaints were forgotten when, next morning, visitors joined us from the deep. Two fifty-foot humpback whales surfaced abeam and then cruised beside us for half an hour or more. Magnificent animals, quite unfazed by the heavy seas, they spouted several times before lofting their immense tails high into the air and sliding with silent grace beneath the waves.

Shortly after they left both waves and wind increased. The Azores low was having one final fling. Aboard, *Johanne*'s crew grew increasingly wretched and worn out, not only from the natural tension associated with a gale but also from the constant physical strain, even in sleep, of keeping one's body braced against the ship's rolling. Added to that was the noise. Along with wind in the rigging and seas pounding the hull, there were odd, disturbing sounds inside *Johanne*—bulkheads creaking, wood suddenly shifting, bilge water sloshing about—and each one increased the tension. On top of that, the decks, shrunk by the scorching sun of the Sargasso Sea, leaked badly and, even with their plastic covers, our bunks were cold and damp. But sooner or later all things pass and, four days after the blow began, a mass of dolphins heralded a new era of fair winds. They dived and leaped and frolicked around our bow. *Johanne*'s narrative log reads: "Just sublime!"

A couple of days later a sharp squall sheered two bolts on *Johanne*'s starboard pin rail. Hastily transferring the halyards from their pins, Edward had new bolts cut and fitted in less than half an hour. Really, the old girl had done us proud. Apart from the mainsail's seams, those bolts were the only things that failed during the whole Atlantic crossing, thanks in good part to David Simmons and Antigua Slipway. (Only much later did I learn that David had given us no more than a fifty-fifty chance of making it safely to England. He might have let me know.)

The following day a noon sight showed us poised on the very edge of our British chart. Traveling at a good 6 knots, we sailed on, silent, through a thin veil of fog. During the night the veil lifted, enabling Edward to take a series of bearings on the Scilly Isles' famous lighthouse, Bishop Rock. At 9:15 A.M. on Sunday, July 20th, a great cheer went up. "Land ho!" Looming darkly through the pale morning mist was the solid mass of Land's End. Too solid. The next thing we knew it had blanketed off the wind. Alone, Edward would have sat it out, but by then I had only one thought in mind: to hug Katy. So, soon after lunch, Edward started the G.M. and in glittering sunshine laid course for Falmouth Harbor. First we passed the Lizard, then Manacle Buoy. Finally, in the far distance, we could see Falmouth's entrance, dotted with a confetti of tiny white sails. We'd arrived in the middle of the Sunday afternoon dinghy races. Weaving between the contestants, Edward luffed *Johanne* up into the wind and then we lowered sail and dropped anchor. We had been thirty-eight days at sea. And it was five o'clock precisely, an ideal time for a cup of English tea.

9. Cossetting and Cruising in the U.K.

BEFORE WE'D EVEN PASSED the harbor entrance I had the yellow quarantine flag hoisted up the starboard shrouds. Surely some eager-beaver customs officer would spot it and come rushing out to meet us. No such luck. We had to wait an age before a launch sauntered out to deliver the boatload of officials needed to give us clearance. As a South African, Don had problems. After much haggling the immigration officer allowed him to stay a mere fortnight, which meant that, at first light, he and John took off bound for John's parents in the north. Next Dave said goodbye, his photocopy of H211 tucked safely in his tote bag. Eventually I too was on my way, off by train across southern England to collect Katy and bring her home. Thus, in a few short hours, *Johanne*'s happy crew of the past three months had scattered like ripe thistledown in the wind.

I'd nodded off from sheer exhaustion when the train, rattling through a tunnel, woke me. Already the more nervous passengers were shaking out their skirts and collecting packages from the overhead racks. We were almost there. My heart thumped in time with the chattering train wheels. How would she be? Would she have changed? Would she be bigger? Hungrily I scanned the platform. There she was, held high on my mother's hip! There was a moment of panic as I fought with the infernal push-down windows of British Rail and then I was out. Dumping my suitcase down the steps, I ran to hug her tightly in my arms. Two yards from Kate's eyes, I pulled up short. I'd been away too long. My only child did not know me. Confused, she clung more tightly to her granny's neck. So I hugged them both and, laughing with my mother, recovered my suitcase from among a press of feet. Gradually Kate unwound, remembered, and started chatting. Then, of her own accord, she reached up to me and, lifting her, I nuzzled my face into her silky blonde hair.

Was it really eighteen months since I'd last wallowed in a bath? Two

NORTH
SEA

IRISH SEA

ENGLAND

WALES

R. ORWELL

SHOTLEY GATE
HARWICH

R. CROUCH

LONDON

THAMES

DOVER

NEWHAVEN

LYMINGTON

POOLE

PORTSMOUTH

COWES
I. OF WIGHT

MASHFORDS

PORTLAND BILL

FOWEY

CREMELL

PLYMOUTH

DARTMOUTH

FALMOUTH

ENGLISH   CHANNEL

1:2,500,000

10 5 0   10   20   30   40   50   60 MILES

whole years since I'd drunk fresh milk from a fridge? Relaxing in such half-forgotten luxury, I watched, contented, as Kate snuggled in my mother's lap. No call for so much guilt. She'd had a marvelous time.

We returned to *Johanne* to find Edward no longer alone. Still slightly awed by *Johanne*'s dimensions, he had found us another crew member. Ivan arrived with a bulky wooden sea chest in tow. Edward, eyeing its size somewhat askance, asked, "And where's the cello then?" Poor Ivan nearly fainted with surprise. "Who told you I had a cello?" I don't think he ever really believed us when we insisted it was just one of Edward's jokes. though he'd left his cello at home, Ivan had brought his antique flute along. Later, to our joy, we discovered that in signing up Ivan, Edward had signed up a truly gifted musician.

Of medium height and about twenty years old, Ivan had shaggy fair hair and high cheekbones with almond eyes set in a strangely delicate square face. Maybe his name, Ivan, was in honor of Slavic ancestors. Even before he joined us, Ivan was something of a gypsy. By his own account his parents disapproved of schools and so had buried them-selves and their large brood of children in the country, educating the lot at home. Every now and then this intensely musical family packed their collection of medieval instruments into a van and took to the road. Together they toured the West Country, a family ensemble playing medieval music long before medieval music was in vogue.

Crew problem solved (at least for the moment—Ivan warned us that he never stuck with any job for more than three months), we hauled up the anchor and the sails and squared away east for Plymouth Sound. Our destination was neither the famous dockyard nor the historic city but a boatyard on the Cornish shores of the River Tamar, a yard which was, in its own way, equally famous—at any rate among wooden boat owners: Mashford Bros. of Cremyll.

Edward had known five of the Mashford brothers since before I was born. They had helped care for several of his boats, and they had one of the finest slipways *Johanne* has ever been on. The base of its ingenious cradle was built in several separate parts joined together by heavy chain. Thus the cradle could concertina together, allowing boats to be launched and hauled up on smaller tides. Above the water vertical metal posts, adjustable to the yacht's width, held the boat upright leav-ing the whole hull free for painting.

In due course Sid Mashford rowed out to *Johanne* to give Edward's latest craft a critical once-over and to discuss what work we should do next. Whereas in the Caribbean our priority had been to make *Johanne* seaworthy, here in England we plotted the first steps of her preservation. The West Indies, with its fleet of ex–Baltic traders in various stages of dilapidation, had provided fine examples of what to guard against. One of the most common headaches was hogging. Sounds beastly and it is, particularly if you're a boat. Hogging is when bow and stern droop so that the center of the keel, instead of being horizontal, arches up as much as eighteen inches above its ends. Quite apart from affecting the shape of the ship's keel, hogging also shows above the water in a sad loss of sheer or curve. The reason for Baltic traders' hogging is twofold.

Originally these traders operated under pure sail. Then, faced with growing competition from steamships, owners had to install engines or go bust. In those days, engines were not the handy things we see today but monsters, one- or two-cylinder jobs, with giant flywheels, and it was the flywheel that caused the difficulty. To accommodate it below, an important strength member, the internal keel (or keelson), had to be cut. Sturdy wooden engine bearers, overlapping the severed keelson by several feet, did their best to make good the damage. But there was a second intrinsic weakness in most Baltics, though not in *Johanne*. Their outside keels were made from two balks of timber scarfed together. Because the main weight and strain of sailing ships came around the mainmast and cargo hold, the scarf had carefully been positioned well aft—exactly where the new engines now hung. This combination of weight pressing on weakness slowly forced the stern down while the mainmast did the same to the bow. Fortunately *Johanne* was well placed to avoid hogging. First, her keel was magnificent, cut from a single log, and second, younger than most Baltics, she was originally built, specially strengthened, to take an engine. All the same, Edward was determined to prevent any possibility of deformity in the future. So he and the Mashfords between them designed a heavy steel shoe, or box, to run the full length of her keel to act as a stiffener. Bolting one-inch-thick steel plates on either side of the keel, they then welded them to a third, foot-wide plate laid full length underneath. This shoe had two further advantages: it would add two tons of external ballast to *Johanne*'s stability and, in any chance encounters with Indian Ocean reefs, it would make an excellent coral crusher.

Even as they finished the last welding on the shoe, men were up forward tapping and prodding around *Johanne*'s stem. There was no denying it, that stem was turning soft. And, just as with the stern dead-wood, the planks nailed to it could cause a serious leak. Temporarily lacking the money to remove the planks and insert a new stem, Edward and Mashford Bros. worked out a cheaper solution. Large steel "aprons" were through-bolted to either side of the bow, covering the plank ends. A metal stem guard, placed down the forward edge of the stem, was then welded to them both. Not only would the aprons hold the planks and stem together, they would also protect the hull when we heaved the anchors aboard.

For the moment, the remaining wormy planks had to make do with make-do measures. At the suggestion of an insurance surveyor—who was, on the whole, impressed with our *Johanne*—we chiseled out the worst patches of wormy planking, hammered small nails into the cavities to help adhesion, and then smeared plastic filler over the lot to form a watertight outer skin. Much more of this treatment and *Johanne* would suffer an identity crisis, what with a half-cement deadwood aft, a steel apron forward, and now plastic patches sprouting like eczema over the rest of her hull.

If *Johanne* was having a rather uncomfortable time at the hands of Mashford's boat doctors, Kate's and my days were greatly enlivened by Pam Mashford and her two young daughters. That autumn England enjoyed one of its best wild blackberry seasons for years and Pam and I often walked with the children through a nearby coppice and on to open fields where bramble bushes abounded. We watched jays and kestrels, marveled over lizards and grasshoppers, and returned home at sunset, our punnets full and our children purple-mouthed and with their bellies bursting.

To make up for the discomforts of the slip, *Johanne* was being spoiled rotten—well, maybe not. But every spare penny we had went into her. She was given a new mainsail (carefully stowed in the hold, waiting till the old one collapsed completely) and new, meatier anchor chain. A new diesel generator, for charging the new batteries and running the new power tools, was an order, to say nothing of a new compressor for diving on wrecks in the Seychelles and a topmast for getting us there. Her greatest need, though, was a better windlass. So while Kate and I wrestled with spelling in the saloon, Edward scoured junkyards until, perched atop a wall several miles from the sea, he found the very thing. Discarded by a magnetic minesweeper, the windlass was made entirely of stainless steel and bronze. Costing £4,000 new, Edward bought it, as scrap, for £150. Clearly the navy had been content to power their fabulous machine with two handles and two strong men. We were not. Once we'd bolted the windlass firmly to the foredeck, a small, 5-hp hydraulic motor, driven by a pump on the main engine, was attached to one of its low-gear arms. We could still use the handles if the engine failed. Quite apart from saving on backache, I saw that motor as a major security investment. When you have an engine to haul in chain you feel free to veer plenty out. In the days of the old donkey windlass we begrudged every rusty link.

Right then I was in a bit of a grudging mood myself, going through a bout of fierce rebellion against the constant, dreary pragmatism that clings, like damp weed, to a seafaring life. Where was color and frivolity and the *olé* of life? Everything was always so damned sensible. At that time, among the normal population ashore, frayed jeans as daywear were out; the Jane Austen look with long, romantic skirts was all the rage. Rummaging through a material sale I bought two lengths of brightly colored, drip-dry cloth (it's hard to become thoroughly impractical all in one go). Dragging out the treadle sewing machine I launched myself into an era of gracious living, or so I fondly hoped. But as soon as I donned my skirts I hit a snag. All very well for Jane, she was never expected to chase down village high streets in pursuit of bloody-minded bus drivers, or climb up harbor ladders inches thick with slime. How Grace Darling, the Victorian heroine who rescued the crew of the *Forfarshire,* managed her rowing feat dressed in all that clobber I'll never know. Each time I rowed ashore, my sweeping skirts swept the bottom of the dinghy like a rag mop. As for leaping over the bow to drag the dinghy up the beach, it couldn't be done, certainly not without risk to life and limb. Defeated, I folded away my glad rags and pulled out my patched blue jeans.

To make up for the flop in the sewing room, Kate and I embarked on a new classroom project—we made a slide-away dollhouse. A tall locker behind the starboard settee had already been set aside for the purpose. Using her own, adult hand tools, Kate sawed up an off-cut of plywood to make the base, walls, and first floor. Marking off more right angles, she cut holes for doors and stairwell. Treated with a coat of red lead followed by undercoat, she finished the walls in white gloss and then glued and screwed them together, leaving the house with an open front and roof. To shut it up she simply slid it into the locker and closed the door. With the walls hung with original Allcard watercolors and the floors painted red and carpeted with Allcard woven mats, it represented our most successful project to date. And by the time Christmas and grandparents had provided furniture, including a lavatory with lavatory paper and miniature lights that really worked, that dollhouse seldom failed to amuse visitors, children and parents alike.

As we finished Kate's dollhouse, so the men completed *Johanne*'s refit. Her topsides returned to their traditional Baltic colors of black planks with two horizontal white lines. An electronic echo-sounder, to measure depth of water under her keel, was inserted in her hull. Also aboard as we slipped smoothly back into the water was *Johanne*'s future topmast, a lovely twenty-five-foot spar, once the sailing mast of a small fishing smack. Riding at anchor off the yard, Edward and Ivan built a lifting sheave into the mast and then, after four coats of varnish, lashed it to the side deck to await some metal fittings. Better equipped and sounder than for many a year, *Johanne* was ready for action.

Friends came to the beach to wave us off—and almost lost sight of us. We'd been blotted out by a disgusting cloud of flies. Unknown to us, they'd been breeding inside the rolled-up mizzen. As we hoisted sail we'd released them in their millions, many of them falling to the deck, dead. But what to us looked like revolting black flies represented a delectable lunch to a tiny goldcrest who came flying out from the shore. Bird replete, we swept the remaining bodies overboard and laid course for the open sea. We planned a leisurely eastward cruise along England's southern shore, introducing our "pirate" ship to friends and relations along the way.

Sailing close to the ramparts of Dartmouth Castle we did a quick reconnaissance of the crowded town moorings and the old stone quay, then headed way up the River Dart, out of sight and sound of the town, to where trees lined the banks on either side. We'd found an anchorage of idyllic peace—until seven o'clock the next morning when, before Edward had even drunk his first cup of coffee, that rural haven was shattered by a motorboat, its driver come to extort Dartmouth's mooring dues. Edward was furious. We were lying to our own anchor, in the middle of an English river, miles from any town. Might as well demand £10 from every car that pulls off and stops in a country lane. The man remained unperturbed, handing us an official receipt in return for our acrimonious payment. Only later did I notice that he'd made a slight error in his work: where he should have written "Allcard" on the receipt he had written "Hellcard."

Breakfast over, we launched the dinghy and motored down river to inspect the town, toward whose upkeep we'd recently made such a major contribution. We found it bursting with life. Overnight a street market had sprung up. Along the quayside were crowds, drawn in from the surrounding countryside, buying everything from fruit and vegetables to coats and household tools. On the outer edge of the market stood a small table heaped high with simple, eight-holed pipes. Ivan picked one up, fingered it, and gave a few tentative toots. Behind us, shoppers surged past. No one so much as glanced at the table.

Then Ivan began to play. From that crude bamboo pipe he conjured up three octaves of pure magic. His fingers hovered like hummingbirds

above the holes, coaxing forth racy Irish jigs and haunting Scots la-
ments. Soon we couldn't move so dense was the crowd. The salesman
sat back beaming and bemused. He'd no idea his pipes could sound like
that. "Say, why don't you play all day? We'd make a bomb!" He was
right. The moment Ivan stopped, a throng of people pressed forward,
all eager to hand over their money so that they, too, could play—just
like Ivan.

On that high note we left the River Dart and set course, up-Channel, for Lymington. The whole area around Cowes and the Solent was,
even in those days, so packed with pleasure craft that there was no hope
of riding at anchor. For the first time in our lives we took our boat into a
marina. Berthed alongside the visitors' pier, she lay surrounded by hundreds of millions of pounds' worth of yachts, 80 percent of which would
never put to sea. Chained to the jetty, we soon learned that we were not
the only people attracted to *Johanne.* One had only to show the top of
one's head above the hatchway to be bombarded with questions: How
old is she? How long is she? Is she a Thames barge? Where was she
built? But, when it came to questions, it was a gentleman from the local
yacht club who took the prize.

Having wined and dined satisfactorily, he and his entourage, his
wife and another couple, decided to take a postprandial stroll down to
the marina—to give that Baltic trader a once-over, you know. Walking
with care along the slatted jetty, our gentleman prepared his opening
speech; always a wise precaution after a good luncheon. First he would
read the boat's name off the stern. Next he would hail her in proper,
nautical fashion. Only when the owner's attention had thus been drawn,
both to his presence and to his obvious understanding of nautical etiquette, would he ask in ringing tones: "Tell me good sir, are you the
master of this fine vessel?"

Alas, poor man, I threw everything into terrible confusion. He
hailed all right but then, you see, he expected a man to answer. Instead
his watery gaze fell on a rather scruffy, not to say disgruntled, woman
emerging from *Johanne*'s saloon (similar calls had had me up and down
those blessed steps all morning). Sadly, our hero's attempts to reorder
his stirring speech became ever more entangled.

"Aha!" he said, playing for time. "Tell me, madam. Are you the
mistress of the owner of this fine vessel?"

"No, sir, I'm afraid not. I'm his wife."

One other stranger we enjoyed talking to came to us straight from
Johanne's past. He had crewed aboard on only her second voyage
under the British flag. He told us how it was a member of the Royal

Lymington Yacht Club who originally bought *Johanne* from the Danes and how the man's partnership with her had been peculiarly doomed. A fortnight after buying her, the owner sailed *Johanne* onto a sandbank in the River Elbe. And then, on the second voyage—and rescue trip—with our new acquaintance on board, they almost ran out of supplies, arriving in England very hungry indeed. Subsequently a fire broke out in the engine room. This series of disasters had a tragic sequel. *Johanne*'s new owner blew his brains out, whether on board *Johanne* or not I did not like to ask. But often in the future, when things went wrong for us too, I wondered if perhaps there was some curse upon her. For the moment, however, this whisper from *Johanne*'s past only increased our resolve to sail her back to Denmark and see for ourselves where she had been born.

Like a fool I had completely forgotten Ivan's itchy feet. His three months up, we returned from a visit to relatives to find an empty boat and a farewell note left that morning on the bar. Above the stove remnants of stew dangled from the deckhead. It looked as if the pressure cooker might have hastened Ivan on his way.

Winter was approaching. After careful study of both charts and pilot books, Edward had picked out the little French port of L'Aber-Wrac'h, near Brest, as a safe and quiet spot to lie. In those days, before Britain joined the Common Market, food in England could be obtained for half the price of that in France. So in early December I devoted one whole day to storing up. That night, worn out by nonstop shopping, I collapsed into bed before everything was properly stowed. Piled higgledy-piggledy on the bar was enough margarine and butter to last us six months.

By morning that pile bore unmistakable signs of teeth—rodent teeth. Timothy Mouse had been on the prowl. Closer inspection revealed a most remarkable fact (zoologists in search of a Ph.D. thesis please note): whereas he had sampled every one of the packs of butter, not one packet of margarine had been touched. Clearly our Timothy was a mouse of considerable discrimination. A bit slow off the mark, it was only after the butter incident that we thought to feed him, partly, perhaps, because we never actually saw him. We only heard him. He had eaten our food, our charts, and my dried flowers, but never, since the West Indies, had we laid eyes on him. There was something a trifle bizarre about adults feeding an invisible mouse aboard a Baltic trader. But that, in the end, is what we did. Each evening Edward or Kate prepared one small dish of raw oats (if Timothy devoured my flowers we assumed, correctly, that he'd also fancy dry oats), and another of drinking water. Each morning the oats had gone. After that Timothy never again ate anything that he should not.

Stored up, *Johanne* was ready. All we wanted now was crew for the crossing to France. Two stalwart friends volunteered: Bodger, who shared his small Cornish fishing boat with a large Alsatian dog, and Hugh, a Rhodesian, who was striving on his own to build a ferrocement yacht. We left Plymouth running before a fresh fair wind. By nightfall the wind had increased to Gale Force 8, turning France's Brittany coast into a treacherous lee shore. It would be madness to continue. We'd already taken the mizzen off *Johanne* and Edward was turning to starboard to bring the gale on the beam and the shelter of Falmouth dead ahead, when there came a thunderclap from the bows. It was followed instantly by the crackle of ripping canvas and the vibrations of flogging sail and sheets shaking the hull. The jib had been blown to tatters. All that night *Johanne* averaged 8 knots under main and staysail alone. Near dawn we entered Falmouth and stayed there for twenty-four hours, waiting for the gale to abate.

At 4 P.M. on Sunday, December 14th, we again hoisted sail for France. All eyes were peeled for ships, all minds concentrated on crossing the world's busiest shipping lanes as near to right angles and as quickly as possible. Above, the skies hung low and overcast. By three the following morning the wind was on the rise, whistling down-Channel from the east-northeast, throwing up an excited sea. Judging time and tide to a nicety, Edward had us off the entrance to the L'Aber-Wrac River at dawn, only to be met by a scene of monochromed confusion: gray swirling sea, gray sky, gray rain, and flying spume blown by a wind that clamored around *Johanne*'s shrouds. And through it all, clearly audible, came the menacing boom of waves bursting upon nearby rocks. According to the pilot book: "Dangers, consisting of above-water rocks, reefs, and shoals, extend nearly 2 miles from the entrance of the river." Also lurking in the gloom ahead there should have been one very tall lighthouse (just visible) plus a buoy and a beacon (not visible at all). Eventually they too appeared through the mist, two lights and two vague shapes, but which was which? The beacon should have been standing still while the buoy rode out the swells but, with *Johanne* flinging herself around like a colt in a swarm of horseflies, the whole world seemed to be heaving about, making identification tricky. Get it wrong, turn in around the wrong light, and *Johanne* would be forced into the embrace of Brittany's rugged shore.

Adding to the predicament of the moment was Hugh. A man of normally robust health, he was lying below prostrate with seasickness.

But we couldn't afford to be kind. After several stentorian bellows of "All hands on deck!" Hugh's pale, unhappy face poked out of the fo'c'sle hatch. We'd located the channel. Now, without delay, we had to hurl all our strength against the gale to haul in *Johanne*'s main and thus, rounding her between the beacon and the buoy, sail into the mouth of the L'Aber-Wrac'h River and safety.

10. Chilly Adventures in France

~~~~~~~~~~~~~~~~~~~~~~~~~~~~~~~~

BODGER AND HUGH, unimpressed by the cold and the gloom, fled France the day after we arrived. In contrast, we looked around our winter quarters and were well pleased. The village of L'Aber-Wrac'h hugs the waterfront at a point several miles from the sea where the river opens into a half-mile-wide bay. In summer the anchorage is crammed with yachts and the village overrun by tourists, but that winter the people of L'Aber-Wrac'h had their village to themselves, apart from us. And we, their sole visitors, were made most welcome. Madame Faure and the postmistress soon had us, perfidious Albions, firmly in hand. The motherly postmistress insisted that Katy must go to school, and Madame Faure, with a son Katy's age, provided the transport. Over the next few months she also provided me with a glimpse into provincial France.

Young David notwithstanding, Madame Faure was a grandmother with grown children not much younger than myself. Always correct and immaculately groomed, I frankly found her rather alarming. And never more so than when she very kindly invited us all to her house for lunch. There I sat, on my very best behavior: back straight, hands demurely folded in my lap. "But no, no, no! Not like that!" cried Madame Faure. "One should always rest one's wrists on the edge of the table, so, with the hands clearly visible." What, I wondered, did the French get up to when their hands were not clearly visible? Was it assassins' pistols or hanky-panky under the tablecloth that they feared? One didn't quite like to ask. Instead I mused on the very parochial nature of most etiquette. What, in the end, does it matter whether you eat peas off one side of the fork or the other, or whether, when you have finished eating, you leave your knife and fork together or apart on the plate or even plunk your dirty cutlery on the tablecloth ready to be used again for the next course.

Returning to *Johanne* after a scrumptious meal, Edward cast an anxious eye at the sky. High above us, clouds raced over from the southwest. Down below, the barometer was falling fast. *Johanne* should be okay—we'd taken enough trouble mooring her. Both her main anchors were out, their chains linked underwater by a giant swivel so that they couldn't foul each other as *Johanne* swung with the wind. To lessen the load, Edward had hooked a heavy metal claw onto the chain a few feet aft of where it came on deck through the port hawse pipe. The claw itself was spliced onto 30 feet of 1½-inch-diameter Dacron line which he pulled taut and made fast around the windlass drum. Most of the strain was thus taken by the line which, unlike chain, could stretch and give as the winter winds gusted and the swells rose and fell. The breaking strain of that line was 42,500 pounds, about 21 tons. Pretty stout stuff, and we had already used it to ride out several normal gales. But this one turned out to be a huge one.

Passing south of Ireland, the deep winter depression made straight for L'Aber-Wrac'h, bringing with it full hurricane-force winds. At the height of the blow, and in pitch-darkness, *Johanne*'s claw line snapped, and the windlass brake failed. Claw and anchor chain rushed seaward, till the claw smashed hard up against the hawse pipe. With a sickening crack of splintering wood, it tore the hawse pipe right out of *Johanne*'s bow, shearing a one-inch bolt as it went. Hawse pipe, claw, and chain hurtled down into the blackness. Only a shackle attaching the end of the chain to a stout ring bolt on deck prevented us from losing the lot. (In the old days ships were occasionally cut to the waterline and sunk, their flying chain transformed into a gigantic chain saw.)

Johanne, evidently disgusted by the whole business, dragged stern first into the nearest mud bank and there sat for the rest of the gale. The next morning the tide left her high and dry and heeled over at a most undignified 25 degrees. As to the cable-stitch knitting on the seabed, it must have been wondrous to behold. Item: one 350-pound fisherman anchor; one 145-pound CQR anchor; approximately 450 feet of ¾-inch chain; a giant claw lashed to it; a giant swivel, which hadn't (so the two chains had tangled anyway); and finally a heavy cast-iron hawse pipe. To add to the chaos we had, in passing, scooped up L'Aber-Wrac'h Harbor's hefty ground chain, which in the summer held all their yacht moorings. Fortunately, along with the moorings, the L'Aber-Wrac'h Harbor authority also laid on a team of most cooperative maintenance divers. Kitted out in their warmest wet suits, they labored for several hours in freezing water before they eventually unraveled the bunch of monkeys we'd dumped on the bottom.

Gale over, Kate returned gleefully to the little village school, where staff and pupils alike went out of their way to make her welcome. She

wouldn't have missed it for the world, but a French tradition, dating back long before "Le Weekend," obliges schools to close all day on Wednesday and open all day on Saturday. So Wednesdays became expedition days on *Johanne*. One particular Wednesday Kate and I climbed into the dinghy and, picking up the oars, set off upriver. We were going bird-watching. I'm no ornithologist, but we had a bird book and binoculars and so, heedless of the freezing weather, we hoped we might spot some birds as foolhardy as ourselves. Half an hour later, in the far distance near some small boats, I saw what looked like a large gull. Resting the oars in the dinghy, I took a look through the binoculars, handed them to Katy, then got out the book.

"Listen to this! 'Great black-backed gull. Head and neck streaked and dusky in winter. Mantle sooty black. Underparts and tail white.' I really think that might be it, don't you? It's certainly black and white. Let's go as quietly as we possibly can and see how close we can get."

Kate's great eyes flashed with excitement as we crept closer and closer, hardly daring to dip the oars into the water. So far, for beginners, we were doing remarkably well. Our quarry hadn't so much as ruffled a feather. Time to take another look through the binoculars. Oh, dear. How does one tell a shiny-eyed little girl that she and her mother have just spent ten minutes stalking a white mooring buoy with a load of black seaweed stuck to its back?

Seaweed littered the beaches of L'Aber-Wrac'h, but it didn't lie there long. After most high tides, horses and wagons trundled down to the shore where, with wide wooden forks, the men loaded up the wavy fronds and carted them away. I thought at first they put it on the fields as fertilizer. Once again Madame Faure was able to put me right. Her husband, a quiet, friendly man, was manager of the local seaweed factory, and one day he took us on a guided tour.

It's quite amazing what can be done with seaweed. Inside the factory the raw weed went from one vast vat to another, churning and bubbling, changing color and texture and stinking abominably. A mass of cellulose was hived off and then, right at the end, a white powder spewed forth. And who wants the powder? Well, the British actually. They eat it. Mind you, most of them don't know they eat it. Seaweed powder is one of the main setting agents for all those instant English puddings that need no refrigeration. And most nutritious it is, too. Monsieur Faure sold 80 percent of his product to the United Kingdom; the other 20 percent went toward the manufacture of commercial glues.

We may have been the only yacht wintering in L'Aber-Wrac'h, but that did not mean there was no marine activity. Apart from the fishing fleet, the village was also home to a large merchant navy college and, in addition, housed the training headquarters of two French sailing teams: Moths and Optimists. A splendid giant of a man coached the Optimist team. At 6 foot 4 inches, Hervé could barely squeeze into an Optimist dinghy. His team, none over fourteen years of age, adored him. Only twenty-one himself, Hervé believed passionately that sport should be fun. The *Gloire de la France* could come later. So he had his youngsters tearing around the bay in the bitterest of winds, playing pirates or tacking like mad creatures as they rescued buoys posing as drowning men.

We never met any of the instructors from the college, though we met any number of their pupils. In those freezing January days the wretched lads would be detailed off to row lumbering great lifeboats around the harbor. Almost every day a boatload sneaked up to the far side of *Johanne* where, out of view of the college and sheltered from the wind, they hung on to her rub rail and enjoyed a quiet smoke before bracing themselves for the long haul home.

Aboard *Johanne* we, too, were perishing, for her hold was never meant for human habitation. We piled on clothes and stuffed towels under the hatch covers to try and caulk drafts which were sometimes so brisk the towels blew right back at our feet. *Johanne* boasted one kerosene stove in the saloon and a wood-burning stove in our cabin. Without doubt, this latter generated the more heat, what with the energy required to saw up the wood and then the hot anger expended trying to light it. Once lit, it did give out an excellent warmth, but by then it was usually bedtime. A more satisfactory source of heat was provided by Edward's "feathers," an immensely bulky, wonderfully warm jacket stuffed with eiderdown and designed for the Artic. In the evenings, relaxing in the corner of the settee, he would open one flap of this jacket and invite Katy to cuddle up inside his "fevvers" with him.

It must have been a month or so after we first met that Madame Faure again took me under her wing, suggesting a new way for me to get warm: join her and a friend of hers at a keep-fit class. We agreed to meet outside her house. Whereas Madame Faure was a trim and youthful grandmother, her friend looked much more her real age. Sliding into the back seat of the car, I left the older woman to enjoy the view and status of the front—and botched it again. In England the front seat may be reserved for the most important passenger, leaving boisterous children, dogs, and inferior adults to scrunch up in the back. Not so in France. There the front seat is known as *La Place du Mort* (the seat of the dead). And, naturally enough, the seat of death is taken, with due humility, by the most inferior member of the expedition. My efforts to mollify the good lady only made things worse: "I'm sorry. You see, in

England we always put the older person in the front." Too late I added "As an honor." The lady was not pleased. And I was left with the tricky decision of where to sit on the way back. In the front and imply she was inferior, or in the back and say she was old? I sat in the front, from where I was well placed to understand the woman's point of view. With French driving élan, that seat sure earns its name.

The actual keep-fit class was great: a large, barnlike hall; a lithe beauty in leotards standing out in front with a group of not-so-lithe bodies facing her. For once I didn't disgrace myself. All that work on board *Johanne* had kept me pretty supple. We rolled away our hips and wrung out our waists; we ran and we leaped and we bent. One hour of such exhausting exercise and everyone was famished, so we crammed into cars and made straight for the establishment of Madame Faure's eldest son. He was patron of an excellent Breton crêperie. Here each of us ordered several of his delicious pancakes, filled with such things as honey or melted chocolate, and proceeded to dig in. In two minutes of munching we had more than replaced the calories so strenuously lost in the previous hour's workout.

Once spring arrives, cruising types throughout northern Europe sniff the air, then, one by one, they creep from their little holes and head south toward the sun. Thus we watched, delighted, as the first two yachts of the new season motored sedately upriver toward us. Where, we wondered, had they sailed from? Would they perhaps care to come over for supper? And, most important of all, where would they anchor? During the past couple of years we had learned to our cost that *Johanne* exerted an almost irresistible fascination on other people's yachts. They were drawn to her like brassed screws to a magnet. This time, however, we really should be all right. L'Aber-Wrac'h Bay was large and we were the only yacht in it. And yet. It did look a bit ominous, the way those two yachts kept coming closer, and closer, and closer—until our initial delight turned to acute embarrassment. Not because they had anchored too near. The trouble was that they hadn't anchored at all. They'd come straight over to *Johanne* and tied up to her, both of them, and without even a by-your-leave. The dismay on Edward's face was almost comical. The last thing he wanted was to be unfriendly, but once the sun shines a boat's deck becomes her sitting room, bathroom, and bedroom combined. Were we now to brush our teeth, cut our toenails, and pee over the side in full view of an audience of strangers? And this was quite apart from the little consideration of anchors. Yachts should carry sufficient ground tackle to hold their own boat in a blow, but not two other boats as well. In the end, however, it was the blaring radio on deck that drove Edward to action. After ten minutes' convivial exchange of news and views, he began:

"By the way, you will be anchoring before dark, won't you?"

"Sorry?"

"I think it would be better if you both lie to your own anchors before dark. If it comes on to blow our anchor won't hold you and there's also the current."

I thought Edward handled it most tactfully. They, alas, looked far from happy.

As woods and hillsides quickened with the first shoots of spring, more and more cruising people called into L'Aber-Wrac'h. They included two family yachts sailing in company and led by Gabor, a marvelously charismatic and bearded Hungarian who, in 1956, had ridden around the streets of Budapest on a captured Soviet tank. Chatting nineteen to the dozen we discovered, by chance, that scattered among our three boats was a rare assortment of firearms. What better way to open the picnic season than with a shooting party ashore?

Edward's chief working exhibit was, inevitably, somewhat different from any piece in our new friends' collections. Besides collecting and restoring old boats, he collects and restores old guns, preferably eighteenth-century flintlocks. He had recently bought a replica of an 1851 Navy Colt revolver (the originals being too precious to fire) and was dying to try it out. The morning of the picnic Kate and I had a practical science lesson: casting shot. Sacrificing a lump of ballast, we melted down the lead in a cast-iron pot, poured the liquid into a special ball mold, and then dropped the shot into the galley sink.

A ruined fort set on a small island near the river's mouth was judged a suitably dramatic setting for our enterprise. Dinghies laden with French bread, sausages, five children, and an armory of guns, our invasion force powered into the seaward beach and leapt ashore. In no time the children had a driftwood barbecue crackling in what must once have been the castle's central courtyard. We were glad of that fire too, not only for cooking but also for warmth. March is not the most popular month for Breton picnics. Appetites satisfied, out came the guns, and immediately the men were as happy as Huck Finn, especially when playing with the Colt. Eyes expertly narrowed, they measured out the black powder, poured it into the six revolving chambers, and then rammed the lead balls home on top. Then they blazed away at a wooden stave as if joining Custer at his last stand or charging with the Light Brigade into the Valley of Death. Of them all, Gabor looked by far the most deadly. Standing square-on to the target, feet wide apart, he took both hands to the Colt's stock—maybe he had Khrushchev in his sights.

As more and more yachts sailed upriver, L'Aber-Wrac'h's harbor authorities began work on their summer moorings. Once all were laid they'd be charging us like everyone else. It was time to leave. But before we did, Hervé rowed over with a request. Would Edward survey an old hull he had found? A possible dream ship? Bundled into the back of Hervé's little van we raced across the farmlands of northern Brittany. Over the centuries the lanes have cut furrows deep below the level of the fields. Primrosed banks flashed by, followed by trees and then pastures dotted with cows, their flanks caked with dung.

A couple of hours later, our bums well and truly numb, Hervé screeched to a halt in the small fishing port of Camouet, southwest of Brest. In front of us stood *La Belle Lurette*. A thirty-three-foot crabber with hardly a speck of paint left on her, she had lain abandoned on the beach for years. Indeed, she looked to me to have dried out beyond reclaim. But Edward, after much tapping, poking, and prodding, checking fastenings and frames and bilges, pronounced her sound. The only major problem that he could see was launching her. She'd been beached on the top of the highest tide of the century. It was going to take someone a hell of a lot of digging to get her off. So Edward made an agreement with Hervé. We would tow her to Lorient—provided he got her afloat. After all, one must work for one's dreams.

Leaving Hervé to caulk the crabber's seams and dig a launch channel, we returned to L'Aber-Wrac'h, said goodbye to our friends, and, with Monsieur Faure volunteering as crew, sailed *Johanne* south for Camaret. We arrived barely an hour before the top of the month's highest tide. Stripped to shorts in the sharp spring air, Hervé was still digging like fury. Finally satisfied that his ditch was long enough, he took *Johanne*'s stoutest line and made fast to the little crabber's stern. Edward maneuvered *Johanne* as close to the shore as he dared, put the G.M. in slow-ahead, and pulled. Nothing happened. Again and again he tried. *La Belle Lurette* refused to budge. Time was flying. Soon the tide would drop and there'd not be another one this high for months. The only chance was a sudden, make-or-break burst of speed (the break being either the crabber's stern or *Johanne*'s tow rope, plus any human limbs that came in range of its flaying end). This time Edward backed *Johanne* toward the beach until the tow line hung quite slack in the water. Then, with a swift movement, he slammed the throttle into full-ahead. *Johanne* charged forward. Her crew ducked. And *La Belle Lu-*

rette, creaking and groaning, shifted very slightly in the sand. Gathering way, oh so slowly, she inched toward the sea. She was afloat! Operation *Belle Lurette*—Stage 1—had been successfully completed.

Monsieur Faure returned home as arranged and Hervé went ashore in search of another hand for the trip south to Lorient. Later he told us how he had found a fisherman at sunset, sitting outside his cottage, contentedly frying up some fish on a portable stove. There and then Hervé persuaded the poor man to abandon his stove and his sizzling supper, to grab some oilskins and an extra sweater, and to join us in mid-April on the 100-mile trip down the Biscay coast to Lorient. Persuasive chap, Hervé.

Spring might have come to the sheltered anchorage of L'Aber-Wrac'h, but out in the Bay of Biscay it was still bitterly cold. Our fisherman stood mournfully by *Johanne*'s helm hugging a mug of hot coffee in his square, red hands and regretting for the tenth time that he had given in to the blandishments of the blond giant astern. Moral press-ganging, that's what it was. But he had only to glance behind him to see that things could have been worse. He could have been aboard *La Belle Lurette*. Hervé, alone on his new love, had no time or chance for hot drinks. His hands were full with pumping and steering. Though to be fair to *Belle Lurette,* she had demanded remarkably little attention to make her seaworthy.

Before leaving Camaret, Edward and Hervé had spent several happy hours pouring over chart and pilot book, discussing strategies— particularly the best way to tackle the Raz du Sein. According to the Admiralty pilot book, the Raz "is never free from danger when conditions are unfavorable." Clearly one's first strategy was to choose favorable conditions. The Pointe du Raz is one of the most westerly points in mainland France, and one of the wildest. In bad weather waves, crashing against its cliffs, can be heard twenty miles away in Quimper. Opposite the point, five miles to the west across the sea, lies the small island of Sein. Known to sailors as the largest and most easterly of a jumble of low-lying rocks and saber-toothed outcrops, the Chausée de Sein on calm days stretches westward as far as the eye can see, but in rough weather a dense curtain of spume conceals the rocks completely. There's also the current. With the tide in full flood, water races through the Raz du Sein at anything up to 6½ knots. So plainly the trick was to arrive on a calm, sunny day soon after the tide had turned. That way there'd be no foul current coming north and the fair current south would not yet have converted into a rampage.

The next day dawned clear and crisp. At the Pointe the first of the fair current was ambling south. A brisk northeaster, throwing a veil of spray over the evil Chausée de Sein, bellied out *Johanne*'s sails from aft. To port, perpendicular cliffs 200 feet high provided a spectacular backdrop to a fantastic tumble of granitic rocks and foaming Atlantic breakers. And then we were clear, scudding south across the wide bay of Audierne.

By 9:30 that night cold was once more burrowing into our bones. This time we sought refuge in the fishing port of Concarneau. Edward, Hervé, and I were cock-a-hoop: *Johanne,* under sail alone and towing eight tons of *Belle Lurette* astern, had averaged 5 knots. It took a hot meal, a bottle of wine, and the knowledge that Lorient was only forty miles to the south before our reluctant new crew member raised a smile.

Dawn again. Outside the thermometer showed 48°F. The strengthening northeaster could only add to our chill. With fingers stiff as ice picks, we hauled up the sails. The old girl surged onward, carried by a quartering wind toward Lorient. At 1:30 P.M. precisely, *Johanne* delivered *La Belle Lurette* to her new home port. At 1:31, our fisherman fled full-tilt for his.

Adventure over, our thoughts, too, turned homeward. Helped by Hervé, it took us twenty-nine hours to sail back to Brest. There, after a series of bear hugs, we parted. Hervé returned to *La Belle Lurette* and Edward set out on foot to buy *Johanne* her most expensive present yet: a Zodiac inflatable dinghy. Big enough to carry six divers and their air bottles and stout enough, with its Grande Raide double skin, to withstand the odd brush with coral, the Zodiac was intended to play a key part in our Indian Ocean diving project. For now, though, we were England-bound and already we had a crewman signed up for the crossing.

Alain first caught sight of *Johanne* anchored off Lorient and, like others before him, had been carried away by her promise of romance. Unlike others, he hired a dinghy and a boatman and rowed out to ask if he could sail with us as a paying passenger. Edward, replying that we took neither passengers nor payment, suggested he work his way instead. Alain hesitated, then agreed. (Later this hesitancy was explained. Owners of large French châteaux, even when in their mid-twenties, do not usually accept work as unpaid deckhands.) Rejoining us in Brest, Alain, openhanded to a fault, came aboard loaded with presents and kitted out in brand new clothes. Realizing at a glance that navy-and-white yachting togs would be somewhat out of place, he had opted for more appropriate gear—army surplus overalls.

A couple of days later Alain disappeared ashore and returned carrying a large and beautifully wrapped parcel. He had heard from Katy that it was my birthday. Inside the parcel was a birthday cake specially iced with my name. Surely only a Frenchman could have made such a delightful gesture. Alain boosted my morale in another way too, though this time unintentionally. Unknown to him, he was the first crew we had had who knew even less than I about sailing. For once I had to teach someone else the ropes, a job made more complicated by the fact that Alain spoke no English. I on the other hand, had learned my French in a Belgium convent when I was ten, and nautical terminology had never ranked high on the nuns' curriculum. From the moment we got under way my mind was in constant turmoil.

Considering that it was still only April, the Channel could have been a lot worse. Nonetheless, the wind gusted to Force 6, the waves slapped at *Johanne*'s hull, and Alain was horribly sick. Nobly he stood his watch at the helm, never complaining as he turned to spew over the side. The rest of the time he sheltered in the stern, his face matching to a nicety those khaki army fatigues. A day and a half after leaving France we were sheltering for the night in Cornwall's Cawsand Bay, and early the next morning we berthed alongside Millbay Pier in Plymouth amid a seething mass of sailboats. We had arrived twenty-four hours before the start of the 1976 Tall Ship Race; then, at the sound of a gun, a great fleet of some forty European sailing ships would race off across the Atlantic to New York, there to help America celebrate two hundred years of independence.

Aboard *Johanne,* Alain packed his bags and left in search of a hot bath, a decent meal, and a drip-free bed. Around us, steel and wooden ships were pouring in from every direction. Old gaffers rafted-up eight deep beside *Johanne.* Some entrants, like ex–Baltic trader *Gefion,* turned me green with envy, they were so immaculate. Others looked their age, and a few must surely have been on the verge of sinking. All at once a buzz flew around the waiting fleet: a certain notorious ex-Baltic was about to berth. In a previous, distressing incident the owner had put his ship's bowsprit clean through the harbormaster's window. Another time the whole engine exploded, sending heavy bits of metal winging like meteorites through the air. Now the grapevine almost snapped under its excited load of gossip: The owner had a large party of charterers aboard. The reconditioned engine had failed. They were adrift off the Devon coast. They were heading for the rocks! The charterers wanted to radio for help, but the owner refused. The charterers seized the initiative, and the ship-to-shore radio. They were begging to be rescued. The rescue tug plus tow would arrive at any moment.

All around Millbay Pier crews stood by their bulwarks. Those with outside berths held fenders to the ready while along the shore a flock of interested bystanders circled like vultures waiting for the kill. No one was disappointed. Tall, weathered masts moved slowly into view. Then the great, and very beautiful, beast cast off her tow and drifted, engine-less, toward her designated berth. As she appraoched, her bowsprit swept the dock, seeking out its prey. Then, lunging forward, she made a wild attempt to pierce to the heart one of Her Majesty's telephonic installations on the shore. Put on its nautical mettle, the crowd fought back and, with twenty or more men pushing with all their might, they narrowly averted an electrical disaster.

Another famous ex-Baltic, *Bel Espoir,* lay right ahead of us along-side the quay. She was owned by Père Jaoen, a Breton priest, admired throughout France for his work with young drug addicts. The good Father would dump a group aboard the ship in Brest and then set out nonstop across the Atlantic to the West Indies. The hope was that, as the addicts worked the ship, they would be both cured of their addiction and infused with a new zest for living. For now, though, *Bel Espoir* had signed on a large, non-addict crew that ranged in age from seven to sixty.

We weren't doing so badly ourselves. Edward had already invited his sister and a few friends to join us in escorting the Tall Ships to the starting line. Wandering around the docks we inevitably bumped into more people we knew—people like Mark Fishwick, present owner of Edward's old yacht *Temptress.* Naturally we invited him along, too. At the last moment, Père Jaoen came over to beg a favor: Could we possi-bly take a French television crew out to film the departure of *Bel Espoir?* I don't know how many people you imagine make up a roving television team. In my ignorance I had assumed no more than three or four. By the time we cast off from Millbay Pier our intimate little party had swelled to thirty-two persons including twelve television personnel and their wives, plus their equipment, plus a miscellaneous collection of children who could have belonged to anybody.

Once clear of the docks, Edward mobilized the troops and we hoisted sail. With the G.M. ticking over, *Johanne* shadowed *Bel Espoir,* TV cameras whirring, while a swarm of local dash-abouts crisscrossed our bows like angry wasps. So great was the number of accompanying boats that it took a moment to disentangle the contestants from their entourage. But they were there all right. Rising high above the riffraff, some of the world's most beautiful ships were heading sedately out toward the starting line. Some were relics from a time past when owners took as much pride in beauty as in profits and sailors could hold their heads high as they pointed to the craft they manned. Empress of our fleet was undoubtedly the Soviet sail-training ship the *Krusenshtern.* Her black hull shone in the watery sunlight. Her creamy flax sails filled in the wind. In her wake swam a flock of fledglings, ex–Baltic traders testing their juvenile tan plumage in the breeze.

The show would have been perfect but for the raucous noise of a hundred motorboats and the sight of a hundred aluminum masts whose tops bristled like a sweep's brush with every electronic gadget known to modern yachtsmen. I know, I know. We were there, so why shouldn't everyone else be. No reason at all, but the spell could not hold. You could not imagine, even for one moment, that you were back in the great age of sail, not when all around you roared, whined, and squealed today's propulsive power.

Across the water the ten-minute gun sounded. Until then we had kept the cameramen close to *Bel Espoir.* Now we bore away—and without warning our own engine ground to a halt. Not the ideal moment for the television crew to announce that they, and their newsreel, had to be on a plane to Paris within the next two hours. We set course for Plymouth under sail alone. Given a fair wind we might have made it, but with a light headwind it was hopeless. Admitting ignominious defeat, we flagged down a passing speedboat. The TV crew were whisked away to catch their plane and we were left to meditate on the undoubted advantages of the internal-combustion engine.

11. *Johanne Returns to Her Birthplace*

As TALL SHIPS winged their way across the Atlantic, a new crewman stepped aboard *Johanne*. Fine-boned, with dark curls and big brown eyes, Andrew looked a cross between Hermes and a choirboy. Add to that an eagerness to help and a willingness to play with Kate, and we were counting our blessings, albeit a mite prematurely. Andrew had joined us at the behest of his mother for what was, to us, our most exciting trip yet. We were off to Denmark—we were taking *Johanne* home.

We'd reached Portsmouth and were in the process of taking on fuel and water when a fair-haired young man cycled to the edge of the dock and paused, one foot on the ground, to watch us. After a time he called out:

"How do you get to crew on a boat like this?"

"You ask."

He grinned. "Say, can I crew on your boat?"

Edward and I looked at each other and then at the young man. We were a bit short on muscle and this chap's bronzed biceps looked more than adequate for the job. I nodded to Edward with my eyes. "Right!" he said. "We're leaving for Denmark in twenty minutes."

"Right! Just give me time to collect my gear and I'm with you"—an arrangement that must surely qualify as one of the quickest crew pickups ever.

An hour later, having stowed our newest crew member's bike in the hold, we cast off from the quay and steamed away up-Channel toward the Strait of Dover. Chatting below over a cup of tea, I learned that Phil, a Canadian, had recently earned a degree as a marine biologist and was taking time off to tour Europe. A genial, intelligent guy, he made an excellent addition to our crew. Absorbed in Phil's story, I quite forgot we were at sea until, faintly in the distance, I heard a foghorn call. In less than half an hour sea mist had slyly turned itself into sea fog—the

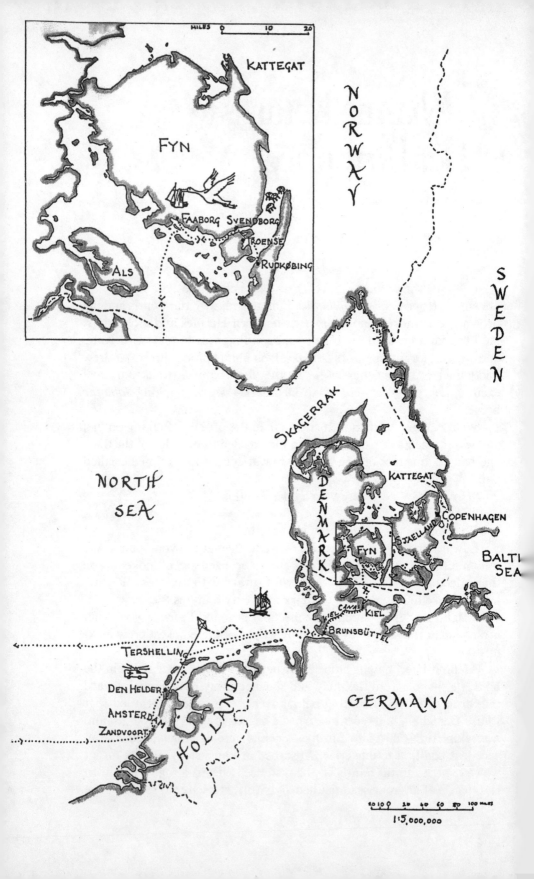

MILES 0   10   20

KATTEGAT

FYN

FAABORG SVENDBORG

TROENSE

RUDKØBING

ALS

NORWAY

SWEDEN

SKAGERRAK

NORTH
SEA

DENMARK

KATTEGAT

COPENHAGEN

JAELLAND

FYN

BALTIC
SEA

KIEL CANAL

KIEL

BRUNSBÜTTEL

TERSHELLING

GERMANY

DEN HELDER

AMSTERDAM

ZANDVOORT

HOLLAND

20 10 0   20   40   60   80   100 MILES

1:5,000,000

first dense sea fog I'd sailed in. I thought it rather fun to begin with, floating around in a silver-gray dream, all sense of motion lost. Our secret world stretched over several hundred feet of flat calm sea to where a soft, smoky curtain of cloud hung down to touch the water and mark the edges of our private universe. But then the curtain began to draw in, closer and closer, trapping us, smothering us till we could barely see from one end of *Johanne* to the other. Only the mournful haunt of foghorns penetrated that thick, silent air.

Somewhere, not far ahead, lay Dover. Somewhere to starboard ran the main shipping lanes. And somewhere close by, hidden in fog, were other ships, all making for the same narrow entrance to Dover Harbor, the busiest cross-channel port in Britain. Edward switched off the G.M. We'd want all our ear-power to detect approaching merchantmen. I sent up an earnest prayer that, on every invisible ship, there was also one dedicated soul glued firmly to his radar screen. Certainly there was no way our own pathetic foghorn would be heard above the thrumming of their engines. In a further effort to avoid collision, Edward sailed as close to shore as he dared. Keeping a sharp eye on the echo-sounder, we inched forward through the shallows, searching in vain for Dover's massive harbor walls. Surely we should have heard the Dover siren by now: two consecutive wails every ten seconds, or so the nautical almanac said. All so simple and precise in a book, but not so easy when you've got to pick out two wails every ten seconds from a whole cacophony of sirens, their cries rising and mingling in the fog.

Andrew and I made our way forward. Maybe we'd see better from there. A moment later I tripped over my own feet with fright as a foghorn, not a hundred yards away, strove to blast *Johanne* from its path. That noise came from inshore of us. Swiveling around, we stared, helpless, into the blanket of fog that hung so soft yet so unyielding a few yards from our eyeballs. Gray-blind, sightless, I was scared. Where was she, dammit! And what was she? A coaster coming up fast? A fishing trawler without radar? She couldn't be anything bigger, not inshore of us, surely? We never did see her. But the vibration of her propeller shook *Johanne* as she passed close under our stern and headed out to sea. My enthusiasm for fog was rapidly evaporating. If only the blessed fog would do the same.

Moments later Andrew called out from the bow—he thought he heard the siren. Everyone strained anew toward the sound. "There! That! That!" he cried before the wails were swamped beneath a quintet of droning foghorns. Another six wails and there was no doubt. The siren was reverberating against our breastbones. Yet still we could not see the lighthouse. Lost and silent, *Johanne* drifted slowly onward.

Then Pilot spotted the ferry, and it was big. We knew that not because we could see her hull low down at sea level, but because we could see the faint yellow glow of her windows, almost vertically above us, where the fog was not so dense. And those windows were doing a good 8 knots. From looking down we now looked up and, following the ferry's projected path with our eyes, made another discovery: Dover lighthouse stood equally high and close on our other side. This fog business was ruddy dangerous.

In an instant Edward had the G.M. pounding full ahead. Now that we had seen the ferry it was vital we didn't lose her. We needed her radar and her stern lights to guide us safely between the harbor walls. Swinging hard to port, hampered by her undersized propeller, *Johanne* churned at the glassy water in a brave effort to keep up. Yet every moment the ferry's lights grew fainter and fainter in the fog ahead. But no matter—she had seen us safely in. Using speed and time to calculate distance covered, Edward carried on a few minutes more, then squared away to starboard, into a featureless world of fog, and anchored.

The next morning, with the fog no thinner, we climbed into the dinghy and made a compass course toward the shore. And, at a stroke, the straight-edged curtain of fog parted and we burst into another land, a land of bright blue skies and beaches spattered with pinkening sun-bathers. Glancing back, *Johanne* was nowhere to be seen.

The pattern of fogs and calms persisted, reducing *Johanne* to working the tides, a venerable art that binds seafarers in closest harmony with the sea. At 9:45 A.M. on the 25th of June, the tide turned in *Johanne*'s favor, carrying her slowly out of Dover Harbor. The current then stayed with her until 3:45 that afternoon. At 4 P.M., with not a breath of wind to help us, we anchored, this time off Ramsgate. Like sailors of yore, we would wait until the foul tide turned fair again.

Late the following afternoon *Johanne* was powering flat-out to clear the shipping lanes off the Dutch coast before dark. Visibility was less than a mile. One ship after another emerged from the fog, each a yacht-eating ogre, only to fade into further mists astern. Using the radio direction-finder, Edward pinpointed the Dutch radio beacons as they passed. (By crossing the beacons' bearings on the chart he got a rough idea of our position.) Freed from the main shipping lane, Edward stopped the motor. The next foul tide was due at 10 P.M., so we tacked toward the shore. At 10:10 P.M. we anchored off what was referred to in the log as "presumably Zandvoort." We could see no land at all.

AT 5:15 A.M. we again weighed anchor to take advantage of the fair tide under us. A warm June sun began to suck away the fog. By noon, for the first time in twelve days, we could see clear to the horizon. An awakening breeze spread *Johanne*'s earth-tan sails against the fresh-washed sky. In a flurry of activity, a Dutch patrol boat sped out from the shore to photograph us. Were they, too, attracted by *Johanne*'s grace, or was it that sinister black hull, smacking of skulduggery, that had galvanized them into action?

That night Edward had difficulty starting the engine. Early the next morning we tied up against the outer wall of Den Helder's yacht marina and an electrical engineer quickly dismantled the starter. He found that not only were its bearings completely shot but the starter itself was a 32-volt machine attached to a 24-volt system. (Even after two years *Johanne* could still spring some surprises on us.) The engineer replaced the starter with one he had reconditioned himself. It has worked impeccably ever since.

Johanne's neighbor on the inner side of the marina wall was an enchanting Dutch sailing barge converted into a yacht. In fact she was too pretty by half, for she was to be Edward's downfall. It was a bit before low tide when her owners invited an admiring Edward aboard. And in Den Helder low water is low. The barge's masts were unstayed and the nearest foothold was the boat's varnished toerail. As Edward's foot landed on the shiny capping he slipped. With no shrouds to snatch hold of, he fell hard. His rib cage, landing full force across the cockpit coaming, took all his weight. I returned from shopping to be greeted by a row of solemn faces and the news that Edward had been carted off to the hospital in an ambulance. We waited an hour or more for news. Then I saw the ambulance returning at funeral pace and with a police escort. No, he wasn't dead—the sympathetic ambulance driver was simply acknowledging Edward's exquisite pain.

The puzzle was how to get the poor chap on board. We couldn't leave him on top of the dock, King Canute fashion, waiting for the tide to come in. In the end the lads rigged up a plank, like a flour shute, and very gingerly we eased Edward down to *Johanne*. At this point another friendly Dutchman arrived to offer some excellent advice. He'd broken his ribs twice. The first time he lay absolutely still in bed, and took several months to recover fully. The second time he was advised, however painful it might be, to get up every hour and walk around. He returned to work in a week. All night Edward sat propped up in the saloon. Religiously, every hour, he got up and, holding himself like a cracked figurine about to break in two, took a few agonizing steps around the saloon. By the end of twenty-four hours he was utterly exhausted. By the end of the week, though still in pain, he was ready to leave.

While Edward continued his hourly exercises on board, Phil and

Andrew took off on bicycles for Amsterdam. Katy and I, remaining in
Den Helder, explored Holland from our doorstep. We climbed to the
top of the dikes and talked of floods and Dutch history and the possible
size of small boys' thumbs (an aspect of that particularly heroic tale that
had always bothered me). Most afternoons we flew kites or bicycled
along country cycling paths. When we wanted food we walked the long
road into town, hauling my "granny" shopping cart behind us. The
shopping precincts were a joy—here was a country that deliberately
included children in its design of life. Toddlers even had their own
attractive form of transport. Instead of being strapped, captive, in a
boring pushcart, Dutch toddlers were pulled along by their mothers in
something I can only describe as a miniature hayrack, or perhaps a
playpen on wheels. Inside, its occupant could safely stand up to watch
the passersby or sit in the bottom of the pen happily delving into
Mama's shopping.

After a week Phil and Andrew returned. I gathered supplies. Edward breathed a little easier and we cast off from Den Helder to head
north, past Terschelling (of *Riddle of the Sands* fame) and on toward
the Kiel Canal in West Germany. We were back in the North Sea, land
out of sight, when *Johanne* plowed her bows into a river of rust-red
pollution. Its edges, running some hundred yards apart, were clearly
defined. A great red river of chemicals was evacuating itself into the
dark gray soup of the North Sea.

The West German town of Brunsbüttel stands at the southern end
of the Kiel Canal. Tying up to the dock, Edward went ashore to ask the
lockmaster about immigration formalities, canal dues, and banks. The
reception was not encouraging. We had arrived direct from Holland
and so, as yet, had no deutschemarks, but we did have traveler's checks
or Dutch guilders with which to pay our passage. Both offers met with
furious indignation. In Germany you use German marks! Naturally—
but where could we get them if the banks were closed? Eventually the
man's nationalistic fervor abated. He took our guilders and we were free
to join a scattering of other yachts moored in the huge lock at the
entrance to the canal. The great steel gates closed and, minutes later, we
were discharged into the canal itself amid a flurry of shouting skippers
and cast-off lines. Edward made straight for the Brunsbüttel marina,
poked *Johanne*'s bowsprit around the corner, and fled. There was no
room for the likes of *Johanne* in there. So then we motored back to the
main dock and, tucking ourselves discreetly into a far corner, tied up.
Within minutes the dockmaster came storming up to us, waving his
arms and shouting. Imagining myself totally unable to speak German, I

tried to placate him in English, which merely enraged the man further. So, remembering my Puerto Rico experience (and with considerable help from Andrew, who had studied German at school), I dredged up an edited version of German gleaned from books and tried again.

The results verged on the miraculous—in an instant the man became quite normal. Yes, he agreed, there was really no room for *Johanne* in the yacht harbor. Yes, if we stayed only twenty-four hours, we could moor alongside his wall. And yes, he did have a tap where I could rinse my washing—whereupon the man picked up my heavy bucket full of soaking clothes and carried it all the way to his own garage, which he unlocked so that I could make use of his tap. An excellent example of how a little linguistic effort, be it ever so incompetent, makes a big difference.

Slipping our moorings the next morning, we chugged off up the famous Kiel Canal. To be honest, I found it a bit of a disappointment as the banks were mostly too high to see over. However, there were always the bridges to admire. Soaring into the sky, they allowed the very tallest supership to pass underneath, while along their surface a procession of minute cars, like exotic beetles, crawled back and forth all day long.

Our pause in Kiel itself was brief, our destination being Denmark, not Germany. Ever since buying her we had built fantasies around *Johanne*'s lines. Most Baltic traders have sturdy, bluff bows and heavy sterns, lines that enable them to carry maximum cargo. *Johanne* was quite different. Her lines were much finer and faster, which was why she was such an attractive boat. Had she perhaps been a smuggler, running gold through tight blockades? Or had she rather slipped spies behind enemy lines in the dead of night? According to her ship's papers she was built by a certain Mr. Anderson of Fåborg. He'd be the one to tell all.

On arrival in Fåborg we quickly proved our Danish to be as hopeless as our Dutch. Unfortunatey, unlike in Holland, we met few Danes who spoke English. But no matter, with the help of a Danish/English dictionary and lots of enthusiastic sign language we established that, though Anderson himself was dead, his son still lived in Fåborg. We set out on foot to find him. Brandishing his address at hapless passersby we were soon totally lost. The snag was that, though we had carefully prepared our Danish to pose the question "Please, where is this?" we could never make head nor tail of the replies. Why did we not take a taxi? Well, I'm not sure really except that taxis are usually the very last resort of cruising folk. There is something decadent, defeatest even, about taking a taxi, and easy option that sidesteps a challenge. And anyway, what a wonderful way to become acquainted with a town, slogging around its outer extremities on foot. Hours later we arrived at the junior Mr. Anderson's front door and, thank the Lord, he was at home. Jamming one foot firmly in the doorway (the man seemed more than half inclined to turn the mad tourists away), we unfolded *Johanne*'s ship's papers and brought out photos of *Johanne* herself. Reversing his original intention, Mr. Anderson entered enthusiastically into the spirit of the chase. A large man, he dived into the bottom of a cupboard and came out with a shoebox full of faded photos—an archive of all the boats his father had built. All, that is, save *Johanne.* Though disappointed, Mr. Anderson did not give up. He promised to come the very next day, accompanied by an interpreter, to inspect *Johanne* for himself.

The next morning he took but one glance at her decks and announced categorically, "This is the *Marie.*" It was the first time we'd heard the name and we wondered whether he really knew. Sensing our doubt, he fought back. "I know it is the *Marie.* I recognize her decks. I was six when she was built. My father was very proud of these pine decks." We gazed down at the wood beneath our feet. We were proud of her decks, too.

So she was the *Marie,* maybe—but we had our first clue. We spent a couple more days in Fåborg, exploring its intricate network of streets. Many of the houses were half-timbered, their wood lovingly picked out in black or brown or laurel green while, in between, the plaster walls were painted in contrasting orange, yellow, or cream. Then someone suggested we visit the curator of the Baltic Trader Museum in Troense, who knew a lot about Baltics and might be able to help us. Much of Denmark consists of islands. Fåborg is on the island of Fyn; just to the south lies the island of Tåsinge and the town of Troense. And so it was for Troense that we now set sail.

The museum, laid out in one low-ceilinged room, was crammed to bursting, a wonderland of Baltic-trader relics. Diffidently we approached the curator: "Excuse me. We were wondering, do you know of a Baltic trader called the *Marie?*"

"*Marie?*" he said. "You mean the one that's anchored out in the bay right now? Yes, I know her. She's in this book here." And there she was, our very own *Johanne,* photographed on her first sea trials. We had uncovered her past.

The curator was a remarkable man and never more so than in his calm acceptance of the reappearance of the *Marie.* According to the book, *Rudkøbing Skibe,* she had sunk ten years before. He told us that the book's author, Emil Gøtfredsen, was still harbormaster in the port of Rudkøbing from where *Johanne,* or *Marie,* had traded for many years. Fantastic! We would go there at once. And, what's more, we'd enter port with a flourish, for the book the curator had shown us stated badly that in 1966 *Johanne* was bought by the British and a fortnight after hoisting the British flag she was lost. We'd show them who was lost!

Two yards of brand-new red ensign streamed defiantly from *Johanne*'s stern when, under a press of canvas, she stormed into Rudkøbing's high-walled harbor; there happened to be a gale blowing at the time. In the bow the anchor hung poised for instant dispatch. Shooting past the enclosing walls, we saw inside the harbor for the first time—not exactly one of the world's major ports, Rudkøbing. Viewed from behind *Johanne*'s eighty-seven feet of deck and bowsprit, it looked positively minute. Three of the docks were already full. The fourth, where we could have gone alongside under sail, had a dinghy tied slap in the middle of it.

"Let go!" yelled Edward above the shrilling wind. We let go. The chain zipped across the deck and out into Rudkøbing Harbor. There'd been no time to point *Johanne* fully head to wind so, as we put on the windlass brake, the chain jerked *Johanne*'s bow around while her stern swung slowly past quays lined with yachts. From every hatch an anxious head poked out. I can't think why. We missed them all by at least a foot, and, after all, it's only the last inch that counts. Once safely anchored, sails stowed, and yachtsmen's heads retracted out of the biting wind, Andrew and Phil rowed a long line ashore to the far quay. Moving the dinghy to one corner, we then had ample room to warp *Johanne* alongside, in much the same manner as she might have been warped alongside years before.

Just as babies are often born in hospitals some miles from their homes, so Fåborg, *Johanne*'s birthplace, proved a red herring in her history. Rudkøbing was her home, the place where she had lived and worked and had her life. Here we welcomed aboard the harbormaster, Mr. Gøtfredsen, author of *Rudkøbing Skibe*. Speaking excellent English, he told us more about our boat.

In the depression years of the late 1920s, Mr. C. P. Jensen could have bought any one of 200 laid-up ships for half the price of building a boat new. But he was adamant. He wanted a new ship and he wanted the best materials he could afford. His *Marie,* our *Johanne,* was the only boat to be built in the area that year. And that meant he had the pick of the timber, hence her fine decks and single-piece keel. And her fine lines? Was Mr. Jensen really a runner of gold bullion? Well, no. As a matter of fact, Mr. Jensen was nicknamed Kartoffel Jensen, "Potato Jones." His trade was carrying potatoes and cucumbers to Copenhagen, perishable goods which had to travel fast or go rotten—not quite the romance my heart craved. Kartoffel Jensen was, sad to say, dead, but his widow lived in Rudkøbing. From our point of view, the only slight drawback was that Mrs. Jensen, a German, spoke no English. But no matter. Dragging Phil's bike out of the hold, we dispatched Andrew, our German speaker, to invite her on board for tea. Mrs. Jensen turned out to be a fabulous person. Possibly in her seventies, she had the enthusiasm of eternal youth, especially when describing her honeymoon spent aboard *Johanne*. Launching into a flood of German, her desire to communicate easily overcame such feeble barriers to understanding as language. Hands, eyes, arms, and legs, all were used in her brilliant synopsis of life on a Baltic trader in the 1930s. Most vivid of all was her description of the honeymoon night. This elderly lady left us in no doubt that those extraordinary bunks, poked away in long low cupboards with closing doors to keep out the cold, afforded very little room for connubial bliss.

Our final visitor from the past was Niels Pils, who brought with him an explanation of *Marie*'s change of name. In 1939, C. P. Jensen sold *Marie* to his brother Richard, and Richard always called his ships *Johanne*. Mr. Pils took command in 1942 and remained aboard, with Mrs. Pils at his side, for the next ten years. He was a thin-faced man, with a bony beak of a nose, his cheeks permanently red and roughened by the wind. Shy with people, his eyes and hands caressed *Johanne*, eager to check on her well-being. How anxiously we followed his progress around the boat. How glad we were that we had repainted her in the proper Baltic colors of black and white. We were thankful, too, that there was no ugly "tomato house" stuck over her hold, ruining her sensuous curves and attracting his censorious eye. But then he came to *Johanne*'s shrouds and all Edward's proud miles of serving were as naught. The old man gave one piercing look at the bulldog clips and turned silently away. Lips compressed, he averted his eyes the better to avoid our shame. We had been dismissed forever as triflers, people who stooped to bulldog clips instead of proper wire splices at the ends of their shrouds. If only we could have explained. We could have told him that those offensive clips were temporary, that we were going to change them right now—well, any year now.

One piece of equipment he was pleased to see was the old ship's lamp. The harbormaster had told us how, when working, *Johanne* had to pass a Board of Trade inspection every few years. Each time she succeeded, the inspector would scratch the date on the glass of the big cooper lantern. Carrying it to the light Niels Pils showed us the markings still visible to this day. That lamp is one of our most cherished possessions, one we carried away with us on *Johanne* when we once again said goodbye.

In a little over a fortnight's time my older brother and his family hoped to spend a holiday aboard *Johanne,* not in Denmark but on the east coast of England, so we prepared to depart. Re-passing the Baltic Trader Museum, we headed north into the narrow Thurø Sound, and a headwind. Sensing the curator's eyes upon us, Edward determined we would not touch the motor but use sail alone to get us through the channel. If the old Baltics could do it, so could we. Boy did we work! Straining with all our might (no winches on *Johanne*), we pulled the headsail sheets hard in to port. Moments later the shore loomed, threatening, over the bowsprit. Edward shouted "Lee O!" and we were off again, letting the sheets fly to port, hauling them in as fast as we could to starboard. Two hours and twenty tacks later we were through. If we thought our hands were burning we soon saw the effects of all that friction on the gear. Unable to find metal thimbles (sheet leads) in Kiel, Edward had, under protest, bought two in plastic—and that one short spell of tacking had worn those brand-new thimbles half away. "Useless modern rubbish!" he cried as he tore them off and flung them in the trash can.

All around *Johanne* the sea had turned to jelly—jellyfish jelly. Denmark's waters were solid with them, and Phil, our marine biologist, fished one out and put it in a bucket of water for Kate to see. Crouching on either side, the two of them contemplated the lovely mauve flesh. Phil pointed out the four nerve centers around its rim and the central stomach working, working, working without cease. That's why those jellyfish were colored—they were constantly ingesting chemicals from the polluted waters.

Helped by a more than adequate wind, we retraced our steps as rapidly as we could. When we reached the canal we took it at a canter, this latter due to Andrew. He and Kate were below together in the saloon when suddenly Andrew let out an almighty yell which was followed instantaneously by a crash. A few moments later he emerged on deck, a rapidly swelling hand dangling painfully from his wrist. In some way never explained, Kate had triggered off one of his fits of blinding rage and he had smashed his fist into a case of beer. Over the past month, Andrew had changed dramatically. Whether it was incompatible chemistry or difficulties with authority figures I don't know, but he had developed a real antipathy for Edward. Nothing the poor skipper did was right. Maybe it was Edward's style of command that bothered Andrew.

Edward is a straightforward guy who runs a straightforward ship

for straightforward people. If he wants a sail hoisted he bellows enthusiastically, "Up main!"—not "Would you mind awfully going forward to
hoist the main?" He himself had learned his seamanship in a more
robust era. Sailing from the age of six he had, as a fifteen-year-old Eton
schoolboy, chosen to spend his holidays as unpaid cabin boy aboard a
Hull trawler. The fishing fleet was delayed off the Faroes, but Edward
had to get back to school. No problem, they said; they'd off-load him
with the fish when the carrier came to collect it. An Atlantic gale was in
full swing when they arrived. The two ships, bucked by twenty-foot
waves, were whizzing up and down like opposite ends of a seesaw.
Utterly unfazed, a couple of fishermen grabbed the boy's arms and legs
and, waiting for that four-second moment of equilibrium when both
boats' bulwarks were level, they flung him across the gap with as much
ceremony as the fish. On another occasion, when working as ship's boy
on a Thames sailing barge, Edward absentmindedly left a winch handle
unattended in the winch. The next moment he was sprawled on the
deck, but it wasn't the flying handle that had sent him there—it was the
captain's arm. "That, Sonny, is t' teach you t' take winch handles out
when you're through with 'em. Them winch handles can kill a man as
quick as I knocked yer down." Not that Edward would ever dream of
laying a finger on anyone, but, like that old barge captain, he didn't
believe in shielding people from their mistakes. Mistakes can kill, especially at sea. Maybe Andrew was used to being shielded.

As I fashioned a splint, then bound Andrew's hand and forearm
firmly to it, my mind was elsewhere, worrying over what he might hit
out at next, wondering what we should do. Obviously the first thing was
to get him to a hospital where his hand could be X-rayed. After that I
felt he should return to his parents.

Advised that the best hospital was in Brunsbüttel, we steamed on
down the canal. Night fell and we were in trouble. There is a rule on the
Kiel Canal: no normal traffic may move after dark. Guard posts all
along its length enforce the rule. The posts were easy to spot: dotted like
distant runway lights along the straight embankment, each guardhouse
stood out, floodlit and warm, in the dark night. And each time we
approached one, the authorities pinned us down with blinding searchlights and shouted at us through loud hailers to stop. We shouted back
"Crankenhausen!" (the gloriously apt German name for a hospital),
and continued full speed toward Brunsbüttel.

On inspection the doctor said he thought Andrew's hand was not
broken, just badly sprained, but he put it in a cast just in case. Sprained
or broken, the accident had a strange effect on Andrew. His whole

attitude changed. He became once again his original charming self, as if all the recent unpleasantness had been some sort of game. But it was a game we didn't understand. Handing him the money for his fare we wished him good speed.

12. A Time of Gales and Topmasts

ONCE SAFELY PAST a heavy barge intent on running us down, we crossed the North Sea in fine style. The wind might not have been exactly the "Force 4 on the quarter" invoked in sailors' toasts, but it wasn't far off. With her sails spread out to catch the breeze, *Johanne* took only three days to reach England's east coast. Turning his back on the noisy port of Harwich, Edward made for the estuary's northern shore, dropping anchor off the village of Shotley Gate, near where the rivers Sour and Orwell meet on their way to the sea. Phil, good-natured as ever, volunteered to stay on another week to help hoist *Johanne*'s topmast.

From *Johanne,* we often watched as local fishermen pulled their open boats up and down the nearby slipway. One foursome in particular fascinated us. Almost every morning they'd launch their immaculate boat and, with nothing but oars to propel them, take off upstream for a day's fishing. But what excited our attention, not to say admiration, was their ages. Not one of those guys could have been a day under eighty. Each time they passed we meant to hail them, but they always looked so intent on getting to their fishing ground or, alternatively, on getting home to a hot bath, that we never liked to intrude. Finding himself alone one afternoon, Phil threw off all such foolish British reticence and called them over for a drink. Now it so happened that aboard *Johanne* we had a very special bottle of rum. Presented to us in an unlabeled bottle by the heir to a family brewery, the contents were 151 proof (Teacher's scotch is 43 proof). At the time the heir warned us to serve it up in very small tots. Phil, moved partly by the "old salt" appearance of his guests and partly, I suspect, by pure mischief, decided their arrival warranted the dusting off of the rum bottle. He assured us later that all four men had been duely awed by the liquor's potency. Indeed, it had warmed their hearts so much that one chap, Chip, invited us up to his home.

A pack of friends joined us for our first short voyage in _Johanne_.

Edward taking a refreshing bucket bath. Deck temperatures reached 104°F in the shade.

Wash day in the Red Sea.

Laundry hanging out to dry on a beautiful clear day. *Photo by Doreen Johnstone*

Above, Edward mending a sail.
At right, the list of jobs was endless.
Here Edward is fashioning a wooden
cleat for the mizzen sheet.

On the facing page, above, I'm paving
the decks with bubbling hot pitch.
Photo by Cecilia James. **Below,** Katy
helping with the chores as *Johanne*
lies, stern-to, to the mangroves in
English Harbour, Antigua.

Loading up with stores for a winter in France.

On the facing page, above, **the mainsail was falling apart at the seams.** *Photo by Rosemary Thompson.* ***Below,*** **a Tall Ship setting off across the Atlantic.**

Halfway across the Atlantic I was still waiting for the galley sinks to be installed.

Johanne on Antigua Slipway, her stern neat and heart-shaped.

First rate carpenters with the job half done.

Using an adze, the Antiguan carpenters worked fast to change twelve of the "softest" planks.

Caulking up the new seams.

Edward Allcard with Katy and her cousin Georgina off the coast of England. *Photo by John Thompson*

Kate wore her new pirate outfit for al fresco lessons aboard.

Looking down from Shirley Heights with Freeman's Bay, Nelson's Dockyard, and Falmouth Harbour stretched below us. *Photo by Edward Allcard*

Guilvinec fishing boats put down "legs" so as to stay upright when the tide goes out.

We'd made it to Denmark.

Corinth Canal, probably the most expensive stretch of water in the world.

From left to right: My mother Rosemary Thompson, Edward, Katy, Martin, Lana, and John.

Johanne moored to palm trees in Admiral's Bay, Bequia.

Drying the main in Fornels Harbour, Menorca.

Anchored in deep water off Foradada, Mallorca.

The man's real name was Chipperfield but as he had worked as a master carpenter most of his life, Chip he inevitably became. When Chip heard that Edward planned to fit roller reefing gear to *Johanne*'s new boom, he suggested he crew with us down the coast to London and help fit the gear there. And that is how, at eighty-two, Chip came to set a record as *Johanne*'s oldest crewman.

But first to the topmast. After putting the job off for months, Edward and Phil took no more than a morning to hoist it into place. In those days *Johanne* had no ratlines on her shrouds, so we had to fist Edward to the masthead in the bos'n's chair. The twenty-five-foot spar followed. First we used the jib halyard, then, when the topmast rose above the jib's upper block, the pulley-hauley was done on a heel line which went through the sheave in the heel of the topmast to a fitting halfway up the spar and then down to Phil and me on deck. Once Edward had the topmast foot trapped securely inside the metal capband (which in turn was clamped to the top of the mainmast), he drove a 1½-inch-diameter stainless-steel fid through the spar to hold its weight. He then lowered the wire topmast shrouds to Phil, who fitted them to rigging screws on deck. Finally Edward rammed specially shaped wooden wedges between the mast and mastband so nothing up top could move and, *voilà,* the job was done. Bundling into the dinghy we rowed out to admire *Johanne*'s new look from afar. With the addition of the topmast, the main now soared, like her original polemast, some seventy feet toward the skies.

Job finished, adventure called to Phil. Extricating his bike from the hold (how people manage without a hold I do not know), he strapped his pack to the carrier and peddled off to investigate the rest of Britain. Edward and I upped anchor and powered a few miles farther south to the River Naze, an ideal setting for a family holiday. A couple more days and we had my brother and sister-in-law plus three pre-teen children safely distributed between fo'c'sle and forecabin. *Wallaby,* our old-fashioned, clinker-built sailing dinghy (bought in a moment of madness three months before), had already been launched and we were just discussing whether we dared visit a nearby, privately owned island when a head appeared. Purple-blue around the lips and nostrils, it was bobbing in the water right next to *Johanne.* Invited on board, the owner of the head turned out to be purple-blue all over. He had just swum seven miles in sea so cold I'd have required a hefty bribe, or a hearty shove, before I'd have put so much as a toe in it. Sitting on the bulwarks making small talk, I nodded casually toward the island and asked what he knew about it. Quite a lot, as it turned out—his parents owned it.

"They breed Arabs there."

"Really! My great-uncle was mad on Arabs. R. S. Summerhays, you may have heard of him." The man looked faintly amused. "Heard of him? He stayed here when we first moved in. Advised my parents on setting up the place." So, thanks to small talk, and Uncle Reggie, we didn't have to trespass after all. We received an invitation to visit the island.

Wallaby's ample form was made for such an expedition. With eight bodies stowed aboard, Edward punted her cautiously up a narrow, twisting channel. At every bend Katy kept a keen eye open for John and Titty, hero and heroine of *Secret Waters,* for it was right here that Arthur Ransome had set his children's sailing story. Of bends there was no shortage, and each brought with it a hotly contested decision as we tried to select the main channel from a confusing tangle of streams and waterways that crisscrossed the island's mud flats. Then someone spied a row of stakes clinging drunkenly by their tiptoes to the bank. That must be the jetty. Making *Wallaby* fast to the most robust of the posts, we scrambled up the mud bank and set out over marshland and dikes toward a low cluster of farm buildings half hidden among trees. Wherever the eye wandered there were horses, majestic Arab horses; cropping the marsh grass, kicking their heels up in the summer sun, or standing, ears pricked, watching with aristocratic disdain as we intruded on their land. I looked back warily. Having inherited none of my great-uncle's empathy with horses, I prayed I would not be expected to pat too many equine noses or, worse still, feel a fetlock.

To say my chief memory of that visit was of flies, not horses, is to speak no more than the truth. The kitchen, hub of activity on the stud, was a large room with a large table at its center. A picture window looked out over rough pasture and near it, seated in a wooden chair, was our host, an elderly man totally absorbed in cleaning his shotgun. A pool of blood, remnant of his most recent foray, lay forgotten on the table. The rabbit hung, skinned and gutted, near the sink. Besides the blood, the table was a repository for open pots of jam, abandoned breakfasts, and a chain of dirty mugs. Offering us tea momentarily drew our hostess's attention to the mugs—and then the blood. The sight seemed to stir a memory of some far distant code of conduct, long since discarded as superfluous. It moved her to pick up a rag and dab at the congealing gore. This was a mistake, for it upset the flies. In an instant a black cloud of them rose up in bitter protest. Efforts to cover the jam jars were no more successful as the wasps, trapped inside, buzzed all the more furiously to be set free. Having thus proved, beyond doubt, the futility of cultivating bourgeois gentility in a farmhouse, our hostess gave up the pretense and made us some tea. The flies settled back, a black scum lapping at the edges of a dark-red pool.

We did not stay long. Aliens, we had intruded unwanted into a specialized world with which we had no solid point of contact. Thanking the couple for their time and tea, we beat a hasty retreat back to *Johanne.* Picnics and games of Frisbee on the beach, sailing and fishing expeditions in *Wallaby,* and exploring the town of Walton on market day all filled the hours and meant that ten days sped by like five. Much against my will, I loaded suitcases, beach gear, and the collected shells, plus four adults and four children, into the Zodiac and we raced up the creek to the town quay, where we hugged goodbye. *Johanne* felt funny on our return. It wasn't often that she had no one but Allcards aboard. The next day the three of us sailed *Johanne* back to Shotley Gate and a rendezvous with Chip.

For years Kate believed that one got smaller as one got older. She had drawn this conclusion from those around her. Her grandmother, her great-great-aunts, even Great-Great-Uncle Reggie, were all little people. And Chip did nothing to refute her belief. At eighty-two he was a tiny hummingbird of a man filled with an immense appetite for life.

We set out, London bound, in early September. Often the least temperamental month in England's notoriously temperamental climate, this time September let us down. The first signs of an approaching gale showed up as we neared the River Crouch, some ten miles north of the Thames estuary. Ahead lay the Maplin Sands, burial ground of many a well-found ship and crew. Not wishing to join them, Edward turned into the Crouch and then its tributary, the Roach, a haven where, since time immemorial, sailors bound to and from the Thames have sought shelter from North Sea gales. Happily this one was short-lived, and seventy-two hours later *Johanne* crept back into the North Sea; after running well clear of the sands, we made course southwest-ward toward the wide mouth of the Thames and London. Along the riverbanks people waved as *Johanne* motored past landmarks of a lost empire. Tilbury Docks, East and West India Docks—once-great trading centers for spices, silks, sugar, and tea—now stood idle, killed by a vicious circle of declining trade and restrictive union practices. To our left lay Greenwich Park. The site, long ago, of Henry VIII's favorite palace, today it houses the National Maritime Museum, home of Greenwich meridian and Greenwich mean time. Beside the park, in permanent dry dock, stands the tea clipper *Cutty Sark,* her masts and rigging rising high above the riverbank. A mile farther and our way was blocked by that quintessential symbol of London, Tower Bridge. A few hundred feet before it and to the right lay our destination.

Maneuvering *Johanne*'s ninety-two feet of total length into the modest lock that links St. Katherine's Dock to the River Thames wasn't that easy. The crowd of onlookers clearly hoped it would prove disastrous. They hovered about, staring straight at us from a few feet away, till I felt like a performing bear, right down to the cheers and round of applause (but no buns) as we docked successfully. Chip, eyes twinkling, whipped off his cap, suggesting I should pass it around for a collection.

Not a bad place as moorings go, St. Katharine's. Visitors' berths ran right beside the river. All around us were Thames sailing barges, immaculately maintained. A few hundred yards away, upriver, the Tower of London could just be seen, whereas on the inland side of the dock the old warehouses were halfway through their up-market renovation. St. Katharine's was spearheading the transformation of London's dockland. Smart city flats rose above expensive delicatessens, and right opposite to where we had berthed, our own yacht club, the Cruising Association, offered us hot showers, cool drinks, and arguably the best private sailing library in the country. With the underground within easy walking distance and the Tower of London next door, Katy and I had a field day. Well, at any rate, I did. Does any child really enjoy visiting places of historic interest?

Aboard *Johanne,* Chip worked flat-out on converting someone else's discarded mainmast into *Johanne*'s new main boom. The spar had been lying, broken, in Mashford's yard for years. Measuring up the longer of the broken bits, Edward found it would make an admirable replacement for the all too natural, and now rotten, West Indian tree trunk which, until then, had served *Johanne* as a main boom. So as to incorporate the roller reefing gear (another secondhand piece of equipment sold to us by a friend), Chip, with infinite care and accuracy, fashioned and glued in long, eight-inch-diameter plugs at each end of the hollow spar. Since then we have traveled the world and sampled the fabled skills of the East, but never have we come across a craftsman with an eye to match Chip's. Everything he touched fitted to perfection. One day Edward presented him with a 1½-inch-thick slab of mahogany. He wanted it cut in half, edgewise. Chip didn't turn a hair. Taking a hand saw he cut the wood down the center, producing two absolutely flat and identical pieces of wood. No machine could have done it better, and yet Chip's own "machine" was eighty-two years old.

Roller reefing gear installed, Chip returned home to Shotely Gate and we awaited our next crew members, Edward's distant "relation" John Campbell. Soon after we last saw John, black with grease on the docks in St. Thomas, he had set sail on another ex-Baltic, *Romance,* and had found it, too. On board he met an American charterer named

Lana. We knew that Lana was joining us too, but what we didn't know was that, the day before they stepped onto *Johanne,* John and Lana got married. For the second time in her history, *Johanne* had honeymooners on board. Both exceptionally intelligent, they were an excellent complement to each other. Lana, tall, artistic, outwardly serene, and blessed with beautiful auburn hair, had married a man who, in contrast, was dark like a genie and had a genie's restless vitality and sense of mischief. They came aboard dragging behind them scuba gear, underwater filming equipment, and a whole trunkload of spare film. They planned to sail with us as far as the Seychelles, shooting a TV documentary on the way.

Once everything was safely stowed, *Johanne* crept through the lock gates and plowed off down the Thames and out to sea, bound some 200 miles down-Channel to Portsmouth where we hoped to collect *Johanne*'s new, tan mainsail and storm trisail from Edward's favorite sailmakers, Lucas.

The Camber at Portsmouth turned out to be a good meeting point for a whole host of friends and relatives. Here single-hander Clare Francis and her husband, Jacques, came aboard to visit John and Lana who, before joining us, had delivered Clare's Ostar yacht, *Gulliver G,* back from the States. From the Camber we went to get our first glimpse of Edward's new granddaughter, Camilla.

New sails stowed below, it was goodbye Portsmouth, hello Poole. And a gray Poole it was, too: slate-black skies, charcoal sea, and rain, dreary rain. Boy how it rained! We arrived on October 1st, blown into Poole's magnificent harbor by a brisk southwester. Edward rounded up into the wind well clear of all other yachts and dropped the CQR to port. A quick tap below the barometer showed it crashing down—the year's first October gale was brewing. Edward ordered us to stand by the 350-pound fisherman anchor. Motoring to windward, and at 20 degrees to the right of the CQR, he waited till *Johanne*'s bow was in line with the first anchor, put the G.M. in astern, and yelled "Le' go!" To starboard the Great Anchor hurtled down through the dusk-darkened water, followed by three times the depth in chain. John jammed on the brake and the chain went taut, dragging the fluke of the fisherman firmly into the seabed. We then paid out more scope until *Johanne* lay evenly balanced between the two anchors. While the rest of us anxiously watched the chains over the bow, Edward gave a final blip astern. The two chains rose steadily, held themselves taut, and then slowly sagged back into the water. (The final sag was due to the chain actually pulling *Johanne* forward. If either anchor had been dragging as we went astern on the motor, the chain would have jerked up and down or else remained relatively slack all along.) As we all concentrated on the chain, Edward lined up two leading marks on the land: one on the foreshore and one in the distance. He then checked that they stayed in line with each other while the G.M. did its best to pull the anchors through the mud. Nothing moved. *Johanne* was ready for the wind when it came— and did it come.

We had only popped into Poole for a couple of days, first to visit two of my favorite relatives and second to discuss our new Seascribe echo-sounder with its manufacturer. For days we did neither; we remained trapped aboard as gale after gale swept England's southern coast. The weather reached its climax on October 14th. You remember that gale off the Azores, the one I said was a textbook introduction to the species, well mannered and orderly with the barometer falling from 30 to 29.85 inches of mercury? Well, the gale of October 14th was neither orderly nor well mannered. As *Johanne* strained at her anchors and I whipped up and down the companionway like a demented poodle, terrified we were dragging, the barometer plunged to 28.65. Outside the winds blasted through *Johanne*'s rigging at a steady 55 knots. All that night we held to our leading marks ashore, yet when Edward looked over the bow the next morning he found that the 350-pound fisherman had dragged right home. *Johanne*'s eighty-five tons had ridden out the gale held only by that most trustworthy of anchors, her CQR. That same night Poole Harbor saw twelve yachts wrecked along its shores; at the same time a Baltic trader, bigger than *Johanne,* sank right alongside the dock. It was a good thing Edward had anchored us well clear of other boats.

Our isolation did, however, have its drawbacks, mainly that of getting ashore, or at any rate getting out again. On the rare days when the gales abated enough for Lana, Katy, and me to make a wild dash for supplies, we were then too far off to hail the dinghy to ferry us home. What we needed were walkie-talkies—and by Jove, we had some. Illegal in England at the time, a friend had asked us to buy a set for him in Denmark. Later he decided he didn't want them after all and so we had hidden them away, another might-be-useful-sometime gadget whose time had come. We just had to be discreet about it, that's all. One machine was permanently switched on aboard the ship; the other lay concealed in the bottom of the shopping basket. When we returned, baskets filled to the brims, to the quayside, I had only to press a button to summon help. It was John who suggested the call sign. Standing there in the bitter wind, carefully shielding my toy from the eyes of the law, I felt like a bit-part player in a B movie. "Calling Kartoffel One!

Calling Kartoffel One! Are you receiving me? Over." And then through the static and the flying spray came the reply: "Kartoffel One to Kartoffel Two. We're on our way. Over and out." What the poor police made of those clandestine assignations between one potato and another we never discovered.

Twenty-two days after we arrived in Poole an optimistic weather forecast and a steady barometer combined with our own impatience to send us on our way. Two hours later a powerful squall ripped the old mainsail asunder. As the heavens opened their sluice gates and torrents of rain poured upon us, Edward hoisted the "iron topsail" and we motored west for two more hours before making Portland Harbor and safety. As to the old mainsail, it was going to require professional intensive care to survive, so we unbent it and shoveled it into the hold, bending the new storm trisail in its stead. Our sail area greatly reduced and the wind once more abating, we put to sea. Next we had to tackle Portland Bill and the Race. There, strong currents churn the water into a nasty chop. Most skippers take their vessels around the outside, well clear of the Race, but that day "most skippers" were notable for their absence. Due to recent gales only two yachts were in sight. One, *Johanne Regina,* had a skipper who was constantly seeking to add a touch of excitement to life. The other skipper, I think, must have been a sadist. At least our route, through a narrow channel inside the Race, was smooth even if it did run nerve-rackingly close to the cliffs. Atop those cliffs a considerable crowd had gathered, but not to follow us—all eyes were uneasily focused out to sea, on the second yacht. And who could blame them. There, right in the middle of the Race, was one of Britain's sail training ships. Pitching and rolling as if about to founder, she shuddered and ground her way with agonizing slowness through a confusion of waves piled higher by the recent gale. No doubt the captain thought it would serve as a good shakedown for his novice crew. Fond mamas and papas perched on the cliff top must have wondered what they had let their precious offspring in for, and so must the precious offspring.

Once past the Bill our own passage was straightforward, and blessed with a fair wind we reached Mashford's soon after midnight. We had a busy schedule ahead: the mainsail had to be sent away for patching and re-stitching, supplies had to be bought, and *Johanne* had to be slipped for one last onslaught to her hull before she left England for exotic shores.

Compared with previous haul-outs this one was swift and painless. The only major new addition was a heavy, galvanized-steel mastband holding in place one end of a steel derrick with a lifting strength of three tons. Slung horizontal, it stowed neatly below the main boom. And what, you may wonder, did we plan to lift with a three-ton derrick? Treasure, of course. How else could we raise those nine-foot bronze cannons we knew were lying off a reef in the Seychelles? We had already bought, and then loaned to the Seychelles Museum, two smaller cannons raised by fishermen from the same site. Derrick in place and the whole hull re-caulked, the painters gave *Johanne* two coats of anti-fouling and she was launched.

Two weeks later, sailing back from a farewell visit to Edward's sister in Fowey, *Johanne*'s bilges suddenly filled with water. Coming so soon after slipping and re-caulking it seemed unlikely that the latter was at fault, which left us to pick a culprit from the several thousand assorted wormholes that still graced the old lady's bottom. We did have one clue. We could see, approximately, where the water was coming in: port side, aft, in the engine room. The difficulty was to identify the exact wormhole on the outside. Motoring up the Tamar we turned into St. Germain's River and beached *Johanne* on a rising tide. The bottom turned out to be mud too soft to stand on, but undaunted Edward and John launched the fiberglass yawl boat and as the tide ran out skidded about like a couple of kids at the fair. Their antics even aroused the curiosity of a pair of swans, who came flapping and paddling across the mud to join in the fun. As well they might, for some pretty strange things were happening to *Johanne*. After probing umpteen wormholes with bits of bent wire, the right one was found—going nine inches diagonally through a plank. First it would have to be drilled out straight, and then plugged with a wooden bung. Mindful of the incoming tide the men wasted no time. Noisy Neddy sang out on deck (our new Petta 110/220-volt generator, though excellent, was well named). Using an electric drill and a one-inch bit, Edward scooped out the hole. Wood for the bung was a cinch—the oak handle from the deck broom fitted to a tee. *Johanne* was to sail for many thousands of miles with that nine inches of broom handle stuck in her bottom—and we were to bend nine inches lower to scrub her decks. Leak plugged, there was nothing more to do; nothing major, at any rate. No cruising boat ever waits to be completely ready before setting sail; if they did they'd never leave. We sold *Wallaby*—she was too cumbersome to stow on deck—and replaced her with a Christmas present for Katy, a super six-foot sailing dinghy that she had already christened *Tinkerbell*. In the hold was a compressor for filling diving bottles and a five-ton lifting bag for raising cannon from the deep. All that was demanded now was to get back to the Seychelles, there to start a properly controlled, scientific dive on the wreck. That inevitably meant saying goodbye to parents, relatives, and friends, and it also meant leaving England in winter. Seven thousand miles ahead of us lay the tropical islands which General Charles Gordon of Khartoum genuinely believed to be the original Garden of Eden. We had but to get there to be in paradise.

13. *"L'abordage!"* (Collision at Sea)

~~~~~~~~~~~~~~~~~~

HALF AN HOUR AFTER MIDNIGHT on December 10th, 1976, we set sail from the United Kingdom bound across the Channel for France, and then the Seychelles. The wind was fair. A night sky, bright with cold, sent us a thousand crisp-edged stars for company. A splendid romping sail brought us off the French coast at first light. Passing inside Ushant, we made for the Gulf de Gascogne, the dreaded Bay of Biscay. Eyes raked the sky for storm clouds and the sea for warning swells. Knuckles tapped furtively beneath the barometer but they found no portents of disaster. Indeed, December 12th dawned remarkably fair.

The four of us were taking equal tricks at the helm and, by mid-morning, it was my turn to steer. Before long a hulking French trawler had me watching apprehensively over my shoulder as she advanced toward us under power. The helmsman must surely have seen *Johanne,* yet still he came on. Losing my nerve, I called below to Edward: "There's a ruddy great fishing boat astern. She looks as if she's going to ram us." Edward was on deck in a flash. One glance, though, and he relaxed, except that my anxiety irritated him.

"Don't be stupid. They saw us ages ago. They won't ram us." And they didn't. Instead the great bully came to within a few feet of our stern and stopped dead—so the crew could get a better photo of *Johanne.* There is little love lost between French fishermen and yachtsmen. Though this time no physical harm was done, that skipper had laid the psychological groundwork for what followed.

All that day Katy wrestled with seasickness and *Johanne* fought against headwinds and a nasty slop. In truth her struggle had begun the night before. The log for December 11th reads "2150 Penmarch [light-house] due east." Nine and a half hours later the log for December 12th reads "0730 Penmarch due east." Stirring stuff. In all we fought for eighteen hours to get south of Penmarch lighthouse and still failed. *Johanne*'s stunted mizzenmast and reduced sail area meant she was

hopeless to windward. We made longer and longer legs out to sea only
to lose what little we had gained when we tacked back toward the
shore—and that infernal lighthouse. Penmarch was getting on our
nerves. Yet Edward, an ardent lover of pure sail and an obstinate cuss
to boot, refused to give in. If fat-bellied trading schooners could get past
Penmarch without an engine so could we.

As luck would have it, I was again at the helm at 4:30 P.M. when
Johanne reached the lighthouse and tacked for yet another long leg out
to sea. Five miles to the south lay the fishing port of Guilvinec, and
coming from the north and heading down the coast across our bows
was the Guilvinec fishing fleet, forty-five- to fifty-foot vessels pounding
home to sell their catch in the evening market. As Edward went below
to plot our latest tack he cautioned me to keep a sharp lookout. In those
days a vessel under sail had right of way, and it was the duty of the
fishing boats to avoid us. Nonetheless, a wise person kept a careful eye
on them. As we cut at right angles through the fleet a couple of fishing
boats did alter course a spoke or two to pass astern of us. For the rest, I
checked each one's bearings, and each one slid safely by. Then I spotted
a fishing boat whose bearings remained steady against *Johanne*'s forward shrouds. Though still far off we were, for the moment, on a collision course. Was he, too, planning to play chicken with me? My pride
was still smarting from the morning's fiasco so I checked and checked
and checked again before calling Edward. And this time he was not
quite so quick to respond, though even then it needed but a slight twist
of the fishing boat's wheel for it to pass well clear of us.

Unable to conceive of a professional seaman deliberately ramming a
yacht, Edward could only imagine that the helmsman had, for some
reason, failed to see us. Seizing the foghorn he delivered a mighty salvo.
Wholly oblivious, the fishing boat continued to bare down on us at 8
knots. All Edward could do was jam the wheel hard over, luffing *Johanne* into the wind to stop her.

The rest was a nightmare, like one of those dreams where you try
desperately to run from certain death but your legs won't move, your
eyes can't see to find an escape, and you open your mouth to scream for
help and no sound comes. I was in that dream. Totally powerless to stop
the thing that was hurtling toward us, I stood suspended in time and
unable to move. Blood pounded in my brain till I could hardly see. I
opened my mouth wide to scream for help—and to my utter horror and
humiliation a scream came out! Even today I blush to think of it.

Seconds later the two boats collided. With a sickening shriek of
tortured wood, the fishing boat's stem smashed into *Johanne*'s side at
the main starboard shrouds. The pin rail broke clear. The main throat

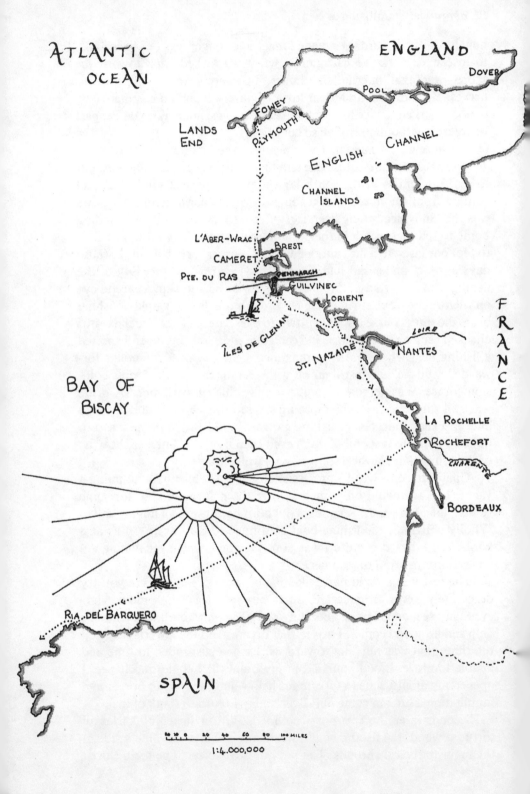

ATLANTIC
OCEAN

ENGLAND

Dover

Pool

Fowey

LANDS
END

PLYMOUTH

ENGLISH   CHANNEL

CHANNEL
ISLANDS

L'ABER-WRAC

BREST

CAMERET

PTE. DU RAS

PENMARCH

GUILVINEC

LORIENT

ÎLES DE GLENAN

LOIRE

NANTES

ST. NAZAIRE

FRANCE

BAY   OF
BISCAY

La ROCHELLE

ROCHEFORT

CHARENTE

BORDEAUX

RIA DEL BARQUERO

SPAIN

20 10 0   20   40   60   80   100 MILES

1:4.000,000

and jib halyards snaked aloft as the mainsail collapsed down the mast, its heavy wood gaff swinging free. John, who had emerged from the saloon clasping a peanut-butter sandwich, hurled it in fury at the fishing boat's wheelhouse. And still the man at the wheel did not respond. The reason was simple—there was no man at the wheel. Every one of that fishing boat's crew were in the hold sorting fish. It was the one possibility that had never crossed Edward's mind; that professional seamen, men he had admired since he was a lad of six, should be traveling at 8 knots in coastal waters, surrounded by a whole fleet of boats, when they themselves were running on automatic pilot without a single lookout on deck. Might as well drive down a highway with your eyes shut. Not that the fishermen stayed sorting fish for long. The crash brought them scuttling on deck, white as cooked cod, and quite as shocked as we were. Their boat, *Bellatrix,* had rammed us with such force that she pushed *Johanne* onto the other tack. That, as it turned out, was just as well, for *Johanne* had been holed to within an inch of her waterline, her bulwarks and planking shattered for several feet. Nevertheless, the old lady had surely proved her worth. In eighteen inches of planking, frames, and deck, she had stopped dead a heavy, fifty-foot fishing boat traveling at speed. Most boats would have been cut in two. Now, with the weight of both sails and booms to port, she was heeled over just enough to keep the lower edge of her holed starboard side above water. Only the wave tops sloshed in.

At the moment of impact Edward threw the G.M. into the fray, its powerful bilge pump working to save *Johanne*'s life—for a few seconds, until its M.P. pump seized up (not the first time it had let us down). In the blink of an eye John was into the engine room tearing the new electric pump from its packaging, connecting it up, and setting it to work. With the starboard shrouds shattered and *Johanne* rolling in a sloppy sea, Edward devoted all his skills to prevent us from being dismasted. John took command of the leak: open hold, grab old sail, grab hammer and copper tacks, over the side and into the gaping hole. Standing on *Johanne*'s internal ceiling with December waves lapping at his waist, John tacked the canvas over the hole and then dashed to the fo'c'sle, dragged out a large mattress, and stuffed it between the ceiling and the temporary canvas hull.

As *Bellatrix* hit, my first thought had been for Katy. Diving below I snatched her, seasick and half asleep, from our bunk. Bundling her into her life jacket, I shoved Womble, her favorite cuddly toy, into her arms and dumped her unceremoniously beside her father on deck. There was no time for child psychology. *Johanne* was sinking and we with her. Abandoning a frightened and tearful Kate, I rushed forward to help operate the powerful hand pumps. And, released from that appalling sense of impotence, Lana and I pumped like things possessed. Water was gushing out on all sides as electric motors and hand pumps sucked from the inundated bilges. Around us, Guilvinec's fishing fleet hovered, sympathetic, waiting to rescue us when *Johanne* sank. But *Johanne* was not going to sink, not if we could help it.

Abruptly both pumps failed. No water was coming out.

"John! Quick! Something's wrong with the pumps. They won't suck anymore."

"Take a look in the bilge. I think you'll find it's empty." He was right. Thanks mainly to his lightning-quick wits, *Johanne* was saved.

Once the avalanche of water was staunched and the M.P. pump working again, I was free, at long last, to comfort my daughter. For the next half-hour we sat together in the stern, Kate curled up in my lap as I held her tight, rocking her to and from and assuring her, over and over again, that all would be well. I left only when, surrounded by her French escort, *Johanne* limped into Guilvinec Harbor. It was time for a show of Anglo-American sangfroid. John, Lana, and I walked calmly forward to unravel the mess of halyards from the mess of shrouds and pin rail. Then, keeping the main gaff perfectly horizontal, we lowered it till it touched the boom and, as Edward brought *Johanne* gently alongside, we stowed it.

Monsieur Pochard, owner and skipper of *Bellatrix,* had clearly decided that aggression was his only form of defense. Hurling words as swift as Exocets across *Johanne*'s bulwarks, he shouted that the whole fleet would back him up, swearing in a court of law that we had tacked right under his bow. Thank God for a good grasp of French. Edward, in reply, commented fluently on the man's seamanship, his morals, and his ancestry. Battle lines drawn, Pochard's parting shot was that he would meet us at nine the next morning at the office of the maritime police.

Sharp at nine, we marched into the police station. Pochard wasn't there. Worried that he might have been before us, we asked at the desk. No, no one had been in that morning. We waited half an hour and then elected to get our side of the story safely recorded before M. Pochard arrived to spin his fine yarn. Edward asked for an interview with the chief. He turned out to be most understanding. This was by no means the first time a fishing boat had rammed another vessel while on automatic pilot. In fact, collisions were becoming so frequent that the maritime police were seriously considering banning their use in coastal waters. Satisfied, we left the police station and went in search of the post office and from there contacted Knox-Johnston, our insurers, who sent out a first-class man, Peter Williams, to help us.

A few days later a conference was convened aboard *Johanne*. Crowding around the chart table, first M. Pochard and then Edward put their cases to a clutch of insurance representatives. M. Pochard certainly tried to claim that we had tacked under his bow but, using his careful plotting on the chart, Edward was able to prove that we had tacked some twenty minutes before being rammed. No one aboard *Bellatrix* could have looked out for at least half an hour. The facts were indisputable. Pochard's insurers took full responsibility for the ramming or "abordage" and agreed to pay the full costs of our repairs.

Conference over, Pochard's insurance agent, a local man, led Edward to one side and asked, in an aggrieved tone, why we had reported his client to the port police. Edward, genuinely confused, pointed out that he had previously never heard of the port police, that it had never crossed his mind to go to any police until M. Pochard himself told us to meet him there. What we had failed to realize was that a visit to the port police was the greatest threat that one Guilvinec fisherman could hurl at another in time of stress—a threat that neither side would have dreamed of carrying out.

Close-knit, Guilvinec was a community embalmed in times past. Many of the older people wore wooden clogs, and some women still favored the time-honored Breton costume of wide skirts and delicate lace caps or *coiffes*. For centuries they had taken care of one another, and once we had cleared ourselves of any vindictive intent the local people took our interests to heart. Every evening M. Pochard brought us choice samples of his catch—not only prawns, for which the port was famous, but fish and crab and squid as well. Following an age-old custom, he was making sure that the victims of his action did not starve while their ship was laid up. If *Johanne* had to be rammed she could not have chosen a better place for it to happen.

Once the rights of the "abordage" had been agreed, the Guilvinec insurers sent their own expert down to discuss the repairs. Graced with the Breton name of Isidore L'Helgoualc'h, we privately called him M. L'Expert, pronounced "L'Expair" in true French fashion. M. L'Expert was a thoughtful man who later invited us to his home for Christmas Eve. On that first visit he merely suggested we take a look at a socialist-style cooperative of local boat builders. If we were satisfied with their work, his firm would pay them for *Johanne*'s repairs.

Inside the boat-building shed they had almost finished the transformation of a beautiful balk of timber into a fishing boat's keel. Molds for frames stood neatly stacked in one corner and the floor was swept clean of debris. Satisfied? We couldn't believe our luck. There and then Edward invited the carpenters over to inspect *Johanne*'s horrid wound.

With M. L'Expert and Peter Williams in attendance, every step of the repair job was discussed. Short lengths of planking greatly reduce a boat's strength so, although the actual damage was spread over only some five or six feet, they agreed that a hole up to fifteen feet long should be made so as to stagger the insertion of the new iroko planks. *Johanne* would also want new bulwarks and covering board. Four broken bits of frame had to be sawed off and new eight-inch oak ones dropped down and bolted in place beside them. The trickiest problem, however, lay inside. *Johanne*'s massive beam shelf had cracked on impact. To scarf in a new length would mean dismantling half the internal structure of the boat. After much discussion they decided to bolt a ¾-inch steel plate, fifteen feet by four feet, across the break.

It was mid-winter and icy cold. The wind, whistling through *Johanne*'s gaping hole, froze us all. M. Pochard arranged for John and Lana to stay in a spare room at his aunt's house. Madame Coice was a dear old lady who spoke mostly in Breton. This led to a few awkward moments, such as the time when John thought she said the stove wasn't working, to which he replied with his engaging grin, "Oh, don't worry about that; it doesn't matter at all," only to find that what the good lady had actually said was that her cousin had just died. Each morning Katy and I walked round to do some lessons and warm up at her kitchen fire. Although a little nervous at the influx of foreigners, Madame Coice was wonderfully kind to us all. When we finally left she gave Katy a sample of her own Breton lacework.

Rather than mooch around waiting for the carpenters to complete the repairs, John and Lana hitched back to John's parents' home in the United Kingdom for Christmas. We remained on board to keep a discreet eye on the work in hand, though in all the seventeen years we've owned *Johanne* we have never met such hard workers as those Guilvinec carpenters. They started on *Johanne* just before Christmas and, ignoring both Christmas and New Year, they took exactly eleven days to complete the job. Possibly helped by much practice, they'd got removing smashed-in topsides down to a fine art. Using a big chain saw, they cut down through the planks on either side of each frame. The cut wood fell away. Next they bashed the remaining wood, still nailed to the frames themselves, till the nails were loose. Finally they pulled out the nails. For the new covering board the carpenters required a piece of wood four inches thick, one foot wide, and twenty-three feet long. After taking careful measurements they went home for the night. Early the next morning they arrived with the imposing hunk of wood already so well shaped that it dropped straight into place. Later, to our astonishment, we learned that that was not all they did in the evenings. When

we returned to their yard to thank them after they'd finished work on
Johanne, we found the new fishing boat fully framed up and waiting to
be planked—a classic example of the motivation provided by worker
ownership, though not perhaps the best route to a merry Christmas.

Shortly after New Year, more distressed mariners limped into Guilvinec. Theirs was a particularly hairy outfit. Mike, an English antiques
dealer of slightly dubious credentials, ran a business in Paris. Wanting
to slip a few of his choicer pieces out of the country, he went to Scotland
and bought himself an old Scottish fishing boat. Enlisting his twelve-
year-old son, Bob, as first mate, and with a battered school atlas as their
only chart, they set out from the Isle of Man and steered for what they
thought was the Seine River and Paris. After many days at sea things
began to warm up. They stripped off first one sweater and then another
until they were steering in their shirt-sleeves—in January. Though they
never sighted it, they must have been close to the African coast. So then
they turned around and drove north again, or thought they did. Part of
their predicament was caused by the compass. Unknown to them, it was
12 degrees out. By the time they sighted Guilvinec they had all but run
out of both food and fuel. Rounding the lighthouse on the wrong side,
they grazed the rocks and then headed into port shouting, "Is this
England?"

On board *Johanne* everything was falling into place. The repairs
were complete and *Johanne* was declared sound. M. Pochard's daily
offerings of free fish ceased. John and Lana returned and Peter Williams
phoned from Jersey to wish us "Bon voyage." The only thing that still
wasn't right was the weather, but then that was no more than one would
expect from the Bay of Biscay in mid-winter.

Leaving Guilvinec on January 7th, we sailed to the small Isle Penfret, part of the Glenan group. There we stretched our legs on barren
windswept turf, turned soggy by recent rain. We walked to the lighthouse, and found a dead lizard on a rock. Returning to the beach we
were waylaid by a slim, dark-haired man in his thirties, one of the three
permanent inhabitants of the island; the other two were the lighthouse
keepers. During the summer things were different; then people
crammed the islet to overflowing for it was the center of operations for
the renowned Isles Glenans school of sailing. Our acquaintance was,
among other things, the school's chief maintenance man. Apart from a
weekly boat that brought provisions, we were the first visitors he'd seen
in three months. Eager to hear more, we turned back with him and
walked uphill toward his whitewashed cottage.

A social worker specializing in the residential care of delinquent children, he had come to this desolate island in search of solitude. Gradually, surrounded by wind and waves, sand and sea, he had found peace and one evening it occurred to him that his past charges might find peace there too. He invited a handful of them to come and spend a fortnight with him on the island. Part of the deal was that they must fend for themselves. They had to trap their own meat (mainly rabbit), and catch their own fish. They had to comb the rocks for edible greens and the foreshore for driftwood. The boys reveled in it. In the social worker's opinion, that fortnight living together on the island brought him closer to the youngsters than all the years they had spent together in the special school.

Lifting the latch, the man led us into his spartan home. Without pausing he reached up to a wooden shelf and brought down a bird book. Aha! An ornithologist no less. Or was he? Turning the pages he certainly carried on enthusiastically about the many different species of birds to be seen on the islands. Coming to one well-thumbed page of photographs he suddenly exclaimed, "Ah, this one we 'have 'ere. He is veery beautiful. A little garlic and he is *fantastique!*"

The next day a northwest wind sent us skimming south toward Spain, El Dorado, and the winter sun. But not for long. By teatime the wind was blowing strong from the west, bringing with it driving rain. We anchored in Quiberon Bay to let another gale sweep past. Two days later, fortified with hot porridge, we took off again for the south. Outside was calm but perishing cold. The decks had iced over and the sail gaskets were frozen to the gaffs. In the forecabin the temperature had dropped to 40°F. But thanks to the calm sea, Kate managed to complete a full morning's lessons.

We started, as always, with fifteen minutes on our recorders, a lesson guaranteed to clear the saloon of any lingerers. Moving on, Kate recited her tables (while I brushed her hair), and labored over her spelling. She read a French children's story aloud, then wrote up our visit to Isle Penfret in her nature notebook. For arithmetic she practiced division sums and for history we discussed the Welsh hero Llewellyn, Prince of Wales. She finished off with a short letter to the Mashford girls before curling up on the settee beside me as I launched into the first chapter of Kipling's *Jungle Book*.

All that brainwork produced an appetite. By the time we'd waded through a lunch of minced beef, rutabaga, and potatoes followed by rhubarb and custard, morale was pretty high—till one cast an eye to the northwest. There, dark clouds brooded, swollen and murky. The shipping forecast confirmed it. Yet another gale was rolling in.

Edward altered course for Saint-Nazaire, the large town guarding the entrance to the Loire River. Four hours later, as the clouds above dumped their load of ice-cold rain, *Johanne* dropped her anchor opposite the town. Next morning icicles, glistening like crystal marline spikes, hung from outside the saloon hatch and *Johanne* was almost hidden in swirling fog, shortly to be followed by swirling snow. Nearby a coaster scored a bull's-eye as it rammed a navigation buoy, putting out its light. Around us, but invisible, Saint-Nazaire's fishing fleet was returning home, going dead slow as they fumbled through the fog. One boat steamed right up to us and someone shouted out: *"Où est la terre?"* (Where is the land?) Nasty stuff, fog.

We lay, holed up in the Loire, for seventeen days. Then came a lull. The skies cleared, the barometer steadied, and we got under way. Almost immediately John was in the wars. As he swung up the last inch on the jib halyard, the halyard broke, dropping him down hard and spraining his ankle. He was understandably annoyed. It was the only halyard aboard that had not been replaced, and we had forgotten to warn him about it. As reparation we had to haul him up in the bos'n's chair so he could reeve a new line. That done, we reached the Charante, eighty miles to the south, without a break, though what with cold and rain all night and swell and rain all day, the trip wasn't exactly your ideal holiday cruise. But then who in their right mind goes cruising in Europe in winter anyway?

Not that we were really cold. No one could be, with all the clothes we wore. My personal preference ran to the following: next to the skin a pair of cotton underpants and a long-sleeved, thermal vest. Over them a T-shirt and tights. After that a pair of stretch tight slacks followed by black trousers followed by baggy blue jeans. On top of the T-shirt went four sweaters, a quilted anorak, and an oilskin jacket. A couple of pairs of thick socks and oilskin trousers and I was ready. I pulled the neck of the polo up to my mouth and I pulled a woolly cap down to my eyebrows. Then I drew the oilskin hood tight over the lot. Sheepskin gloves covered my hands and Wellington boots my feet. It's just as well there were no keen anthropologists around for they might have mistaken me for the missing link.

By the time we entered the Charante the tide was already ebbing, so we anchored close to the riverbank off the Rochefort Yacht Club. There we stayed, gale-bound, for another twenty-eight days. Far from being bored those were days of intense activity. Lana and I spent much of our spare time thumping typewriters—free-lance journalism featured high in our latest plans for boosting our respective family fortunes. Whenever the muse failed, which was often, I treadled away at my new Reeds Sailmaker, turning out a growing stock of boys' shirts and trousers (I'll explain why later). John and Edward had already dismantled and completely redesigned the M.P. bilge pump: gluing specially shaped bits of wood inside it, they radically altered the internal water flow and the pump never troubled us again. That job out of the way, Edward kept himself happy turning Chip's two slices of mahogany into a fine baize-lined gun case to hold his favorite pair of flintlock duelers. Lessons over, Katy painted, drew, read books, and played endless private games of imagination with whatever props were to hand. In the evenings, crowded around the saloon's kerosene heater, we all joined in better-known games such as chess and checkers, de Bono's "L" game, and Cluedo, and we admired the latest progress John had made in constructing two scale models of their dream boat, the one he and Lana hoped to build on our plot of land in the Seychelles. If we ever got there. At our present rate—220 miles a month—the 7,000-mile trip would take us about three years.

And then, glory be, the sun came out! On the last day of February the clouds dispersed, the barometer rose, and not a single gale was forecast. We really were off. A swell left over from the last blow made Kate dreadfully sick and the lack of wind forced us to motor-sail, but we weren't worried—we'd escaped. Our spirits soared so high that we defiantly stripped down to sunbathe in temperatures that a couple of years before we would have faced in woolly jumpers.

The sun was setting when I sighted Spain for the first time. Far away, on the southern horizon, the jagged teeth of the Cantabrian Mountains poked up above crimson clouds. The next sunrise tinted their snowcaps pink. A morning mist, rising from the sea, flowed into the cleavage of the hills and gradually moved upward until we could see only the mountain peaks, quite separate from the earth, floating way above us like some other world. Eventually the mist covered the mountains completely and, as we bashed on westward toward Cape Finisterre, we did not see Spain again all day.

That night a land breeze brought with it the smell of recently dampened earth—Spanish earth. Katy was beside herself with excitement, and I hurriedly turned to "Week Four" of Hugo's *Spanish in Three Months*. Then the wind died and it was another two days before we dropped the hook in Ria del Barquero, one of many splendid fjords along the Galician coast. We'd made Spain at last!

14. Adios: to Timothy and the Mainsail

ROWING ASHORE to the village, we flushed out a clutch of Guardia Civil propping up a sun-washed wall with their specially designed, wall-propping-up hats (surely the only conceivable reason for the flat bit at the back). Having heard some pretty grim reports of the Guardia Civil, we approached them with great politeness and asked the way to the immigration office. Unhitching themselves from their wall, the three young men replied by asking how long we planned to stay. Only a day or two? Why, they said waving us cheerily on, in that case don't worry. So we didn't. Instead we investigated the village's steep alleyways and pushed through bead curtains slung in front of doorways to search for meat (tough) and vast disks of bread (also tough). Our chosen loaf, certainly not the biggest, weighed three and a half pounds. The few scarce vegetables were of doubtful quality, unlike their vendors. Those Galician fisherfolk may have been materially poor but they were wonderfully rich in spirit. Everywhere we went they smiled and laughed and seemed to take genuine pleasure in helping us learn their language. I've loved Spain ever since.

But we had no time to linger and, next morning, we moved on. Afternoon calms gave way at dusk to a rising southwester. Six hours later the winds, whistling round Galicia's pitch-black cliffs, had us casting around for a bolt hole. Blindfolded by the night, we nosed anxiously forward. The moon rose. *Johanne* crept on and into an uninhabited bay. All of a sudden strange vessels loomed ahead. Eerie vessels. Like a ghostly fleet of galleons, their square yards glinted in the moonlight. What could those specters be? Dawn revealed all. We'd anchored on the edge of a mussel farm. Fifty-foot-long hulls had sprouted up to six "masts" apiece, each mast crossed with a metal "yard" which in turn helped support, through a series of wires, horizontal metal platforms that stretched many feet beyond the hulls, like ballerinas' tutus. From these platforms a thousand dark-blue strings dangled down through the

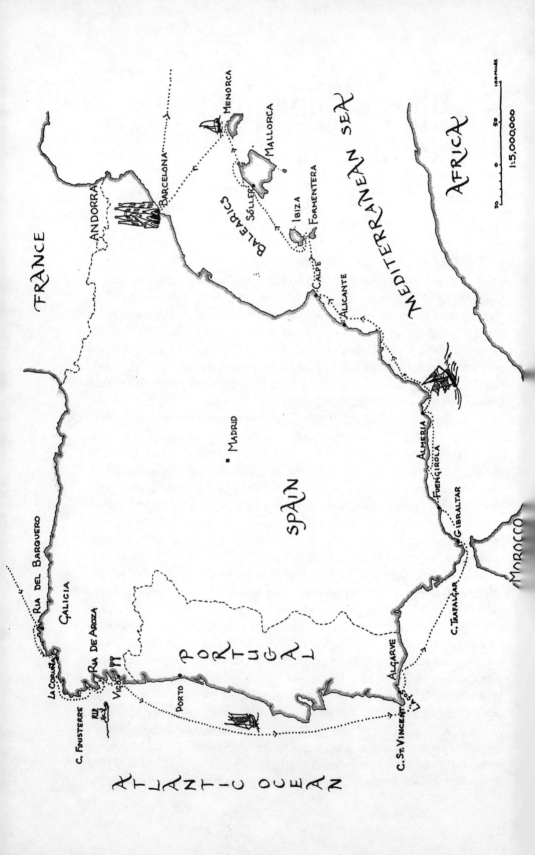

dark-blue water, and up each string grew the mussels.

Ashore we found a countryside sucked dry, where once green pastures rolled. As generation after generation divided the land among their many sons, so the plots grew ever smaller, the people ever poorer. One such plot was being cultivated as we passed. An old man, plodding behind a single ox, steadied his wooden plow. Behind him, his equally ancient wife, dressed all in black, sowed seed by hand in a timeless, biblical rhythm. Only the plastic bag that held the seed acknowledged the advent of the twentieth century. Watching them, I wondered: Did that couple ever raise their tired eyes and see the glories of the bay stretched out below them? Did they pause a moment to admire the bright abundance of spring flowers run rampant because costly chemicals were scarce? Did they reach up with pride to touch the swelling lemons on the trees? Or was it all too familiar and were they too weary?

Donkeys, hidden under loads of freshly cut grass, ambled past us, driven by sturdy peasant women in long skirts and thick wool stockings. Each carried a sharpened scythe across her shoulders. In the center of the village stood one tiny shop and, unlike those in the fishing village, this one was stocked with fine fruits and vegetables. A friendly señora smiled at my faltering query and then broke into voluble, and totally incomprehensible, directions on how to reach the bakery. We finally located it by smell. It was as we walked back to the bay and the dinghy that Lana and I spotted the waterfall. We grinned at each other—washing! We would return the very next day with every dirty sheet and towel we could lay our hands on.

By then yet another gale was blowing, throwing a mean swell against the jetty. We had to be mighty nimble, scrambling out of the dinghy and up a vertical ladder clutching our overflowing buckets, an oilcloth, scrubbing brushes, and soap. After that we had but to scale a forty-foot pile of rocks to the waterfall and the job was virtually done. Roping Katy in as forced labor, we carried everything up in relays. Okay, so it wasn't one of the world's most convenient wash places but, for sure, it was one of the most spectacular.

High above us the freshwater stream shot, suicidal, over the cliff to dive into a deep rock pool at our feet. From there it somersaulted over more rocks to fall into a wrecked rowboat twenty feet below. By starting work in the lower "tub," the rowboat, we could keep the upper pool clear for the final rinse. Dumping the suds-soaked laundry on the oilcloth, we all three set to work scrubbing the clothes on the weathered, rounded rocks, wringing them out, then plunging them into the boat for a rinse. Icy water and gale-force winds could easily be ignored amid such stunningly wild and vibrant country. A last rinse in the crystal

waters of the upper pool and all was done. Back on board, I slung the
washing line low across the deck and stuck four pegs on every garment.
They wouldn't take long to dry anyway—the wind was now gusting to
Storm Force 9.

Ever since we'd bought *Johanne* we'd suffered from her lack of
anchor-chain stowage. So as the storm raged outside John set to work in
the forecabin, building two big chain lockers directly below the windlass. Edward worked on deck, cutting out chain pipes to lead down to
the lockers. This addition to *Johanne* brought another revolution: no
longer would we have to lay out 240 feet of ¾-inch chain in great
snakes along the deck. Nor would we have to leap for the bulwark
capping as, with the anchor falling free, the chain lashed out across the
deck, threatening to shanghai any feet left carelessly in its path.

Two weeks holed up along the Galician coast and we'd had enough.
Regardless of the weather, we'd go to La Coruña. Outside, unnecessarily large swells meant that, with the G.M. grinding flat-out, it took
Johanne four hours to cover the six miles to the town moorings. From
there we could get in touch with the outside world. Catching a bus to
Vigo, John and Lana returned bearing a tantalizing bundle of mail,
kindly held for us by the Vigo Yacht Club. It was our first news from
home in eight weeks. The next day we again weighed anchor, and at
11:20 A.M. on March 21st we had Cape Finisterre bearing east and
Johanne pointing south. We'd quit the Bay of Biscay. Two days later
we zigzagged into the picturesque inlet of Ria de Aroza. Dotted as it
was with low islands, Edward waited till high tide before steering *Johanne* between them to find shelter off Isla Toja.

Others may remember Ria de Aroza as a beautiful holiday resort.
For us it will always be the place where Timothy died. Recently his
habits had changed. From being the most elusive of all crew members,
he had appeared several times in the past few days, usually crouching
near the gas rings as if trying to keep warm. Had he perhaps caught a
chill? He was, after all, a West Indian mouse. Sadly he gave us no time
to concoct a tonic. Kate and I returned from shopping to meet him
tottering across the floor. Even as we watched he keeled over and lay
twitching in a shaft of sunlight. Quickly I propped a sheet of cardboard
over him so that he would not feel vulnerable and alone. A few minutes
later he was dead. Katy and I both wept over that mouse. Invisible for
most of the past two years, he had nonetheless become an integral part
of our lives. The least we could do was give him a proper send-off.
Lining an old shoe box with blue silk, we laid Timothy inside and rowed

over to the uninhabited island of Beiro. There we buried him with full honors and a wooden cross. Timothy Mouse R.I.P.

What a difference the sun makes. Did I really go out in mid-Atlantic and deliberately stand in the rain? I must have been nuts! After the Bay of Biscay our sail to Vigo was pure magic: a sparkling, sun-filled day, a temperature in the high 70s, and, with a fair wind behind her, *Johanne* bowling along at 7 knots.

Knowing Vigo Yacht Harbor to be small, Edward anchored outside and then rowed round with John to reconnoiter. A large, very smart ketch had tied up in the only possible berth. The owner did offer to have us alongside, but then he hadn't seen *Johanne*'s steel rub rail or the collection of old automobile tires which served her as fenders. We concluded that, in the cause of future harmony and his immaculate white topsides, we had better decline. Instead Edward dropped anchor out beyond the high yacht club wall. Taking a stern line ashore in the dinghy, we then warped *Johanne* in and made her fast to the far corner of the wall's walkway. Happily the whole operation went smoothly. Standing on the jetty, critically assessing our every move, were most of the fancy yacht's crew.

After two months of being cooped up, hiding from wind and rain, I had developed a bad case of wanderlust. I wanted to see the inside of Spain, not just her outer wrapping. So early one Sunday morning Katy and I packed up a picnic, stuffed a Spanish dictionary and a local road map into a rucksack, and caught a clatterbang bus into the hills. The weather was superb; everything was golden with sunshine yet nowhere was too infernally hot. Around midday the bus stopped to let out passengers. Katy and I hopped off too and ambled down through some trees to where the map indicated a river. Men and boys dotted the shallows while women spread out picnics on the grass. Sometimes I wondered if there was a man or boy in Spain who did not own a fishing rod. They might give the outside world the impression of a nation obsessed with soccer but, in reality, the Spanish male's true, if secret, passion is for fishing.

Lying back in the supple grass I squinted through half-closed eyes at the sunlight flickering through the bright spring leaves—and woke to hear Kate rummaging in the rucksack for food. Picnic over and fearful that we might miss the last bus home, we packed up and retraced our steps, walking into the town.

A bare, ugly little place, the houses were walled with raw concrete. Roadworks formed wide-open litter traps beside the road while the citizens waited for mañana and the promised installation of proper sewers. But venture a few steps past the last drab house and you are confronted by acres of terraced land laboriously cut from the hillside. There knotted vines and neatly furrowed vegetable plots leave not an inch of the precious soil unused.

In the interests of progress we voted to give Portugal a miss and sail straight on to Gibraltar. But, by keeping close in to the shore, we were still able to admire in full the weird and wonderful coastline of the Portuguese Algarve. There Atlantic rollers and Atlantic gales have combined to erode the sandstone cliffs into delicate archways and lone pinnacles of rock while black-mouthed caverns run in deep under the land. Sand martins nest in the cliffs and occasionally one swooped aboard. In the sea a group of dolphins came bounding over to frolic with *Johanne* in the waves. A land breeze brought the scent of spring flowers and Katy stood her first whole trick at the helm.

It took us four days to reach Cape Saint Vincent, that sharp point of land at the bottom left-hand corner of the Iberian peninsula. Rounding it, *Johanne* altered course 90 degrees. At ten o'clock on the night of April 28th we passed Trafalgar Point (of battle fame), and steered southeast toward the Rock. As I came off watch, the lights of North Africa blinked, clearly visible, off our starboard bow. At 2 A.M. on April 29th, we dropped anchor at the end of Gibraltar's airport runway.

Gibraltar, "Port of Lost Hopes"—one doesn't have to look far to find the reason for the epithet. We'd moved *Johanne* into the old Destroyer Pens, a relic of Britain's now-defunct naval dockyard. Moored all around us where *Johanne*'s sisters and cousins and aunts, a whole tribe of former trading craft sliding inexorably toward death. One had a rudder with holes right through it, Chinese style, only it was worms and not Chinese that had made them. They were decaying ships, yes, but home nonetheless to their owners, people who many moons ago set sail from northern Europe with such Utopian dreams: of sun, and sand, and turquoise tropical seas. By the time they reached Gibraltar many of those dreams had already been shattered, cracked and then broken in the constant sniping between people confined in too small a space. In other cases it was the boat herself that had proved unequal to the task. Occasionally, perish the thought, there was trouble with both. So there they stay, especially the Brits, who find in Gibraltar all their favorite food from home—chunky marmalade, chocolate digestive biscuits, cheddar cheese—but with none of home's foul weather.

I did not expect to like Gibraltar; after all, a rock is a rock is a rock, and Gibraltar really is just a rock. The whole colony covers no more

than two square miles of land. And yet it grew on me, and it grew on
Katy too. For the first time since leaving Guilvinec she had friends to
play with, hordes of them. From the look of it, the chief occupation of
all those adult Lost Hopers was producing platoons of Lost Hope children. Kate and Julie, from the boat next door, became inseparable. At
night they slept on deck in Katy's Wendy House. During the day they,
with a gang of others, bicycled around the dockyard or swam in Gibraltar's saltwater pool, decamping in the evenings, by special invitation, to
watch films aboard *Samson,* a German tugboat said to be the largest in
the world.

Gibraltar proved equally kind to *Johanne,* showering her not with
friends but with charts. A complicated tale, it had a strange scent about
it. Channel No. 5 had decided to sell their 150-foot luxury motor yacht
to Channel No. 6 (unless maybe it was the other way around). For
reasons best known to themselves, and possibly the tax man, the new
owners were not only ripping out every interior fitting in sight, they
were also shifting their base from the Mediterranean to the West Indies.
Some 200 charts had become redundant—200 charts that included virtually every anchorage in the Med. And they actually asked if we would
like them! (At today's prices that windfall was worth approximately
£2,000.)

The next excitement to hit Gibraltar was the arrival of *Dar
Pomorza,* a 270-foot Polish sail training ship and one of the grandest
full-rigged ships in the world. Holding hands, Katy and I ran along the
dock to beg permission for a quick look around. Two minutes of conver-
sation and we were trotting back again, permission refused. I should
have known better. Next time we traveled in John and Lana's wake. As
Kate and I merged into the background, John worked his usual charm
and in no time he and Lana were invited to step aboard. (Kate and I
sneaked on in their slipstream.) If, from the shore, her three masts
seemed to pierce the sky, from close up *Dar Pomorza*'s wheel looked no
less impressive. Kate's head barely reached its central hub.

Having conquered the first mate—*Dar Pomorza* carried 120 cadets
and 49 crew members—John further flabbergasted the latter by not
only getting permission to climb the rigging, but taking his shoes off to
do it. It must have been agony on his winter-softened soles, but as we
walked back to *Johanne,* John would admit only that it was a bit tricky
high up—where one had to hang out over the deck at 45 degrees to
reach the "top."

Holiday time or not, there was no reason to abandon education
altogether and, anyway, how could one possibly leave Gibraltar without visiting the only remaining band of wild apes in Europe? Very

easily, according to the rest of *Johanne*'s crew. So, with Kate as companion, I rode the cable car 1,400 feet to the top of the Rock. Way below us the waters of the Strait glistened blue-black, streaked here and there with the thin white line of a ship's wake. Farther still, over to the south, was Africa. And somewhere in the haze between were John and Lana on a day trip to Tangier.

We waved in their direction and then returned to the project in hand: apes. We hunted everywhere for those wretched beasts but not one did we find. This was serious! Someone should cable the British government for, as no doubt you known, once those Barbary apes leave Gibraltar the British reign on the Rock will end. No, I'm not joking. No lesser person than Winston Churchill himself is said to have taken the ape situation most seriously. During World War II when Britain stood alone as the only nation fighting against Hitler's armed might, he heard that the ape population was dwindling. At once he dispatched an urgent message to the Officer Commanding Apes, Gibraltar, urging him to do everything possible to rebuild their population. As the fortunes of the apes improved so, too, did those of Britain. Indeed, a couple of years later the war was won. So you see what I mean. The situation was serious.

Just as I was debating whether to hurtle down the hill to raise the alarm we chanced on a notice pointing to St. Michael's Cave. I'd never heard of St. Michael's Cave but, with no apes to be seen, it seemed like a possible second-best outing. How wrong could one be. After only a few moments inside the immense entrance cave, Katy declared it the most beautiful place in the world.

The cave is so large that it has been converted into a full-size theater. Permanent seats cover one sloping rock face while the floor serves as a stage where international orchestras play and international ballet companies dance. What more magical setting could there be for *A Midsummer Night's Dream* than among that fantastic forest of stalactoes? From somewhere high above us, "Amazing Grace" fanned out into the cold damp air. Below the first cavern a whole network of smaller caves burrow into the rock, their hanging gardens of stalactites shimmering, crystalline, in the white spotlights. (By the way, if you are ever puzzled by stalactites and stalagmites, try this one. Stala-*C*-tites Come from the Ceiling and stala-*G*-mites Grow from the Ground. Stalactoes are the ones where the two have joined together to form a single, waisted pillar.)

Back in Gibraltar town we found most of the free wall space liberally sprayed with anti-Spanish slogans: "We're British" and "Franco is a Fascist war criminal" were both popular at the time. I am told that

Gibraltarians in fact dislike the British almost as much as the Spanish, but, so long as Britain offers better social security and greater autonomy, 98 percent of the population of 28,000 will continue to vote to stay British.

At 8:30 A.M. on Friday the 13th of May (Edward thought it was Saturday and I didn't have a clue what day it was), *Johanne,* for the first time, plunged her stem into the waters of the Mediterranean. And Katy, for the first time, cried at leaving a place. She'd made good friends in Gibraltar and was old enough now, at almost eight years, to realize she would probably never see them again. We began to think seriously about finding an easygoing boarding school that could offer her lasting friendships and a less nomadic life.

Despite Franco's death, tension still ran high between Spain and Gibraltar. Yachts, clearing from Gibraltar, were warned to go as far north as possible before entering a Spanish port. So we ran north. On Saturday came half a gale of wind and a heavy following sea; rollers swept under us, crushed to perpetual froth by *Johanne*'s mighty hull. Now she was head down. My God! Hang on! She'll plunge her bowsprit into that sea ahead. But no; with seconds to spare, *Johanne* rose, shuddering—and then slewed around, her keel tight-hobbled in the next wave's grip. Edward, at the helm, fought back. Grasping the wheel with both hands, he turned it spoke by spoke, just enough to send *Johanne* skiing, straight and true, down the blue-black silken curve of the next roller. All much more thrilling than a fun fair.

Above us Force 7 winds played around *Johanne*'s "soft" mizzenmast. It was time to lower the mizzensail. Earlier in the day, in response to the following breeze, we'd let the mizzensheet right out. Now the wind had the sail pinned at right angles to the boat and hard up against the shrouds. We slackened the halyards—but nothing moved. We'd have to heave down on the cloth itself. How I loved those clashes: standing high on the cabin top, exposed yet free; fighting the sail, fighting the wind; stomach skydiving as *Johanne* swooped like a swallow over the ever-rising seas. Inch by inch, fingers crying out as they scrabbled at the harsh canvas, we dragged it down. We had won. Life was great.

By eleven o'clock that night life was no longer so great. We'd had enough. Kate was being violently ill and the rest of us were exhausted. A few hours ahead, tempting as the devil, lay the Gulf of Almeria and a safe anchorage. But to reach it we would have to jibe.

"If we jibe in this wind the mainsail will go," said John on the foredeck.

"Of course, if we jibe her in this, the old main'll probably go," said

Edward at the helm. Lana and I, standing near the break of the poop, nodded our heads sagely.

"You know, that main's going to go if we jibe."

"Jibing stations!" yelled Edward above the hungry howl of the wind. The three of us took up our positions at the mainsheet. Lana and John were to heave with all their might and I was to tail the sheet over the cleat, standing ready to make it fast at the very last moment. John and Lana heaved. I tailed. And the boom did not budge one inch.

"Come on! Let's try again. One! Two! Three! HEAVE!" shouted John. We gained six inches. Only twenty feet to go. The more mainsheet we could get in, the less distance for the sail to slam over and the less danger to mast, sail, and boom. Doing his best to help us, Edward ran as close by the lee as he dared in the dark, thus taking the pressure off the sail—and onto his skill and his nerves. He, too, had to get it right. A foot too close, a sudden surge of a wave, and the wind, coming from astern, could catch the wrong side of the sail and send it smashing across the deck with us still hanging on to the sheet—or not, as the case might be. Eventually the boom came to within a few feet of amidships. I quickly made fast and we jumped back, breath held, as Edward called "Jibe O!" and eased the helm around to bring the wind on the other side of the . . .

WHAM! CRASH! RIP! Rip—rip—rip-rip-rip! How gratifying that all four of us could say, "I told you so!" That really was the death knell of *Freelance*'s faithful main.

Under headsails and engine we reached smoother water and, while the rest of us stowed what was left of the mainsail, Edward did his best to identify Almería Harbor from the confusion of lights along the shore. At 4:50 A.M. we anchored off the breakwater. Edward went to bed fully clothed, convinced that the authorities would be after him at the crack of dawn. More optimistic, and probably less tired, I pinned to Kate's cabin curtain an envelope containing her week's pocket money (15 pesetas, or 15¢), a square of chocolate, and a note asking her to play quietly and get her own breakfast. Bribery thus blatantly offered and willingly accepted, the rest of us slept soundly until midday.

That afternoon we unbent the mainsail for the last time, a sad moment for a brave old sail. Still, one couldn't help but feel excited as the new sail emerged from the hold. *Johanne* was going to look pretty smart now that all her sails were tan.

From our anchorage we gazed across to the town. Originally founded by the Phoenicians, Almería is dominated today by an eighth-century Moorish castle. Below it and to one side squat a group of cottages, each a modest flat-roofed home gleaming with whitewash. The

hard-baked earth around every house is swept and spotless. What un-
common spirit allows these people to draw pride from the oppressive
landscape of southern Spain? Behind them, hill upon hill of crumbling
white rock glares in the sun, featureless as the moon, pitilessly dry and
naked of vegetation save for a few bent olive trees struggling, on narrow, man-made terraces, to survive. Yet out of that land sprang fla-
menco, a gypsy rhythm born right there in Andalusia, and a music well
fitted to transport its people's burden of love and sorrow and injustice.

A gentle breeze from the southeast pushed *Johanne* slowly north
toward her next port, Alicante. Before midday the wind had backed 70
degrees. *Johanne* was plunging into head seas, this time accompanied
by thunder and horizontal rain which stung our cheeks like flying sand.
When it came my turn to take the helm, visibility had dropped to a few
hundred yards. By then the "abordage" off Guilvinec was a fading
memory for everything except my nerves. They, alas, had fallen prey to
a terror of moving ships—any moving ships. Time and again I had
awakened poor Edward in the middle of the night to pass judgment on
vessels that must have looked to him as harmless as glowworms inching
their way along the horizon. But he never complained. Now, as I stood
at the helm, the curtain of rain parted for one short moment, just long
enough to reveal a cargo ship making straight for us. Then it vanished,
hidden by more driving rain. Till that moment I had presumed that
knocking knees were a Gothic novelist's device used to represent fear.
Let me tell you, those knees are no invention. They're for real. What's
more, if you're so scared that your knees knock together, chances are
you can't stand up either—your legs turn to jelly. I remained upright
only by hanging on to the wheel with both arms. And then the visibility
improved. The ship had passed and so, miraculously, had six months of
a quite irrational fear that never troubled me again.

The log entry for midnight on May 17th reads "Looking for San
Pedro. *No está!*" (It isn't here.) What with the rain and the lack of
moon, we couldn't find the wretched inlet anywhere. Baffled, Edward
motored up to a brightly lit fishing boat to ask the way. But what with
the roaring wind, roaring engines, and Spanish delivered with the speed
of a racetrack commentary, we were basically no better off. There is,
after all, a limit to the number of times you can ask a chap to repeat
himself. So we set off blindly in the direction indicated by half a dozen
hands. It was like sailing into a whale's maw so black was the night, so
uninhabited the shore. Cliffs loomed everywhere. We lost our nerve and
turned back to the fishermen. This time the captain gave a broad shrug
and shouted for us to follow him. Opening up his engine, he led us
unerringly through the blackness for some fifteen minutes till we

reached Escallos Bay and safety. Wishing to thank the fishermen for their generous help, Edward waved a bottle of scotch in their direction. But the men simply laughed and shook their heads and called *"Adios!"* and *"Buenos noches."* Our *"Muchas gracias!"* and *"Buena pesca!"* drifted tamely after them on the thin night air.

We woke to find the bilges full of water. Hey ho! Here we go! The previous day's pounding to windward must have shifted some caulking or given a fat worm the extra "umph" it needed for a final break-through. Either way, we'd have to slip. Encouraged by a fresh breeze from the southwest, *Johanne* skimmed up the coast under a hot sun and cloudless sky. This was more like it, this was what sailing was all about! Dusk came, the sun forsook the sky, and Venus rose; the blue above turned black. *Johanne* sailed on, silent, beneath a galaxy of stars. And, still under sail, we dropped anchor at dawn off Alicante's breakwater.

15. Mediterranean Spain

ALICANTE'S WATERFRONT stretches for more than half a mile. Yachts tie stern-to to the promenade and, close by, nonstop city traffic belches up fumes to smother the straggle of the city's famous date palms. High above, in the monotint of a stone edifice built on a bare stone hill, stands the great bastion of Santa Barbara, another castle of Moorish origin despite its Christian name. Until one sees these castles one forgets that, for 750 years, Spain was ruled by Islam; forgets that, when the rest of Europe lay buried in the Dark Ages, here in Spain. Arab scholarship shone out doing its best to keep the fires of civilization alight. In at least one section of Alicante society we found that civilization was still facing an uphill struggle.

Shortly after we re-anchored *Johanne* inside the harbor, Lana and I rowed ashore to buy supplies. We made the dinghy fast and had started up the steps to the promenade when, without warning, two gun-toting policemen barred our way. "You come from the black boat, yes? What is in there?" The leader, boorish and overbearing, thrust his hands toward my shopping basket. I was furious. Brought up in England to regard policemen as friends and protectors, not to say servants, of the community, I felt outraged at the man's efforts at intimidation. Who the heck did he think he was anyway? Already he was trying to force open the basket. Right! He wanted to know what was in my basket, so I'd show him what was in it. Pushing his prying hands away, I snatched up the basket myself and jabbed it close up under his nose. There was no need for further discussion. I was bringing ashore four days' worth of rotting garbage. The man fell back and we swept past in high dudgeon. Maybe a bit late in the day, but I was at last learning to assert myself. And rather enjoying it too.

Probably they had received a tip-off. Drugs were on the move, and what, I ask you, could be more suspicious than a black "pirate" ship? But there's a right way, courteous and firm, and a wrong way, aggressive and overbearing, to go about a drug raid. One wins the cooperation of any honest citizen; the other instantly raises his hackles and makes him determined to defend his rights and be as bloody-minded as possible. Those men went about their raid the wrong way and John and Edward were indeed as bloody-minded as they could be.

For a start, the drug squad leapt aboard *Johanne* without either permission or a search warrant. Then one particularly loutish fellow pushed his way below. Nosing under the settee, he dragged out a tin filled with an off-white powder. " 'Ello, 'ello, 'ello, what have we here?" John didn't know the Spanish words for "custard powder" and Edward wasn't telling, though he did suggest the man try some and see. Next, Lout demanded all the floorboards in the saloon be torn up. John brought a screwdriver but, when Lout pointed imperiously at the boards, he quietly laid the tool down and walked away. If Lout wanted to look under the flooring he was welcome to, but he'd have to get down on his own hands and knees to do it. Lout, it transpired, was in fact only interested in exercising the petty power of an armed man over unarmed civilians. The floorboards stayed put.

The final object of his zeal was the Zodiac. He ordered it deflated and then, pointing at a lower minion fully kitted out with guns, whistles, and I know not what, told the man to roll all over it. Not surprisingly he punctured our brand-new, £2,000 inflatable. But that was minor damage compared to the destruction of a previously excellent impression made on us by that other branch of Spanish police, the Guardia Civil. (Spain has come a long way since then. Ten years later we were again in that country when there was an expertly coordinated swoop on all yachts along the Mediterranean coast. Our police raiders could not have been more courteous and charming, nor more thorough. In all the years we've owned her, they were the first police to find *Johanne*'s hold—a space twelve feet by eighteen—unaided.

That first, Alicante drug raid was an inauspicious start to what should have been a very happy day—Kate's eighth birthday; a day on which some of the fruits of our industrious, television-free winter went on display. The theme was pirates. First came a complete pirate outfit, cut out and sewn in secret after Katy was asleep. A red silk blouse contrasted with black crepe knee breeches and waistcoat, all fastened with mock-pearl buttons. To arm the pirate John had made a most ingenious "flintlock" from painted wood and metal and thick rubber bands. Edward had bought his daughter a real telescope as much to encourage her to study the stars as to pick out likely victims on the high seas. To finish everything off, Lana had designed a wonderfully evil Jolly Roger to hoist in *Tinkerbell*'s stern. By the time I'd added some of Katy's favorite Matchbox cars to the hoard I was wondering whether we'd gone a bit over the top with our daughter's unisex upbringing. The final offering, a handmade card from John and Lana, bore the following poem:

> Whose birthday dawns this morning fair;
> Is it the angel with the long, blonde hair?
> Whose dulcet tones make each morning glow,
> Till the sound is replaced by the piccolo.
> Whose conversation is often witty,
> But it never stops! More's the pity.
> Who makes us treats in cookery class,
> And sometimes beats us at draughts, alas.
> Who is it that gives us all such pleasure?
> None other, of course, but the little treasure!

Remaining supremely indifferent to both louts and birthdays, *Johanne* continued to leak. Donning his scuba gear, John slid over the side into the murky waters of Alicante Harbor. Careful inspection showed one plank butt where paint was suspiciously absent—the caulking had worked free. Pounding in more oakum stopped the leak, but if that bit had come loose so, too, could another. Ahead stretched the 600-mile crossing to Italy. It would still be wise to slip before leaving.

Calpé was, in those days, a small fishing village thirty-five miles north of Alicante. A light but steady headwind meant we took a leisurely twenty-four hours to get there but with little danger of missing our destination. It lay right at the foot of an amazing rock, Peñon de Ifach, which, not unlike Gibraltar, sticks up some 1,000 feet into the air, a gigantic bolder dropped right at the end of a long flat finger of land.

That Calpé slipping was something of a milestone in *Johanne*'s recent history. We didn't change a thing. Just up and paint and down. Well, with a bit of caulking in between. And how good it was to hear an expert at work, hardening up every seam before it was puttied over. Work complete, *Johanne* rumbled down the slipway and straight out to sea, destination the Balearic Islands and some cousins I hadn't seen for years.

Lying sixty miles to the east of peninsular Spain, the four Balearics have an extraordinarily varied topography. Formentera, the smallest island (thirty-seven square miles), is dry and relatively flat. Fields of thin corn stand interspersed between parched limestone rocks more inviting to the legions of basking lizards than to humans. Ibiza, a couple of miles to the north, is bigger and boasts hills up to 1,500 feet, plus a myriad of small inlets and natural anchorages, though none that give

all-around protection from the wind. For that you have to sail northwest to Mallorca, an island on a grand scale. Here mountains peak at
4,740 feet and the rugged northwestern coast confronts Spain with a
line of towering cliffs and steep hillsides punctuated with ruined watch-
towers. Along its whole forty-seven-mile length this coast offers just one
bolt hole, Puerto Sóller—but what a place to bolt to. Thickly wooded
slopes reach down to the small town that garlands an almost landlocked
bay. Now overrun by yachts, when we were there *Johanne* lay at anchor
alone. My memories of the final island, Menorca, are, in contrast, of a
low rolling land and few trees. Reminiscent of proud Scottish moorland
but without the proud Scots mist, Menorca has a spiritual quality about
it that was sensed by prehistoric *Homo sapiens*—there on Menorca
those early humans left a greater concentration of artifacts than anywhere else in the Mediterranean. But island memories are not just of
topography any more than cruising memories are only of sailing from
one anchorage to another. Equally important to both are the people one
meets on the way.

We found my cousins and their three delightful little girls clearly
thriving on Formentera, their chosen islet in the sun, and we too loved
the austere beauty of Ensenada del Cabrito (Little Goat Cove)—though
after the dreary concrete of Spain's man-made ports that was hardly
surprising. The surprise, or shock, came on June 5th, 1977. That morning I woke early and, opening one eye, peered up through the skylight.
It was going to be another flawless day. The sky was blue. The sea felt
calm. Slipping headphones over my ears (Edward loathes canned
noise), I settled back, eyes closed, to listen to the BBC World Service
news.

"This is London. Here is the news. James Mancham, president of
the Seychelles, has been overthrown . . ." Snatching off the headphones,
I shoved the radio toward Edward. Jimmy Mancham, flamboyant, popular, and democratically elected, had been overthrown by his own
prime minister, Albert René, in a Tanzanian-mounted, Communist
coup. A coup! In the Seychelles? In a country with a total population of
60,000 (less than that of the English market town of Bath), surely no
one could be that power hungry? What could it mean? What of our
friends, were they safe? And what of our own plans and dreams, were
they to be shattered before they had even begun by one man's greed for
power? Surely not. Good heavens, no. Nothing much would change,
and anyway, maybe it was all a mistake. Probably some journalist had
got his facts wrong. And whatever happened, there wasn't anything we
could do about it. By the time *Johanne* got there all would have re-

turned to normal. And so, like small children, we covered the coup with our fingers and pretended it wasn't there.

We spent a couple more days off Formentera with parties and swimming and picnics on the beach. Then, reluctant to say goodbye to our rediscovered cousins, we carried them with us to Ibiza, an island where pines thrived on the hilltops and hippies overran the main town—for, along with Formentera, Ibiza was then one of Europe's hippie homelands. They came from all over the Western world to sleep on the beaches by day and people Ibiza's street market by night, when a motley array of trestle tables, carpets, easels, and chairs transformed the town's narrow side streets into an instant craft fair. Around each display flickering candles broke up the darkness, creating intimate circles of light that echoed the gentle gaity of the market itself. Today it is fashionable to deride the hippies as shiftless pot smokers, but originally theirs was a movement of ideals. The spirit of caring and nonviolence that blossomed with the flower children of the sixties led later to the founding of such worldwide organizations as Survival International, Médcinssans Frontières, and Friends of the Earth. Ibiza's night market, for its part, saw a flowering of the arts. Here young people sold finely wrought anklets, paintings, and pottery, tooled leather belts and sandals, and long flowing skirts, each item unique and handmade. I have regretted ever since that I forgot to take along my purse; Edward probably has not.

Once she had returned my cousins to Formentera, *Johanne* took another eight days to cover the 200 miles to Barcelona for we traveled via the islands of Mallorca and Menorca. My favorite anchorage, Fornells Bay in Menorca, was less glamorous than the lush tourist bays of Mallorca but to me far more attractive. A fishing hamlet guarded its narrow entrance. Farther around the foreshore a solitary hotel kept a flotilla of sailing dinghies drawn up on the beach alongside it. The only other habitation, a bleak monastery, gazed down from a distant hilltop. Edward and I discussed staying in Fornells forever and then stayed two days, swimming and walking and watching Kate's first efforts at sailing *Tinkerbell* single-handedly. After several months of shared adventures, Katy loved that dinghy with the same ardor that other children love their teddy bears—and that regardless of certain mishaps they'd suffered in the past. Like the day when Kate's father told her not to row down-tide of *Johanne* and she did. Edward refused to rescue her saying that, for her future safety, she must learn to do as she was told. I wrung my hands and didn't know what to do. John, bless him, took action. He got into the yawl boat and rowed over to where Katy, plying the oars with all her might, was barely stemming the current. "Katy? Do you want a tow back?" he asked. Her reply came over the water tough and clear as a bell: "No thank you!" Heaven preserve us! She was going to grow up as stubborn as her father. "Okay. How about we race back together, then?" Kate's little face relaxed and together, very slowly, they returned.

Every now and again the uncertainties thrown up by the Seychelles coup sneaked past our blind optimism. Would John and Lana be allowed to stay long enough to build their boat? Would the boat be safe? And what of our Seychelles home, our Ant's Nest? Would the Communists seize it out of hand? It was the sort of thing Communists did. Suddenly we had to know. We had to reach Barcelona and collect our Seychelles mail.

Two days after leaving the peace of Fornells, *Johanne* was moored stern-to in Barcelona's overcrowded harbor. We had no time to dally: we were due to rendezvous with my parents in Greece in six weeks' time. We'd collect our mail, spend a couple of days sightseeing, and then we'd be off. Innocents abroad! We had as yet to confront the Spanish postal service. Day after day we traipsed to the yacht club to ask for the mail we knew my mother had forwarded. Day after day we returned empty-handed. Unfortunately that mail was important or we would have left. Not only should there be news from the Seychelles on which we would base all our future plans, but we were also waiting for *Johanne*'s insurance papers, my pain-killers, and Kate's school assignments from W.E.S. (the World-wide Education Service, able providers of her correspondence course).

The delay did have its compensation. We fell in love with Barcelona. A city founded 2,000 years before, it is still vibrantly alive today. Lana, Katy, and I visited everything: a Picasso exhibition, a remarkably interesting museum of shoes with exhibits dating back to Roman times, and a Museum of Mankind that bizarrely included shrunken heads. We strolled through the Barrio Gótico where graceful stone archways spanned the ancient streets and dark-fronted houses faced each other across sunless alleyways made gay by pots of flowers slung from wrought-iron balconies. We all went to the Maritime Museum to peer at model ships and princely galleys and together we visited the replica of Columbus's *Santa Maria.* (It was to Barcelona that Columbus returned for his royal reception.) There we marveled at the cramped space between decks. Either his men were very small or life was horribly uncomfortable in those days. The half-finished Sagrada Familia Cathedral (exotic brainchild of the Catalunyan genius Gaudí) had me entranced. Its multitude of earthcolored spires seem to grow right out of the ground, a group of fine-carved stalagmites, or fingers, of delicately honeycombed coral stretching high into the sky, each one crowned, totem-like, with a glittering halo, a mosaic of gold and red, silver and green.

In Vigo we had been amused by an English gentleman who had bemoaned the apparent lack of "four-fork" restaurants; he could find only less impressive "two-fork jobs." One night John and Lana returned home jubilant after a night out in Barcelona. "We've found it! It's fantastic! Your first ever, genuine, 'no-fork job.' We'll take you there tomorrow night." And they did and they were right. It was great. Hidden down one of Barcelona's back alleys, the restaurant was housed in a dimly lit warehouse with hams hanging from old rafters and hogsheads of wine ranged along the bare brick walls. The place was packed solid with Spaniards, some standing, others seated at simple tables whose dark sheen bore witness to years of human handling. And then there was the food. Small squares of thick brown paper held piles of sardines, fresh and fried to a crackling perfection. We ate them with our fingers. There was not a fork in sight.

After seventeen days of waiting our patience was rewarded with just one letter: from our neighbor in the Seychelles. But what a relief it brought. Everything was fine, or so he said. The coup had made no difference at all. We were not to worry but to come and see for ourselves as soon as possible. With a deadline to meet in Greece, we could delay no longer. Requesting the yacht club to forward any further mail to Italy, we cast off from Barcelona on July 4th and, in flat calm, motored out to sea. Away went *Spanish in Three Months* and out came *Pocket Guide to Italian.* The language appeared to be a mixture of Spanish and French. The challenge was going to be to get the mixture right.

They say that, in the Mediterranean, either it blows a gale or there's not a breath of wind. We'd had our gales so it was only reasonable that, for the next 350 miles to Corsica, the Med should, for the most part, be glassy calm, often with a fog bank or two thrown in. The whole would have been a lot more bearable if we hadn't been cruising in a cesspit. Land had sunk well below the horizon when we entered the river of filth. Several hundred yards wide, it twisted out of sight, an evil serpent crossing a landlocked sea. Discarded light bulbs, plastic bottles, solid gobs of oil, and flip-flops bobbed and jostled together, a vulgar pressing mob propelled by an invisible current. And when we slithered clear of the current we still had the bags to look at, two whole days in constant sight of at least one plastic bag—and they're not easy to spot, floating as they do a few inches below the surface.

The approaches to the French island of Corsica lay shrouded in fog yet, right above us, spread a sky of periwinkle blue. A couple of ticklish sun sights gave Edward our position, after which he allowed the freshening wind to carry *Johanne,* tan sails billowing, right into the heart of Corsica's southernmost anchorage of Paines. Silently and efficiently, *Johanne*'s crew went into action, for by now we really were a crew. Each one of us had our station and each knew what to do without a word being spoken. As Edward brought *Johanne* head to wind, we let fly the jib and staysail halyards and pulled like fury on their downhauls. In seconds the headsails were off. Edward meanwhile nipped forward from the helm to lower the main peak and so cut the gaff-sail's driving power by one-third. With the way taken off her and headsails stowed (rather than flapping dangerously about our faces), Edward ordered the anchor down. Only after we'd anchored did we lower the main- and mizzensails and lash them neatly to their booms. All in all it had been a most satisfying bit of teamwork—until the anchor dragged.

Most reluctantly, Edward trudged aft to break our silence with the G.M.'s whine. The CQR came up covered in weed. Clearing it, we again dropped anchor but this time went astern with the engine to make sure it dug right in.

"Great!"

"Not so great!" The ruddy thing had dragged again. What a pain, but thank goodness for the engine and the winch. In the end we nosed *Johanne* really close in to the shore where a light-turquoise patch of water promised a sandy patch of bottom. Down anchor; astern engine; anchor chain rise (this time it did); hold still, leading marks; sink back chain. The anchor had gripped. We were safe.

As soon as the next day's sun rose enough to light up the underwater world, John and Lana were off scuba diving. On board I scrubbed a bathful of dirty clothes, baked some bread with Katy, and then we too were ready for a ramble ashore. We had no more than a glimpse of a beautiful craggy corner of a wild and rugged island but it seemed a fitting birthplace for one Napoleon Bonaparte. Flowers bloomed everywhere and, guided by an excellent tree book, a present from John and Lana, I made a stab at identifying the shrubs as we passed. Perhaps this was Spanish juniper; they say it's quite common. And this one I think must be Balearic box, unless that's found only in the Balearics. At least the book didn't say it was rare. You'd be surprised at how many rare birds, shells, flowers, and trees I used to "identify" (some indeed so rare they were not mentioned in my books at all), until I lit on a simple rule of thumb. If the book said something was rare then that was not what we were looking at. Casual amateurs do not stumble upon rare shrubs beside well-worn footpaths.

At 3 P.M. shore leave was at an end. We had stopped off in Corsica only to stretch our legs, and in no time we had *Johanne* racing before a strong fair wind, carrying us, straight as a die, toward Naples.

16. The Good and the Bad in Italy

~~~~~~~~~~~~~

FOR THREE INCREDIBLE DAYS *Johanne* ran, arms outstretched, under a cloudless sky. Gliding easily over the following seas she sailed direct to our next port of call, Naples. Collecting together our passports and the ship's papers, Edward went ashore to clear us into Italy. The rest of us stood guard around *Johanne*'s decks. What with the Mafia and Godfather's splashed in lurid Technicolor across our imaginations, we didn't linger long in Naples but left the moment we could for Portici, a suburb a few miles south across the bay. There a man, his face deeply rippled with age, rowed over to show us the best spot to drop a stern anchor so that *Johanne* could swing round and nudge up against the short town quay. Satisfied that our boat was safe, the considerate old fellow then warned Edward, with further signs, to watch out for thieves. He was but the first of many. Sharing the dock with us was a Danish coaster, and her crew told the same story. Keep a powerful light on deck all night and have someone visibly on watch at all times; if this was not done, everything, including the very mooring lines, could disappear.

As if to emphasize the warning, the Danish skipper pointed across the harbor to where a fleet of some seventeen speedboats bobbed innocuously on moorings. All painted a uniformly dull gray, I had assumed they were a fleet of hire boats owned by a rather unimaginative hire-boat man. The Dane laughed. "I thought so too. Why, I even asked if I could rent one! You should have seen the guy's eyes when he turned me down. They're smuggling boats! Every one of them owned by the Commara [local Mafia] and kept right here in the harbor under the eye of the customs office." We looked again and now, for sure, we saw a group of sinister powerboats, their streamlined bows snatching like dangerous thoroughbreds at their moorings. Every boat was identical, and therefore impossible to identify individually in a court of law.

But we couldn't stand around all day staring at powerboats, we had work to do. A mile or more back along the coast, half hidden in a haze of heat and pollution, stood the focus of our visit, a large, red-pink building. Once a summer palace for the princes of Monaco, today it houses Casa Materna, in translation and in reality, "A home filled with a mother's love."

I first heard about Casa Materna when, in Antigua, I read a paperback called *Take This Child: The Santi Story* by Cyril Davis.* The book related how a fatherless boy, Ricardo Santi, was brought up in a Methodist orphanage in Italy and how, at the turn of the century, he himself became a Methodist minister, married, and went to work in the slums of Naples. There, on his thirty-fourth birthday, two small children accosted him in the street, begging him to buy some matches. Instead he invited them home with him to share his special birthday tea. What else could a compassionate man do? With their father dead the children, aged four and six, were sleeping at night huddled under a stone archway.

Angelo and Rosetta were the first of an estimated 15,000 children who have found love, security, and the chance of a decent education within the Santis' fold. By the time we arrived in Portici, Mama and Papa Santi were dead but their own four children had expanded the Santi movement far beyond their parents' humble dreams. Constantly fighting for funds, those children of a poor pastor have yet managed to build a modern 160-bed hospital in the heart of one of Europe's worst slums. They have created a day-care center, "Casa Mia," for up to 400 city street kids and provided clinics and temporary housing for earthquake victims. Best of all, in Casa Materna itself they provide a loving home for up to 100 children, with primary education for 250 more. Throughout they have kept in touch with the American Methodist movement. Much of the funding for their work flows from the generosity of ordinary Americans, for the Santis are not unknown in the United States. A number of years ago, Dr. Teofilo Santi of Naples, Italy, son of Papa Santi the pastor, was the subject of the American television program *This Is Your Life*.

Thinking of their work made my meager offering of homemade shirts and trousers look more and more paltry. Nonetheless I packed them into a battered suitcase and set out with Edward in search of Casa Materna. Corso Garibaldi is a long, gray street running in a straight line from Portici to Naples. High tenements on either side block out the sun. Below, cars driven with Italian panache hurtle back and forth stirring

---

*The latest, updated edition is called *Casa Materna: The Santi Story* and is available in the United States from P. O. Box 176, Tuckahoe, NY 10707.

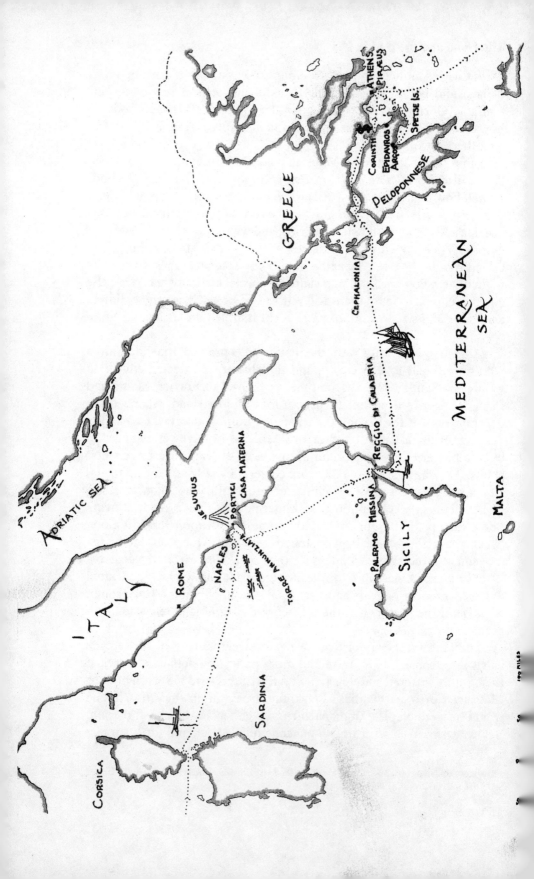

up private whirlwinds of litter, whipping them momentarily to life before depositing them, exhausted, in the dust. The pavements of Corso Garibaldi are narrow, the shops small. And the suitcase was growing heavier by the minute as we hunted up and down the long street for Casa Materna. Somehow I had expected something more arresting than a simple plaque on the wall that stated baldly "No 235." I suppose I had expected a summer palace.

The entrance to Casa Materna is through a stone archway which tunnels darkly under the full thickness of the street-side building. That tunnel leads directly into a secret garden. Less than twenty feet from Corso Garibaldi lies a seven-acre domain filled with sunlight and color and life. A driveway sweeps around and down toward the Bay of Naples. Mediterranean flowers bloom on every hand. Classic statuary, left behind by the princes, grace the pathways and, at the far end, near the sea, a fountain plays. Behind it stands the mother house. Above its door, picked out in white letters against the palace's faded red stucco, are the words that best symbolize all that the Santis stand for: *"Lasciate i fancuilli venire a me"* (Suffer the little children to come unto me).

The sufferings of the poor of southern Italy are hard to credit in what is now the fifth-wealthiest industrialized nation in the world. Unemployment is rife yet unemployment benefits are scarce. Those speedboats in Portici Harbor provided an important source of income to an impoverished people whose central government levied taxes on southern cigarettes but returned little of the revenue to the south in the form of better housing, hospitals, or schools. Many thousands of southern children have no formal education at all, for there are not enough schools and teachers to go around. One little child was brought to Casa Materna's door with some of his toes missing. Not a birth defect or an accident, the baby's toes had been chewed off by rats.

As we sat chatting in Emanuel Santi's office, children made constant use of his open door: bringing him paintings to admire or questions to answer or just calling by for a quick cuddle on his lap before continuing with their daily lives. Yes. Casa Materna knows all about mother's love.

Half the stack of mail waiting for us in Portici was for John and Lana. That night they broke their news to us. Due to the restrictive practices of the British television industry, no film shot by non-union members could be screened in Britain and, due to unemployment in their ranks, the union was refusing to accept new members. John and Lana's film would be banned by the union from British television, and their backers had withdrawn their funding. John and Lana were out of a job. They would have to leave us in Greece to hunt for work. It was shattering news for us as well as them. Through ten months of fun and laughter, frustration and disaster, we had lived together in remarkably warm harmony. Neither their company nor their expertise could be replaced.

Clothes delivered and mail collected, Edward was keen to press on at once to Greece. I, on the other hand, was determined to go sightseeing. Hang it all, we were moored in the shadow of Vesuvius, only ten miles from Pompeii. John and Lana backed me up and *Johanne*'s culture vultures won the day. Blasting a farewell to Casa Materna, we sailed past Torres Anunciada and anchored off the coast about a mile south of the port. To be absolutely safe (and, no doubt, to emphasize his disdain for sightseeing), Edward remained aboard. The rest of us caught a bus to Pompeii. My diary entry reads *"What a place!* If only we had more time. . . ."

Mind you, ruins usually bore me to tears—all that jumble of fallen masonry laid out on neatly coiffured lawns. Pompeii was different. For a start it is so large, its streets and houses cover such an enormous area, that fellow tourists actually enhance the wonder of the place. You bump into no more of them than you would strolling shoppers in any small town. And therein lies the magic of Pompeii. Regardless of the lack of visible residents, or roofs, Pompeii is a living town. I felt genuine diffidence, even guilt, as I nosed about her houses, fearful that at any moment the rightful owner might return, demanding to know what I thought I was doing. But even then, for me the most dramatic sight of all was to be found not in Pompeii's houses or her theaters but out in her streets. There, deep narrow ruts dissect the paving stones, ruts made by the friction of a thousand passing chariot wheels driven century after century, over the exact same route. Iron-clad wheels they must have been, eating millimeter by millimeter into the hard, unyielding stone.

And then, in A.D. 79, *whumph!* One mighty rumble from Earth's belly, one belch of gas and flames, one gush of boiling lava spewing out of the mouth of Mount Vesuvius and 20,000 people were buried alive. Is it their spirits that haunt Pompeii still and make it feel alive? Suddenly Kate's hand was snatched from mine. A dark-jowled man had whisked my daughter from me, but a moment later she reemerged from his kiosk, a smile lighting up her face. He had given her a charming mosaic brooch. I don't know why, but strangers were always giving Katy presents. Only a fortnight ago an artist in Barcelona had given her a large print of one of his works. Maybe it was due to the smile that set her green eyes dancing. Or maybe she carries with her some invisible, friendly essence. To this day it is from her that strangers ask the way and to her that old tramps chat on buses.

We arrived home in the late afternoon and, as if to make up to Edward for the delay, spent the next hour zealously lashing down everything in sight, getting *Johanne* shipshape and ready for sea. We gave special attention to the Zodiac. Stowing *Tinkerbell* inside, we zigzagged stout line back and forth to hold them down. No sea could wrench those dinghies free. As we worked, one of Portici's smuggling boats zoomed past and we pondered idly on their mission. Soon after supper everyone turned in—we all wanted a good night's sleep, for at dawn we'd be off on a nonstop voyage to Athens.

At 2:15 A.M. John woke, uneasy, and listened. There! He heard it again—a spine-tingling sound of stealth on deck. Stark naked, he leapt out of bed and up the ladder, bellowing at the top of his lungs as he went to wake the rest of us. He arrived just in time to see two men hurl the Zodiac, plus *Tinkerbell,* into the water. A few feet away in the darkness, an accomplice stood by with a getaway boat. As the men jumped after the dinghies, the accomplice yanked on the outboard cord. *Phutter! Put!* Silence. He pulled again. And again. It wouldn't start. Quick! Leap after them! Stop the bastards! Just in time I remembered that they'd be armed. Now the outboard spluttered to life and they were on their way.

Everything aboard *Johanne* was stowed for sea: outboard locked in the hold, yawl boat lashed to its davits aft. Unlash it then! Get after them! As the thieves puttered toward the shore, *Johanne*'s crew darted hither and thither in a frenzy of activity. Lana and I grabbed every offensive weapon we could think of: crowbars, sheath knives, an air pistol that didn't work, even an underwater floodlight. Edward and John grabbed clothes. While they opened the hold and hoisted up the outboard, we unlashed the yawl boat and launched it into the sea. Another minute to dump everything, pell-mell, into the boat's bottom and they were off in a chase worthy of James Bond, or perhaps Inspector Clouseau of *Pink Panther* fame. By the time our heroes reached the shore all sign of thieves and Zodiac had vanished. Turning toward town they scoured the beach in vain, then went to the police to demand immediate action. The police promised a thorough search at dawn. Tired and dejected John and Edward doubled back to the boat.

In the meantime, on board *Johanne,* Lana and I played out the woman's part. We waited. Frustrated by the impotence of our role we pressed binoculars to our eyes and scanned the blackness. We bit our nails. We worried that our men might catch up with the thieves and be hurt. We worried that, angry as they were, they might catch up with the thieves and commit murder. As for Kate, when she learned that her *Tinkerbell* had been stolen, she burst into tears. In her sometimes lonely, nomadic life, *Tinkerbell* had become her dearest playmate.

Further sleep was out of the question so, soon after sunup, we took *Johanne* into the middle of Torres Anunciada Harbor and dropped anchor. Leaving Lana and Katy on guard, the rest of us strode off to the port police. But what metamorphosis was this? Men who the previous day had overflowed with warm Italian charm had turned taciturn and uncooperative. They didn't give a damn about *Tinkerbell* and the Zodiac. They cared about one thing only: when we were going to leave their harbor. We told them: as soon as they found our dinghies. Then they turned nasty and raised their voices. They threatened us with heavy taxes, not to mention dangerously impassioned gestures, if we didn't leave at once. Without doubt, they had something on their minds. When anger failed to move us they tried bribery. If we left the port before midday they would forget the taxes and wave the harbor dues as well.

Furious, we stomped out and marched uptown to the main police station, a place remarkable only for the pulsating silence of its inactivity. No, the dawn search had not, as yet, been carried out. They needed another statement and, anyway, the dinghies were insured, right? So why not forget about them and leave? They looked anxiously at their watches; they, too, had something on their minds. So did we— in our naïveté we believed that every moment spent arguing with the police was a moment longer for the thieves to cover their tracks. Come to think of it, that was probably what the police were thinking as well.

Some three hours after we hit town a senior police officer entered the station.

"What happened?" His tone was brusque.

"We had two dinghies stolen last night."

"Did you see the thieves?"

"Yes."

"Why didn't you shoot them, then?"

"We didn't have a gun."

"So. What do you want now?"

"We need a police car to help us search along the shore."

"But why? Surely you were insured?"

"Yes, but we're leaving Europe. We haven't time to replace the dinghies. And anyway, we all saw the thieves' boat. I'm sure we'd recognize it again." The man shrugged and ordered a police car and two men to go with it.

Another half-hour's delay and we were on our way, or their way, for they drove us miles down the coast to a place where the boats could not possibly have been. When, on our return, we passed the track where the dinghies must have come ashore, the police flatly refused to drive down it for, they said, the uneven surface would damage their car. After that we gave up. The whole operation was a farce.

Abruptly, with a screech of tires scraping curbstones, we came to a halt. Our police officer had spotted the man he wanted. Winding down the window he gave a hearty handshake to a lean, loose-limbed pedestrian. They chatted for quite a while, casting an occasional backward glance at the three foreigners sitting hot and squashed together on the car's rear seat. Another friendly handshake and the officer nodded to our driver and we drove off.

"That," he said, turning to us with palpable pride, "was Al Capone. Head of the local Mafia!" We were not impressed. Somewhat deflated and quite possibly baffled, the police officer went on to inform us that Al Capone had confirmed that our robbery was a professional—that is, Commara—job. We should claim our insurance money and forget about it. Case closed.

From then on the day's events grew more and more surreal. Heading back toward the dock our police escort was halted at an intersection—not by traffic police, but by more Mafia, or Commara, this lot armed with walkie-talkies. We appeared to have hit town on a busy day. Our driver listened carefully to the mafioso's instructions, nodded a couple of times, and then set off down a series of side streets. Clearly the Mob wanted to keep the direct route to the docks free for more important traffic.

Inside the harbor the police drew up in the shadow of a large coaster. Out! Out! Out! Barely waiting for the back door to slam shut, our escort fled. Were they afraid to witness what followed or merely worried they might be accused of snooping on the Commara if they stayed?

Thanks to the heat and the crush of the car our clothes stuck wetly to our backs as we walked past the tanker's bow—and stood stock-still. Torres Anunciada Harbor was in turmoil. The seventeen gray speedboats from Portici were out and running. One after another they roared into the port. With a great flourish of macho power, they tight-cornered up to the dock, their rainbows of spray threatening to douse the customshouse windows. Crowds, eagerly lined up alongside the quay, caught the cases of contraband cigarettes as they were tossed ashore, then loaded them into waiting cars. Once full, each car sped off through town down thoroughfares kept open by those walkie-talkie-toting mafiosi.

We rowed back to *Johanne* totally bemused, watching as boat after boat, having completed its smuggling run, did a noisy circuit of the port, the crew clasping their hands high above their heads in a salute of victory. No wonder the port police had given us a deadline of midday to quit their harbor. The time was 1:15.

17. A Greek Holiday

BACK ABOARD *Johanne* gloom, like a cold-eyed octopus, wrapped its clammy limbs around us all, though it stuck to none so tenaciously as to poor Edward. He'd been against us going to Pompeii in the first place. Now, with the theft of the Zodiac, he saw his future plans in ruins. Without the rugged inflatable how could the Seychelles diving project go ahead? No doubt the insurance money would come through one day, but we couldn't afford to wait. Even the seasons were conspiring against us. *Johanne* had to reach Suez by the beginning of September or risk weeks of headwinds at the bottom end of the Red Sea. Add to that the Communist seizure of Seychelles and the impending departure of John and Lana and I suppose our future did look a wee bit bleak. But brooding wasn't going to help. We had to get moving.

Two days of light airs brought us to the Strait of Messina, that narrow stretch of water which divides Sicily from the Italian mainland. There, belching at us through the strait, came a southerly gale direct from the hot deserts of North Africa. With darkness approaching we anchored off Sicily's sheltered lee and settled down for the night. Not that we slept much, not anchored there. If Naples is the brain center of the local Commara, then Sicily is the breast from which the worldwide Mafia sucks its mother milk. Aboard *Johanne* lights blazed and her crew took turns to pace the decks, brisk as sentries—and backed to the hilt by a formidable armory of deck brooms.

By dawn the wind had dropped and *Johanne* nosed cautiously forward, into a strait that has, since antiquity, played host to mythic beasts. Though, in the event, it was neither the notorious sea monster Scylla, with her six barking heads and twelve feet, nor the terrible whirlpool of Charybdis, but the Sicilian fishing boats themselves that most impressed us. Forty feet on deck, there is nothing exceptional about the boat's hull—it's the bowsprit that is so striking. Like a water diviner's rod, it stabs forward, rigid and horizontal, and quite as long as the boat itself. Along each great probiscus they build a catwalk with a seat at the outer end. From there the wiley fishermen can cast into the very heart of the Messina whirlpools and still leave their boat motionless, forty feet astern. *Johanne,* too, avoided Charybdis's hungry maw though I couldn't resist a slight shiver of revulsion as we watched the monster slowly churn and swirl a yellow-spittled froth around her lips.

No sooner had *Johanne* cleared the mythic hazards of the strait than an all too real wind hurtled down on her from the highlands that pace the instep of Italy's southern shore. A bandit wind it was, a screaming Fury, swooping without warning from out of a clear-blue sky. It would have thrown a lighter boat on her beam ends. Even on *Johanne* we leapt for the cabin top like scalded cats to drag the mizzen down. At once she slowed and came more upright. Soon after, we anchored off the coast to let the wind blow itself out and to get some sleep and then we were off again for Greece.

By noon the next day we had sighted the Greek island of Cephalonia. With little wind and a firm deadline we pushed on, mostly under power. Around us the air sparkled in its purity and the Gulf of Corinth, leading to the Canal, seduced us with its peace and splendor. To the south, a coastal plain reached out to peaks that rose 8,000 feet into the sky. Close on the northern shore, purple-shadowed mountains ranged one above another toward heaven or slid into the water in a fluted network of inlets and bays. Edward's spirits soared, his normal lust for life miraculously revived by such unspoiled beauty. Why not forget the Seychelles and their wretched coup? Why not stay on here in Greece? Where in the world could you find a more idyllic cruising ground than this?

The idea of digging a canal through the Isthmus of Corinth was first debated in the seventh century B.C. It would reduce by 150 miles the journey from Italy to Athens. Julius Caesar and Caligula both studied it. Nero even forsook his fiddle long enough to seize a golden pickax and have a go at digging it himself. He didn't get far. Not till those great canal diggers, the French, came along did the concept turn into reality. Cut into a solid mass of limestone, the canal is 3.2 miles long and, I believe, the most expensive stretch of water in the world. In 1977 it cost *Johanne* £67 to traverse that 3.2-mile stretch or, put another way, the cost per mile to travel down the Corinth Canal was almost exactly 100 times the official charge for traveling through Suez. (Suez's unofficial charges were something else!)

The Canal traversed and payment extorted, *Johanne* reached the Piraiévs, the port of Athens, the following afternoon. Weaving through a multi-tonnage of laid-up ships, she berthed in Zea Marina and her crew let out a mighty cheer. The G.M. had fallen silent. We'd made it in time. My parents weren't due for another two days.

Zea Marina had three things in its favor: its ship chandleries, its proximity to Athens, and its prices. Apart from that it was, and no doubt still is, a sump. There's no through flow of water so raw sewage pumped from yachts stays, and settles, in winter. In summer the gases rise to fill the air with a quite appalling stench. We arrived in high summer. Zea Marina stank.

Learning that my father would be unable to get away, John and Lana immediately volunteered to stay another fortnight so as to help us sail *Johanne* for my mother. A few hours later Martin walked into our lives. We first noticed him, laboring under a mountainous rucksack, as he wandered from boat to boat looking for work. But there, already I exaggerate. One thing Martin never did was look for work. A young man in his early twenties, he had been told by friends back home that there were yachts in Greece just dying to take unemployable young men on a cruise of the Mediterranean in exchange, as far as we could gather, for nothing save the honor of their company.

Johanne was moored at the far end of Zea Marina. By the time Martin reached us, very hot, very pink, and very exhausted, we hadn't the heart to turn him away completely. No, we said, we did not want crew but if he wished to dump his pack and come back for it when he had found a suitable berth that was okay with us. We soon learned our mistake. Give an inch to the Martins of this world and they'll take a long vacation. After a good night's rest and a good breakfast aboard *Johanne,* our Martin took off, ostensibly in search of work, but in fact to tour the sights. He returned aboard just in time to tuck into a hefty supper before retiring to the fo'c'sle bunk for another good night's sleep. We should have been tough and chucked him off but we were weak and so got our deserts.

I had been saving our own tourist forays for my mother's arrival. I always love traveling with Kate and her grandmother though I sometimes wonder if we're an endangered species: three generations of females who get along together. This time we visited the Acropolis. That extraordinary upsurge of rock, rising sheer and square 200 feet above the surrounding plain, was certainly an imposing site on which to build a fortified citadel and sanctuary to the goddess Athena. But if you're after a sense of reverence for the Parthenon's splendid marble columns, forget it. It will be killed by the guides' raucous cries. Ignore, too, the sanctuary's magnificent views that stretch, like the temptation of Christ, at your feet, for now that sanctuary swarms with people who, like scavenging gulls, pick at the rocks and ruins, hunting for crumbs of "culture" to carry home while leaving behind them their own dead droppings of litter. The place is a disaster, a summer sale in the discount store of packaged culture.

Next day, casting off the sapping heat of Athens (temperatures were over 100°F), we sallied forth for a short cruise of the adjacent islands. What bliss to slow down and relax, to know that when there was no wind we did not have to start the engine but instead could drop the headsails and dive over the side into the cool Aegean. For a few marvelous days we swam, read on deck under the awning, and rowed ashore and went for walks amid gnarled old olive trees where once a donkey scared the wits out of us by braying loudly from behind a dry stone wall. We visited Metapi. A dab of an island, small and flat and uninhabited, it had, at one time, been given over to the grape. Now the ground was matted with wild herbs which filled the air with a sweet pungency as we inadvertently crushed them underfoot. At the far end of the island stood two wattle huts, their thatched roofs rotten and half blown away. Inside, a waist-high wall divided the single room in two; the floor of the larger part was pebbled several inches thick with dried goat droppings.

Toward the center of the island, and quite separate from the huts, was another minute house, a house of God. Finding the door on the latch we tiptoed in. Simple icons graced the whitewashed walls, and a deep window embrasure held a random collection of candles, lamps, and oil. A faded cloth of orange silk, emblazoned with a golden cross, hung in front of an arched doorway. But who, we wondered, worshipped in this chapel on an uninhabited island? Was it used just once a year on some special feast day or did fishermen and goatherds drop in to light a candle and say a passing prayer?

Far too soon we were sailing back to the heat and stink of Zea Marina. Far too soon we bundled baggage and bodies into a clapped-out taxi and escorted my mother to the airport, and hugged her and kissed her goodbye. It wasn't going to be so easy to pop over for a visit when 7,000 miles divided us. Aboard *Johanne,* John and Lana were also packing their bags as their life was taking a new turn. Undoubtedly, we wished them well, but we wished even more that they were staying with us. Dear friends, over the past eleven months they'd spoiled us. We were going to find it hard in the future to accept lower standards from the people who shared our lives.

Sorrow at their departure was somewhat lessened by the arrival on board of my much loved brother, another John, and his much loved wife, Helen. The weather was irreproachable. A cooling breeze took the worst edge off the midday heat and in the afternoons the local Melteme blew strong enough to give us several rousing sails through the rash of islands that spot the waters south of Athens. We visited Spetsi and Návplion and a remote monastery high above Mandraki Beach. At Argos we found a completely deserted amphitheater with seats for 20,-000 people and a back-street bakery where, for a few drachmas, old women in long black skirts and shawls brought their Sunday lunch to be roasted in the baker's oven. We drove in local buses past exhausted land from which Greek farmers still managed to coax forth oranges, lemons, olives, figs, pomegranates, and peaches. Finally we headed for Epidaurus, planned as the climax of our cruise. The theater at Epidaurus is said to be the finest example of classic architecture in existence as well as the best preserved of all Greek theaters. Here, each summer, Greeks and foreigners alike flock to see the classical Greek dramas reenacted in their classic, Greek setting.

Beating back against the Melteme it took us two hard days of sailing to reach the town. By then Martin's free-riding ways no longer amused but frankly irritated. Never once during his stay did he volunteer to do anything: row ashore, do the shopping, scrub the decks, or wash dishes. If it was a charterer we wanted we could have had one—at £500 a week. As to offering to guard the boat so that Edward too could go on expeditions, such a thought never crossed his mind—until we told him that he could stay behind and look after *Johanne* as Edward was coming to see the Epidaurus theater. Our young "crewman" looked utterly astounded and then positively aggrieved. I pointed out that he was welcome to go on his own on the following day but he didn't. Who, after all, would pay for his bus fare and his lunch?

Epidaurus theater lies some thirty minutes by road from Epidaurus port. At my insistence we took a bus. Bus rides are so much more exciting than the cultural quarantine of private cars or taxis. For a brief moment you come in contact with the real spirit of a country. All around you faces, costumes, and personal interactions fight for your attention. Odd-shaped packages dig you in the ribs arousing wildest speculation. And then there are the smells. Not just those of washed and unwashed bodies, but the tempting wisps that rise from exotic foods nibbled en route, and from fresh produce packed in baskets or crammed into plastic bags in racks above one's head. In some countries it is the smell of the farmyard that predominates. Livestock stand tethered to the seats and the odd chicken roosts on a neighbor's knee.

Soon after our own ramshackle bus took off, tightly packed with peasants returning from market, a Greek woman, bent with years, flagged us to a stop and pulled herself painfully up the steps. John offered up his place and, in return, she rewarded him with a beatific smile. Once seated, perched well forward, she kept her eyes fixed resolutely on the side of the road. Suddenly a chicken claw of a hand whipped out from her enveloping clothes of black, and she crossed herself three times in quick succession. She repeated the process at every wayside shrine we passed, and not without reason.

Our bus driver was of the extrovert persuasion—a man who saw life as a challenge and bus driving as an art form through which he could express the individual beauty of his soul. We hurtled around corners and down the wrong side of narrow country lanes. We rattled through small villages scattering infants, chickens, and stray goats from our path. Beside me the old lady's hand was rarely still. Was there perhaps some connection between the inordinate number of roadside shrines and the driving skills of our chauffeur? Our fears were not allayed by the realization that he too sought protection from above, though happily this did not involve removing his hands from the wheel. Instead an icon, illuminated by a red lamp, was permanently installed above the windshield. All around the icon dangled everything that could possibly be made to dangle. There were nylon tassels in fluorescent pinks and greens, red cloth parachutes, and black plastic bats. There was even a large shamrock, left behind, perhaps, by an Irish traveler who felt the bus's need for good luck was greater than his own. From loudspeakers above our heads Greek folk music twanged forth. Jaunty rather than jarring, it provided the ideal accompaniment to the swirls of dust that followed our wild passage through the Peloponnese.

Epidaurus was my favorite monument in Greece. No heap of old marble lying about on the ground, it still had a "feel" about it. Like good tourists we climbed the fifty-five rows to the top of the theater. From there, for the first time, I was actually glad of a tour guide. A bony Englishwoman, she stood right in the center of the circular stone stage and imperiously commanded everyone, client and non-client alike, to silence. (Looking like a nineteenth-century governess, she was probably in fact a twentieth-century professor.) Once silence was established to her satisfaction, she tore a piece of paper in two and then dropped first a small coin and next a small twig onto the ground. Every single sound could be clearly heard from the fifty-fifth row of that open-air theater. But even that marvel could not compare with the view. Ancient Greeks must surely have worshipped their countryside. Every amphitheater I have visited (be it in Greece or Asia Minor) has been built with a stunning view. From where I sat I could see a long, straight valley green as emerald which stretched to the very feet of distant mountains glistening silver where they touched the flax-blue sky.

Aboard *Johanne* time was running out. John and Helen had work and family to return to and *Johanne* herself had a wind to catch. Before we could leave Greece there were crew members to find, supplies to buy, and another hard decision to make about Katy.

Back in Zea Marina, as John and Helen and Martin disembarked, others hovered, eager to take their place. A fortnight before, we had pinned an advertisement up in a quayside bar asking for experienced crew. The luxury of sailing with John and Lana had made us choosy. We no longer wanted to face the long haul to the Seychelles with a pack of novices. Nonetheless, the first two to approach us were exactly that. Tony and Paul, a couple of London lads, admitted that they lacked experience but claimed to be eager to learn. We said we'd think about it. The moment they left another couple stepped forward. According to Jean Louis, he had "skippered a charter boat for two years," and Lola's father owned a yacht. Both were French, quiet, small. We took them on. The next morning two more hopefuls arrived. One, a woman, would have been ideal. Australian, she had already hitchhiked halfway around the world on yachts. The other, a lad of eighteen, was mad about old sailing ships, but what about Tony and Paul? They had asked first and we certainly didn't want six extra crew. With two experienced people already signed on, it seemed a bit unfair to turn down our eager, and brawny, beginners. We accepted Tony and Paul. I'm sure somehow we should have known better.

Prior to buying supplies to feed six people for up to seventy-five days (fifty days to get there plus twenty-five days' reserve), I checked with everyone for any pet aversions in the food line; Jean Louis and Lola looked suspiciously like vegetarians to me, but happily they all claimed they'd eat anything. I then did a tour of the supermarkets to study their prices. One, close to Zea Marina, had a huge sign painted right across its outside wall: "10% DISCOUNT FOR ALL YACHTS!." On closer inspection I found out why—all their prices, before discount, were 15 percent higher than elsewhere.

Recruiting Lola's and Katy's help, we went ashore to store up, with a very long list in one pocket and a great deal of cash hidden in another. "Twenty-five large and twenty-five small cans of tomatoes," I called out and Katy dived into the canned-tomato display. Seven jumbo carts, wheels sagging under their weight of cans, caused chaos at the checkout counter. And we hadn't started on the uncanned goods yet. Upstairs was a gastronomic wonderland: barrels of glistening black olives, streamers of thin salamies, and tubs filled with luscious feta cheese. The grocer insisted the feta needed a fridge but it looked so tempting we bought four pounds anyway and, in spite of the torrid heat of the Red Sea, it stayed good to the very last dollop.

Having blocked the checkout counter for half an hour, boxed up the stores, and handed over the cash, we were faced with another frustration. No shopping carts were allowed off the premisis, not even to go across the road to the quayside. Mentally shattered, I had to rake up enough smiles, patience, and Greek to alter the decision without making the manager lose face, which was particularly difficult as my own ego had just received a painful left hook: the checkout woman had asked if Lola (five years my junior) was my daughter! To be fair, Lola looked nothing like her age. Five foot four and a little plump, she had long dark ringlets and big expressive eyes set in an innocent, lightly freckled face. The Arabs were going to adore her and the Greeks appeared to be not entirely averse either—certainly the supermarket manager was persuaded to lend us his own store-handling cart to trundle our stack of cartons to the dinghy.

Almost ready to leave, we had once again to face the question of what was best for Katy. She'd been much less sick during the past few weeks, but then the sea had been less rough. Besides that, on this trip there was another danger—pirates. In 1977 there were some pretty grisly stories coming out of the Red Sea. Yachts were being attacked not only by real pirates but by Communist government gunboats behaving like pirates. Some people had already been killed, others imprisoned. I reckoned that one collision and one Mafia raid were about as much as a small child could cope with in any one year. What Katy needed was a safe haven.

Sue Pick and I spent our infancy in the same village. We shared prams, walks, and babysitters and, after leaving school, planned to drive together to India. Instead I met Edward and, while he and I drove a Land Rover to Singapore, Sue took an overland bus to the subcontinent and stayed on, marrying Partap Sharma and settling down in Bombay with their two small daughters. Now it was they who came to Kate's rescue, generously offering her a home until we reached the Seychelles. Not only would she be safe and loved, she would also be traveling in vaguely the right direction.

Booking a seat on the only direct flight from Athens to Bombay, I was left with one last-minute poser to solve: shoes. Boat children go barefoot for most of their lives. When forced, they slip their feet into plastic flip-flops, footwear that can get wet and that floats when it falls in the water—and which in no way inhibits the spread of their toes. It must have taken us two or three hours, hunting through the shoe shops of the Piraiévs, before we found a pair of sandals wide enough to fit Kate's uninhibited feet.

Soon all was packed. Her rucksack, full of felt-tips, books, and games, was topped by her beloved Womble, who stood with his long nose sticking out so he could breathe. Tucked in his arms was Peter, her favorite bear. How, I wondered, would our eight-year-old react to flying 3,000 miles to stay with people she could not even remember having met? I need not have worried. Clasping her tough little arms tightly around my neck she gave us each a passionate farewell kiss. No clinging, no tears, her face was radiant with excitement. She was on her very own adventure. The next moment she was chatting nineteen to the dozen as the Swiss Air hostess walked away with her to the plane.

Back at the boat we still had a couple of things to shift aboard. We had bought a replacement inflatable. Nothing like that BMW of rubber dinghies, a Zodiac, it was a cheap and nasty shade of yellow, and it would have to do. The other aquisition was more controversial. Edward, determined to be armed when he faced the Red Sea pirates and the Communist gunboats, had bought a semi-automatic shotgun. The Greek customs officers didn't bat an eye. I, on the other hand, loathed the thing.

18. The Suez Canal

On August 20th, the day after Katy left for India, we cast off from Zea Marina and turned *Johanne* south, bound for Port Said and the Suez Canal. Hauling on halyards and sheets, Paul and Tony soon showed their strength, a strength we'd be glad of in the days ahead. Beside them, Jean Louis looked as skinny-kneed as a young colt. Five foot six or seven, he had the slender frame and sensitive features more often associated with poets than with sailors. By comparison, Lola, the dominant one of the pair, looked almost sturdy.

In all, it took *Johanne* four days to amble her way south through the Mirtoan Sea to Crete, four days in which to remember all the reasons why, this time around, we had agreed to sign up an experienced crew. It is seldom the major tasks—steering, sail trimming, and navigation—that cause difficulties. Given enthusiasm and that all-important streak of practicality, their rudiments can be quickly learned. For me, anyway, the strain comes from the constant background fear that, through ignorance, someone aboard would seriously injure either themselves or others.

"Hey! I wouldn't stand on that chain. We're about to anchor." "Let me hold the boiling water. You keep the cups. There, now we've both got one hand free if the boat rolls." Sometimes I felt I was mothering a bunch of nine-year-olds let loose in a farrier's, especially when it became evident that common sense was none too common among our handpicked crew. Disappointing, too, was the discovery that Jean Louis and Lola had been somewhat economical with the truth when describing their previous sailing experience.

By the time we reached Crete Paul and Tony had had enough. At first seasick, they later became bored without their television, pub, and motorbikes. As soon as we dropped anchor in a creek opposite Áyios Nikólaos, they announced that they'd be off. A spot of grape picking might be fun. There was no apology, no hint that they'd let us down—just broad grins and genial waves as they stepped ashore, taking with them not only their brawn, on which we had been depending, but also, alas, my small collection of best-sellers.

Oddly enough, the loss of Tony and Paul filled the rest of us with a feeling verging on elation, a camaraderie of survivors which had not been there before.

Beyond our sheltered creek, light airs gave way to a full-flown gale. *Johanne* was once again weather bound, but her crew were far from idle. While Edward fixed a rotten knee (*Johanne*'s, not his own), the rest of us lavished grease on her blocks and stays. Alarmed to discover that our "experienced" crew's knowledge of bends and hitches stretched no further than a reef knot, we spent one whole morning teaching them the essentials. They were quick to learn, and we were soon racing each other to complete bowlines and rolling hitches, figures of eight, and the double sheet bend. Already behind time, we gave up waiting for the weather. Loading up with thirty pounds of potatoes and thirty more of onions, we left Crete on August 28th.

Outside, great cresting waves, twelve to fifteen feet high, came charging down on us from behind. *Johanne* loved it. Crushing roller after roller beneath her, she bowled south toward Africa. Lola, too, was in her element. Her fine dark eyes flashed with excitement as she took the helm and steered us on our hectic course. Jean Louis's expressive features were, in contrast, timorous with unease. I sympathized. Running before the wind was still my bugbear. Hours spent trying to detect the slightest shift of wind on the nape of one's neck left me as tense as a snap trap. And what if a sea crashed against the rudder and I couldn't hold the helm and *Johanne* slewed around broadside on? What if she jibed? Already I was dreading my night watch—three hours alone at the helm with nothing but a half-smile of moon for support. How I admired Lola's sangfroid, standing up there so relaxed and carefree. It was several weeks before she accidentally jibed *Johanne* and one source of her sangfroid was revealed. Lola had been blissfully unaware that an accidental jibe was possible and we, still half-believing in her experience, hadn't thought to tell her.

Before the final pink brushstrokes of day left the sky, Edward called out "Down mizzen!" We certainly missed Paul and Tony then. The following wind had again pinned the sail hard against the shrouds. It took us three weaklings a good half-hour to carry out that simple order. But the instant the sail was down conditions eased. The helm lost the worst of its weight and *Johanne*'s crazy flight turned into a more seemly progress. Even so, our first noon to noon showed us a heartening 134 miles nearer Port Said. And then the wind died, leaving those same large seas to play with *Johanne* as they willed. They willed vilely. They rolled her every which way. Her gaffs and booms, preventers, blocks, and sheets all took a battering. So did her crew. Gripping the kicking

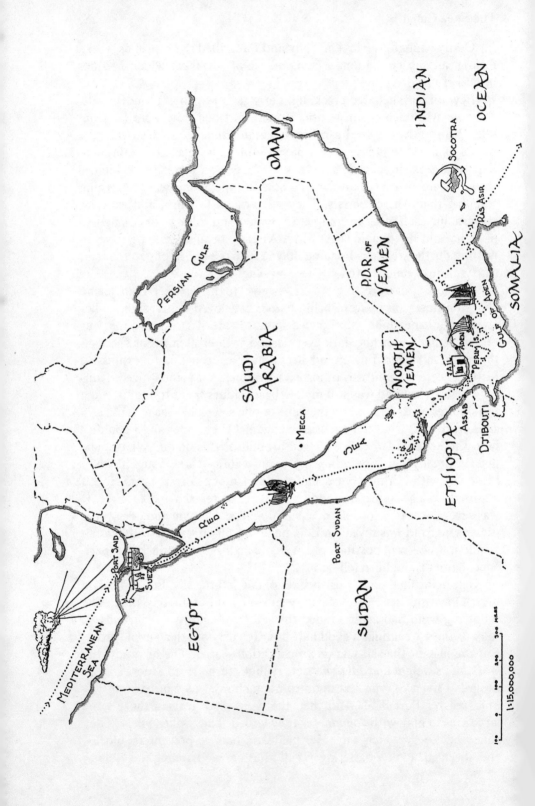

MEDITERRANEAN SEA
EGYPT
PORT SAID
SUEZ
RED SEA
SUDAN
PORT SUDAN
MECCA
SAUDI ARABIA
PERSIAN GULF
OMAN
P.D.R. of YEMEN
NORTH YEMEN
TA'IZ
ADEN
PERIM IS.
ETHIOPIA
ASSAB
DJIBOUTI
GULF OF ADEN
SOMALIA
RAS ASIR
SOCOTRA
INDIAN OCEAN

1:15,000,000
100   0   100   200   300 MILES

wheel in both hands I cursed it and cajoled it and begged it to calm down. Struggling alone in the dark, I singularly failed to prevent *Johanne* from rolling beam-on to the swells and pointing miles off course. In those days I was still obsessed by course. It had yet to dawn on me that, with no wind, traveling zero miles with *Johanne* pointing west was no worse than traveling zero miles with her pointing south. Either way we were going nowhere.

That night the masthead light bulb blew. Recently installed, it was from a new, more powerful batch we had bought in England in compliance with the latest international maritime laws. Remember those faulty bulbs—they were to play a small but significant part in our trip.

Dawn brought with it a welcome breeze from the west-northwest, a fair wind that stayed with us for five whole days, five days of peace and splendid sailing with *Johanne* heeled slightly from the wind and the soft hiss of bubbles as they rushed past her hull. Sun and breeze tempered our bodies and here and there a sheerwater tipped its long, tapering wings to skim the sea. Five glorious days.

At midday on September 2nd we sighted Port Said. Edward's entry in the log reads "1230. Fairway Buoy, Port Said. Here comes plucking and diddling of yours truly." How right he was. We were still outside the port and lowering sails when an enormous tug, the *Antar,* drove to within a couple of feet of our yawl boat, dangling and vulnerable on its davits aft.

"You want agent?" demanded the captain, a rascally fellow with a two days' growth of beard.

"No thank you!"

"You must have agent!" he yelled.

"No!"

"You must anchor here!" Outwardly we ignored him. Inside he had stirred up an explosive mixture of anger and fear. *Antar* was a very big tug. As if sensing our fear, the captain revved his engines, inching his bow to within a hairsbreadth of the dinghy. He'd got his version of extortion with menaces down to a fine art.

"You give cigarettes to my crew, huh!" Luckily we came forewarned. Although none of us smoked, we had several cartons of cheap cigarettes stashed below. I threw one carton over *Antar*'s bows and onto her deck. The crew surged forward, one man snatching up the carton, others bawling "You gi' Chicklets!"; "Chocolates!"; "Coca-Cola!" They were like children, stamping their feet for sweets in a supermarket. I exploded. "No!" I yelled. "I've got nothing more. Now bug off!" As if by magic they stopped. From threatening pirates and clamorous brats, they became charming people, full of genuine smiles.

"Okay! Okay! Thank you very much." And they laughed and waved and reversed away from *Johanne*'s stern. We did not wave back.

Our first obstacle cleared without much credit, we edged on through a mob of small, besieging boats. One after another we drove them off, but somehow one man managed to leap aboard. His accomplice rowed swiftly away leaving us with little alternative but to carry the gate-crasher with us. Uninvited and unwanted, he proceeded to get in every-one's way, and then demanded U.S. $12 for our pains.

Once moored in the yacht basin we shoved a packet of cigarettes into his hands and pushed him ashore, only to find him replaced almost at once by an immigration officer. Already exhausted, we steeled our-selves for more graft but the man could not have been nicer. We offered him drink—tea, coffee, beer, whiskey—but he refused them all. We had arrived in the month of Ramadan when pious Muslims fast from sunup to sundown and then celebrate with a large meal under the stars.

Transiting Suez was, and still is, a matter of scaling one colossal pyramid of corruption. The official charge for yachts was set at a most reasonable U.S. $30. There were even a few brave and determined souls who managed to transit for precisely that. They lined up and haggled, pleaded and shouted and smiled. They demanded to see the boss and the bank manager (bosses and bank managers from the apex of the pyramid with most bribe money climbing automatically to the top), and finally, after three to five days, they collected all their papers together and left.

We arrived to be told that a new law had been passed: everyone had to have an agent. Too late, we found out that that too was a lie. By then we had already taken on an agent, and, once in an agent's clutches, you were lucky to get through the canal for less than U.S. $120: $30 went to the authorities for the upkeep of the canal and to pay the obligatory pilot, $90 went to the agent to distribute up and down his personal chain of corruption.

In Port Said foreign yachts were herded together and watched over by Ali, the guardian, who lived in a far corner of a wooden shed ashore. Small, dark, and thin, with shining black hair, Ali was always gentle and helpful and never begged. In sheer gratitude, visiting yachts loaded him with presents. On our arrival he handed us several letters, includ-ing two from Bombay. Katy was safe and happy and, at her own re-quest, about to enroll in a school in the city. Ali, as well as acting as postman, also loaned us the yacht club visitors' book, a truly amazing chronicle of the trials and tribulations of cruising people as they ap-proached Suez.

The most memorable tale came from a single-hander who had been boarded by pirates in the Gulf of Aden, north of Socotra. They had stripped his boat of everything; even his sails and halyards went. The man, utterly alone and faced by a horde of brigands, was convinced he was going to die. But Allah was with him. He recorded in the visitors' book that the attack came on the one day of the year when Muslims are forbidden to kill. His life was spared but he was left adrift in a yacht stripped of all means of propulsion. We voted to give Socotra a miss. Though the book included several more tales of attack, by both pirates and Communist gunboats, the most common stories of all were those of being ripped off by people right here in Egypt. There is a well-known saying among yachtsmen: "You'll find no sharks in the Red Sea. They all stepped ashore at Suez."

The yacht pen in Port Said is but a short walk from the terminal where, day in and day out, government ferries ply back and forth across the canal. On the opposite bank lies the heart of one of Egypt's largest cities. Squeezing with difficulty aboard the nearest ferry, Edward and I dodged between bicycles and donkey carts, horsedrawn carriages, cars, steaming trucks, and men: men dressed in flowing desert robes and turbans to protect them from the sun, men in Western shirts and trousers—men everywhere. A quick look around confirmed it; I was the only female in sight.

Once arrived at the far bank the cars vanished, spewing clouds of pollution over the more impoverished foot passengers who, pressed on all sides by livestock and handcarts, made their way into the alleyways and open spaces of the market. Here everything was tumbling into rubble and decay. Everything except the Egyptians themselves, who were a vibrant people struggling, and surviving. Hell-bent on the big rip-off, they could still laugh uproariously if you caught them at it. One presumes they laughed more discreetly if you did not.

First we had to lay our hands on some Egyptian pounds. We chose as our money changer an old man of great dignity. Sitting outside his shop on a simple wooden chair, he had, balanced across his paunch, an ornate fly whisk which, every now and then, he waved in a vague, regal fashion around his head. He could not be more accurate for his ears were deaf and his eyes almost blind with cataracts. Egyptian pounds bought and safely buttoned into Edward's front pocket, we roamed the market, drinking in the scene of dust and color and laughter and shouts of simulated anger. I bought fifteen cans of Quaker Oats from off a rickety wooden table and remembered, too late, that we were supposed to bargain for them. No wonder those gorgeous black-eyed children were giggling as we left.

The Suez Canal has room for only one line of shipping at a time, so, each day, the waiting vessels at either end are organized into convoys: supertankers first, yachts last. Three days after our arrival our own convoy was ready to depart. At 9 A.M., a canal inspector came aboard bringing with him Mohammed, our pilot. Surely a most auspicious start, notwithstanding the yacht club book's warnings about pilots and canal. One snag for yachts was that, bringing up the tail end of a convoy, they were often still in the canal when the first supertankers of the opposite convoy appeared. Pilots would then become agitated and, quite unnecessarily, force yachts' crews to tie up to piles at the side of the canal. Those obedient to the command often found their yachts badly damaged as the passing wash pounded their hulls against the posts. The most common warning in the book was "NEVER allow the pilot to take the helm." With the best pilots reserved for the supertankers, the yacht pilots were not always competent.

Before leaving, the inspector of pilots admonished us to take good care of Mohammed—and to pay him $10 to cover his return fare from Ismailia (the convoy's overnight stop, halfway along the canal). How much of that return fare went into the inspector's pocket and how much to poor Mohammed was anyone's guess.

Edward turned to Mohammed, a timid little man, and said, "Right, Mohammed. We will take care of you but I will steer. Okay? Otherwise I'll eat you for lunch."

"Oh, but I don't eat lunch! It is Ramadan."

"You may not eat lunch"—Edward paused dramatically—"but I do!" We had no trouble from Mohammed and we took good care of him.

First we rigged an awning over the break of the poop, well away from the helm. Then we got out a canvas deck chair and sat him in the shade. And there he stayed for most of the voyage. Occasionally he came aft to say something to Edward, and three times I brought him a bowl of water to wash in before he said his prayers toward the Kaaba. Undeniably, Mohammed was a good and pious man. The Prophet Mohammed, in his wisdom, gave his followers a dispensation. Travelers could, if they wished, eat normally during the month of Ramadan. But our Mohammed preferred to make his act of fast. Reaching Ismailia at 6:30 in the evening, he replaced his shoes on his feet and prepared to leave. Keeping our word, we handed over $10 knowing full well that little of it would remain his.

We spent that night anchored off Ismailia and, shortly after 4 A.M., our new pilot arrived. It was cold on the canal before the sun rose and, seeing the man shiver, Edward peeled off his own jacket and handed it to him. By the time that second pilot left, I almost wished he'd let him freeze. For the next eight and a half hours we were a captive audience to his demands: whiskey, *baksheesh* (money handouts), canned food, clothes, shoes, handbags, toys—you name it, he demanded it. A large, corpulent man, he was, by Egyptian standards, well off, except in pride. Of that he had none at all.

The eastern bank of the canal, where the Israelis had invaded Egypt, was still littered with the detritus of the Yom Kippur War. Dead tanks, gutted by fire, lay with their single cannon pointing skyward like an arm flung up in supplication to the heavens. On the western bank all the ruined Egyptian tanks had tactfully been cleared away. A train clattered past, riding the crest of the sand dune with people perched, cross-legged, on its roof, their thin djellabas flapping like prayer flags in the wind.

On the second leg of the trip the canal passed through the Bitter Lakes, the only part of the canal on which a pilot was really called for. Beneath the lakes' cloudy waters lurked sandbanks waiting to catch unwary yachtsmen. Not that our pilot evinced much concern for sandbanks—by then his sole interest was in Lola. He was the first of many to show us just how attractive Lola's dark and fulsome looks were to Arab men. The man was quite dotty about her. He wanted to carry her off to his lair there and then and kept discussing bride money with us, much to Jean Louis's irritation.

By 1 P.M. we were tied alongside in bombed-out Suez Harbor. By 1:15 P.M. Moses had contacted us. We had read about him in the yacht club visitors' book. As Edward said, "If one has to be fleeced by someone, you couldn't ask for a nicer rogue than Moses to do the fleecing." The other agent, Moses's chief rival, went under the colorful name of the Prince of the Red Sea. He was, however, a disappointingly greasy individual. Several stories told of how he came alongside northbound yachts imperiously demanding passports and ship's papers as if he were an Egyptian official. He then refused to return them until he had milked the owners of all they had. Moses could be infuriating but, nonetheless, we came to like him enormously.

Reaching the shopping center of Suez called for either a taxi or a knowledge of bus routes. Moses owned a taxi, a marvelously dilapidated affair with the number "100" painted large down either side. In this he drove Lola and me into town to buy fresh food. The port of Suez had suffered severe bombardment during the Yom Kippur War, leaving many of the houses a heap of rubble. As we passed, Moses pointed across the canal: "Israeli tanks come right to there."

"Did you see them?"

"Me? No! I run away." This latter was said with all the pride of a
sane man secure in his wisdom. When it came to buying supplies Moses
was worth his considerable weight in fresh Egyptian dates. He took us
first to a street lined with wooden booths, each stacked high with vegetables. But, with a gesture worthy of a Grand Pasha, he rejected all. For
us, his special clients, the stallholders must open up the back of their
booths so we could select from the very freshest supplies—a piece of
showmanship that I relish to this day.

What an amazing cornucopia we found. There we were, on the edge
of a vast desert, yet we bought lettuce, cabbages, tomatoes, cucumbers,
mangoes, green peppers, fresh figs, carrots, grapes, pears, guavas, and,
most delicious of all, fresh dates. Taxi 100 had difficulty fitting it all into
her trunk. Next we went to the government rice store where we were
again in luck. Normally rice was rationed and foreigners had a hard
time buying it, but now, with Ramadan, rice rations had been suspended.

On our way home we gave a lift to two elderly Americans. Wiry and
tanned, they had been living aboard a tramp steamer for the past year.
Charming people, they had all the calm forbearance so attractive in
liberal-minded Americans. As we bumped along the potholed road,
Moses announced that he would take Lola and me back first and drop
the Americans off afterward.

"Oh, I see," drawled the old boy, a smile warming his voice. "You
plan to take us for a little ride, do you?" and we all hooted with laughter. "Yes! Yes! Like a little thirty-dollar ride!" Poor Moses, he had to
protest most vehemently before any of us would believe him innocent.

Unloading the trunk of the taxi, we bid the Americans good luck
and, with help from Jean Louis and Edward, moved our booty aboard.
Bought fresh from a stall, not sick from a supermarket, that food was to
survive the rigorous heat of the Red Sea with no trouble at all.

Our next chore was to buy diesel. In spite of its world renown, Suez
had no quay where smaller boats could take on fuel. One had to order
one's diesel through Moses and wait (the donkey, you see, was getting
old). But by late afternoon McGregor the donkey had covered the long
road from town pulling behind him a rickety cart loaded with a tank of
fuel. There was no proper pipe for transferring the fuel and no gauge for
measuring it. By then, any illusions we might have harbored about
Egyptian honesty had long since vanished. Here all business was a
game, one side trying to outsmart and outdiddle the other. To trust
anyone was simply stupid. So we took two jerricans ashore and transferred every drop from the tank, through a gauze filter, into them and
then, through another filter, into *Johanne's* tanks and spare fuel drums.

That way we cleaned out impurities and checked the quantity at the same time.

Once fueled, we slipped our lines and, minutes later, *Johanne* was swinging comfortably at anchor. Around her, lateen-rigged open boats fluttered like white-winged butterflies, their skippers handling them with utmost skill as they wove through the crowded anchorage, offering a door-to-door service in fresh vegetables and fish, ship chandlery, ship agents, and even tourist souvenirs.

19. An Incident off Ethiopia

FOUR DAYS after docking in Suez, *Johanne* set sail again, her hold weighed down with the six extra drums of diesel. Within an hour a hardy wind swooped down from the northeast and picked her up and sent her romping south, racing to catch the last of those precious fair winds through the Gulf of Aden. We made an excellent passage with but one complaint: the following wind kept pace with us, denying us a cooling breeze. In the Red Sea you do need a breeze. The Red Sea is hot. On *Johanne,* on deck in the shade, the temperature hovered around 104°F. Below, in our cabin, it reached 110°F. That did it. Dragging a spare mattress on deck, I put it in the bottom of *Johanne*'s inflated inflatable and climbed into bed. I've slept in inflatable dinghies off and on ever since. With the stars and sails above and a mattress underneath, an inflatable makes the ideal tropical bed. The cool night air wafts over you yet the sides of the dinghy protect you from the worst of the flying spray.

Our *Ship Captain's Medical Guide* (issued by Her Majesty's Stationery Office for captains of ships with no ship's doctor on board) served as my bible on health. Now it gave us dire warnings about heat stroke, with the Red Sea given pride of place as the most villainous environment of all. At the helm, Jean Louis and Lola wore damp towels tied turban fashion around their heads. Edward protected his handsome nose with a peaked cap while I favored a broad-brimmed hat and a thin long-sleeved shirt. When becalmed I added a bucket of seawater to cool my feet and a fan to cool my face. Fighting dehydration, we strove to drink the recommended eight pints of liquid a day. By adding a pinch of salt to each pint, we kept up that other bulwark against heat stroke, body salts. Cooking was the worst. A few minutes in the galley and rivulets of sweat began trickling down the backs of one's legs, dripping off one's elbows and chin and onto the floor; that is, when it wasn't dripping into the bread dough.

We weren't the only ones to feel worn out: the swallows were on their way south. Arriving on board with a great flurry of blue-black wings, they perched precariously on the handrails, hopping up in alarm each time *Johanne* rolled. We soon noticed that the ones that did not swiftly fly away died. Were they already too exhausted by their flight, or did *Johanne*'s motion make them ill? Should we drive them off or let them rest?

Each morning brought with it a new crop of almost weightless corpses, their dark feathers still gleaming like midnight silk. Maybe they were starving to death. Quickly Lola put out a saucer of water as I ransacked *Johanne*'s stores for suitable food. "I've got it! The rice!" And we laughed at the neatness of the solution. The rice bought in Suez was already heaving with a groundswell of weevils and their maggots. For us those maggots were unwanted protein but we reckoned, for a peckish swallow, they might be just the thing. Tipping the grain out in handfuls, we poked through it for the tastiest, fattest grubs we could find. These we placed temptingly before our latest guest. Poor wee chappie. He politely ate seven of the proffered tidbits, then keeled over and died. Maybe from a surfeit of worms.

Not that all *Johanne*'s guests died. Along with worn-out swallows other, more robust, land birds called by to visit us—zebra-striped hoopoes and ospreys, green parrots, and dainty desert wheatears. What they were doing living in such an inhospitable place with desert on either side I could not imagine. Unbelievably tame, one bird landed straight on Edward's arm and twice I was awakened from a doze by a desert wheatear walking nonchalantly over my back.

Whatever its effects on local birds, the Red Sea is notoriously confusing to navigators. A combination of heat haze and dust-filled air has been blamed for sight errors of up to ninety miles, though I cannot in fact remember any of our own sights being more than a few miles off. Nonetheless Edward was taking no chances. By going only slightly off our course, we could pick up a series of lighthouses en route and so gain a positive check on our position. A fine idea provided you can find the lighthouses. One night we couldn't. It was like hunting for an industrial diamond at the far end of a cow's fourth stomach. For hours we raked that inky-black horizon. Anything could have accounted for its nonappearance: it could have been lost in poor visibility, we could have been out in our sight, or the light itself might be out of order. As it stood at the head of a chain of reefs its whereabouts were of considerable interest, a point sharply underlined when dawn revealed breakers to the southwest.

"All hands on deck! We've got to jibe!"

The wind had lost none of its ardor and the seas none of their lift but, urged on by those breakers, *Johanne*'s crew fell to with a will. Swiftly casting off the mizzen foreguy we hauled in the sheet as far as we could before turning our puny attentions to the main. What puffs and grunts we made! What shouts of "Come on!" and "Heave ho!" and *"Allons-y!"* as we inched in the mainsheet and made it fast. An instant later Edward snatched advantage from between two following seas and eased over on the helm. Even before the vibrations of the jibe had ceased, we had the sails let out and drawing on the starboard side. *Johanne* turned her back on the breakers. But where the heck was that lighthouse?

In the end it was Lola who spotted it. *"Le voilà!"* she shouted, her face alight as she pointed into the haze off the starboard bow. Edward and I peered through binoculars, and still saw nothing. But Lola was right. As we drew closer, a lighthouse did emerge from the cloak of desert dust. With one ticked off we could head confidently south and east for 250 miles in search of the next beacon, this time on the Arabian shore.

If anything, the strong northwesterly was increasing, whipping up waves behind us till, compressed in the narrow confines of the Red Sea, many stood well over ten feet high and with scarcely a breath between their foaming peaks. Edward, surveying that saw-toothed water, commented dryly, "Remind me never to sail north in the Red Sea." Even steering south down those rollers called for considerable concentration. Added to that, every ten minutes or so one had to glance back to make sure no tanker was poised to pounce on *Johanne* from astern. I soon learned to do my glancing when the old lady was riding on the crest of a wave. Looking back when she sank, stern down, in a trough not only failed to show any tankers, it also scared the pants off me.

Anyone who has done a bit of sailing will tell you airily that ten- or twelve-foot waves are nothing. And in a way they are right. It's all a matter of familiarity. Once you have steered before twelve-footers for a while and the end of the world has not come and the blue-green gurgling swirl of water has not swallowed you up forever, you naturally become more confident. It then takes sixteen-foot waves to impress you. As to those twenty-footers, essential ingredients of all good sailor yarns, or worse still those monsters that reach above a large yacht's mast, I reckon one needs either one hell of a lot of experience or no imagination at all not to be frightened.

Although we towed a fishing line all the way down the Red Sea, we had few clients on our hook. One handsome, ten-pound barracuda went into the pot (once we'd convinced ourselves of the odds against its being poisonous). But most of the fish that found their way into our frying pan jumped aboard of their own volition. Flying fish are found throughout

the tropics. A flash of silvered belly, a glistening dark-blue back suspended between outstretched, vibrating "wings," and they're away,
skimming over the water for twenty valiant seconds before subsiding
back into the sea. Only at night, startled by some predator, do they
accidentally fly aboard. So each dawn we combed the decks for flying
fish as farmers search their fields for free-range eggs. Often we found
two or three, stretched out in the scuppers or lying lifeless among the
gas bottles. With any luck there would be enough for each one of us to
savor a few mouthfuls of their delightful, crumbly white flesh.

The Red Sea is not all nature in the raw. It also plays host to two
extremely busy shipping lanes. Among those ships, supertankers
roamed like drunken hippos, a red light permanently flashing from the
bridge: "I am out of control. Keep away." It takes them so long to alter
course, let alone stop, that it is safer for everyone else to steer well clear.

Three more days of hectic flight and then, for the first time since
leaving Suez, the wind quit. And the most extraordinary thing happened. The steep, following seas simply vanished. In minutes *Johanne*
was floating on a duck pond, no rolling or crashing about, no jerking
and wrenching, nothing but peace, perfect peace. But if *Johanne* was
floating on a duck pond then we were the ducks, slowly grilling under a
tropical sun (we'd crossed the Tropic of Cancer the day before). Like
ducks, what we craved was a swim and a wash. So, lowering the headsails, we backed the mizzen and, with *Johanne* thus hove-to, we flopped
over the side. A quick inspection and it was clear that *Johanne,* too,
could do with a scrub. White goose barnacles were sprouting like an old
tramp's stubble along her waterline. Wielding wooden wedges as if they
were paint strippers, we launched our attack. In seconds we were surrounded by a shoal of tiny fish, each darting at the falling debris in an
excited orgy of nibbling.

That shoal of small fry were contented with their diet. Jean Louis
and Lola were not. Regardless of those assurances back in Greece that
they ate almost anything, and in spite of helping me to spend $600 on
canned food, they announced that they did not, in fact, eat canned
food—or dried food, or sugar, or butter, or meat, or any of the other
fashionable "poisons of the month." That established, they happily did
eat what remained of *Johanne*'s fresh fruits and vegetables before concentrating their attention on feta cheese and cereals. Toward the end of
the voyage they existed almost entirely on spaghetti cooked in milk and
garlic.

Edward, haunted constantly by the fear of changing winds, dared
not wait for our own fair breeze to return. After a few hours of peace he
started the motor. Talk about sauce for the gander. That ghastly whine

acted like a siren's song to dolphins. All around the horizon they
erupted, cutting toward us through a sea that, a moment before, had
been as flat and lifeless as polished steel. Crowding forward, we watched
as the biggest dolphins played in *Johanne*'s bow wave. Farther off, the
smaller ones bounded about like seaborn puppies. They leapt and dived
and belly-flopped. They flipped their tails and clapped the sea and, I'm
quite sure, they laughed.

That night, far away on the horizon, I spotted a ship steaming
north. I knew her direction from the heights of her two white masthead
lights: the one at the back shone well above the one near the bow, which
reminded me—I lashed the wheel and went forward to check our own
navigation lights. Already, after only six months, we had reduced our
ten-year supply of bulbs to two solitary spare lights. Forced to ration
them, we switched them on only when other ships could be seen in the
vicinity. Each night I checked to make sure no more had blown.

By dawn on September 19th *Johanne* had reached the Hanish Islands near the exit to the Red Sea. My diary records: "These islands are
supposed to be dangerous. Don't know why. Communists or pirates?"
The chart showed two shipping lanes, one running either side of the
islands. The main bulk of supertankers and container ships were heading down the eastern side so Edward chose to play it safe and take the
less-frequented western, or Ethiopian, side, a course that would carry
us some twenty miles from their shores.

At 1:30 A.M. on September 20th, I was alone on watch when, somewhere toward the land, I heard the hum of a marine engine. I stared,
straining, into the blackness. Where were the lights? There were no
lights. There must be lights! The hum came closer and closer. Pinpricks
of fear buzzed my neck. I called below to Edward and then dashed
forward to wake Jean Louis and Lola and to check, once again, that our
own lights were glowing. Grasping the shrouds, I climbed onto the
bulwark capping and peered into the starboard lightboard. It wasn't
possible! Yet another bulb had blown. Now we had only one spare bulb
to last until Seychelles. With no time to dally, Jean Louis changed the
bulb. I retrieved the helm and Edward went below to load his new
shotgun. Pirates or Communists, either way it might come in handy.

As soon as Edward got back to the helm I ducked below to fortify
the rest of *Johanne*'s fearsome crew. Jean Louis took the old and rusty
rifle. Lola chose the air pistol; it looked menacing enough even though
salt water had seized it. That left me with the replica Colt revolver
clutched in my clammy little hand—you remember, the gun that operated on percussion caps and a spoonful of black powder. *Johanne*'s
crew was ready for action. Or almost. Once more I darted below, re-

turning with one further weapon held in my other hand, my ultimate deterrent. Convinced that we were dealing with pirates, not navies (what self-respecting navy would steam around in international waters without its lights on?), I had brought up from the galley my kitchen timer. Once triggered, that thing gave off a shriek guaranteed to scare the wits out of any band of Ethiopian pirates. And, in a tight corner, I'd back wits over firearms any day.

Guns at the ready, Jean Louis, Lola, and I crept forward to crouch behind the dinghy and the bulwarks. We knew exactly what to do. We'd seen it all at the movies. At *Johanne*'s helm, Edward stood upright and exposed. Four pairs of frightened eyes blindly swept the darkness. Four pairs of ears throbbed in an effort to comb the void for clues. I tried to swallow and failed. So this was what it was like, being hunted.

WHAM! A fiery tail of rocket arched high above *Johanne* and exploded, and the next moment they were on us, a great bow rising out of the night. And on that bow, in huge letters, was its number—P204. We were being attacked by an Ethiopian gunboat. Feeling a trifle foolish, I slid my ultimate deterrent beneath the dinghy—under the circumstances, it appeared to be somewhat inadequate. As for our pathetic firearms, they were worse than inadequate. Seen through the eyes of the Communists of Ethiopia, those weapons could prove a quick passport to heaven, as in "Shot while smuggling arms to Eritrean bandits."

Beneath the roar of the gunboat's powerful engines no one heard the G.M. spring to life. Surreptitiously Edward turned *Johanne* so that her stern davits pointed straight at the gunboat's hull, because Edward, wearing his "naval architect" hat, knew that hull well. Built during World War II, of double-diagonal wood planking, P204 was a 110-foot British Fairmile B. If her old wooden hull came into contact with *Johanne Regina*'s stern davits, there was a good chance the davits would win. And double-diagonal planking is notoriously expensive to repair. Unfortunately the captain, edging dangerously close, showed a reckless disregard for such costs. Turning angrily in their searchlight, Edward waved them off.

"What do you want? *Que voulez-vous?*" we shouted. A voice, clenched tight with hatred, came back at us through the darkness. "Shut up!" it screeched. We did. There followed what could best be described as a duel of captains. Try as he would, the Ethiopian could not get his ship alongside *Johanne*. Giving up to windward, he shifted downwind off our port quarter and someone shouted through a loud hailer:

"Who are you?"

"English yacht *Johanne Regina*."

"Where you from?"

"England."

"Where you going?"

"Seychelles."

Then came a phrase we could not understand but I felt it included "other ports."

"No other ports. Suez. Seychelles." This was not what they wanted at all, and the Ethiopian's next words left little scope for misunderstanding.

"We order you to Assab Port!" Nothing could have been clearer than that. But Edward fenced on.

"No other ports!" he repeated in his best, irritated-Englishman voice. "We go Suez, Seychelles." And so the game continued—"I'm sorry. We didn't hear." "I'm sorry, could you please repeat." "English yacht! English!"—until they were as sick of it as we were.

Finally they shouted, "Can we come alongside your ship?" We knew then that we had almost won.

"No!" replied my valiant husband.

"Why not?"

"Because you will damage my boat." The truth of this unkind thrust pierced them to the core. The enemy was routed. A mighty revving of naval engines and churning of international waters followed (we were way outside their legal jurisdiction). One last long scrutiny under searchlight, one final insult spat across the waters that divided us, and then they yelled at us to go.

Five minutes later Edward cut the engine and we listened. Nothing. They had vanished into the night.

20. Jail

At last there comes a paleness in the east that, rising, slowly washes out the stars. Ships' lights fade. Now it is their hulls and not their lights you see. Far to the east the sky flushes red, straining with the effort of new birth. Then, above a bank of morning fog, a crescent peeps. At first deep crimson, the crescent grows; and growing, pales. Molten steel. Orange. Yellow. The sun has risen and the heavens brighten to the blue of day.

Johanne spent most of that day becalmed. The next day she twisted and tacked, back and forth, back and forth, between Perim Island (part of the People's Democratic Republic of Yemen, or South Yemen for short) and the stream of shipping bottlenecked at the entrance to the Gulf of Aden. After thirteen fabulous days of southward flight our goal, the Gulf, was in view, yet now a steady headwind held us back. Was this the change? Were we too late? Or was it merely a warning of the change to come?

"This is hopeless!" called Edward. "Lower the headsails and tighten in the main. We'll motor out of the shipping and into the Gulf before it gets dark."

As night fell we plowed past the uninhabited island of Perim. "Look at that for an anchorage!" Edward pointed to the chart. There, right in the heart of Perim, lay a grand, landlocked harbor. "How about popping in for a quick shower and a steak in the yacht club?" We laughed. We knew there was no shower, no yacht club, and no steak. It was one of Edward's jokes. Perim, tomb-black against the night, was obviously uninhabited.

Once safely into the Gulf, Edward stopped the engine and set a course some four miles off the South Yemen coast. A British compromise, it put us safely clear of the main shipping yet comfortably within the Gulf's special international waters.

I was below, cooking supper, when Jean Louis called.

"Edward! I hear a motor coming from the shore. No lights." This was getting tedious. I turned off the stove and tumbled on deck to join the others as they squinted into the sooty blackness. Hidden by the night, someone was powering toward us at high speed.

Edward took the helm and switched on the precious stern light. "Check the navigation lights are working forward." Out of the darkness searchlights strafed our decks. Through binoculars I spotted a black bow and, poised above that bow, a gun emplacement.

"Edward! It's another ruddy gunboat!" Even the script was the same.

"Where you go?" Their wash foamed in the blackness a few feet from our own.

"Seychelles." They too had never heard of them. "Islands! Indian Ocean!"

"Where come from?"

"Suez." Our attackers seized a megaphone. A retrograde step as it mangled all they said beyond reprieve. Two and a half hours of incomprehensible shouting later, they discarded the fiendish machine and ordered us to follow them to Perim. Perim? That deserted island we had passed a few hours back? Why take us there? Edward inched closer to the shipping.

Abruptly, all parallels with Ethiopia ceased. The Yemeni captain knew his powerful gunboat inside out. Though *Johanne* crept forward she was quite unable to escape. Outmaneuvered, I ducked below. Maybe the old, double-sideband radio had enough life in it to summon help.

"Mayday! Mayday! This is British yacht *Johanne Regina.* Calling all shipping. Calling all shipping. We are a few miles east of Perim Island in the Gulf of Aden. We are being attacked. Repeat, we are being—" Two loud reports echoed through the cabin followed by a *thwack* as something hit the hull. "Mayday! Mayday! We are being fired on! Repeat. We are being fired on. Please help! Over."

Static chased silence in the darkness. There was no one out there listening. Climbing slowly back on deck, I gazed at the changing patterns of the large ships' lights: red, green, white. Lights heading east, lights heading west on ships blithely ignorant of our fate. Edward might have a brand-new five-shooter, but the gunboat had a 20-millimeter Oerlikon mounted on her deck. Protesting bitterly, he turned *Johanne* around and pointed back toward Perim.

As we closed the blackened shore thoughts, like Gaderine swine, ran madly around my brain. Why were none of the crew in uniform? Thank God Katy wasn't with us! Maybe these were the same marauders that stripped the single-hander and his yacht. Why take us to an uninhabited island? Was it to loot and sink *Johanne,* rape and kill her crew?

"Edward?" I felt suddenly shy of my own husband. "If they try to rape me—promise you'll do nothing. I couldn't bear to see them beat you up." Edward steered on, silent in the gunboat's wake. How he must have longed to dash for freedom. But what chance had we? They could do 30 knots and we no more than 7. They had some twenty-five armed men aboard and we were four. God damn it! How dare they seize a yacht at gunpoint? Pirates, that's what they were, barefaced pirates. The thought triggered off such a storm of rage that it stifled every ounce of fear. I'd make them sorry before they were finished. Once alongside, they'd demand to see below. Right!

"Come on, Jean Louis. Let's make 'em boil!" Together we dragged the cargo hatch over the exit to the saloon. With the G.M. pounding away at full throttle the saloon would quickly turn into a sauna. They wouldn't stay long.

A couple of hurricane lamps glowed yellow on the foreshore, bringing with them a quite irrational relief. Maybe the island was inhabited after all. Maybe the gunmen weren't pirates returning to their den. They might even have a commanding officer. He wouldn't let them loose to rape and murder. No. As we'd already been accused of spying, he'd probably call out the firing squad instead.

Three bodies deep, dark-shadowed ruffians lined the gunboat's rail. Once the two boats touched, those men would swarm aboard to snatch up anything that caught their eye. We touched. I braced myself. And no one moved. The men's civilian clothes might be bedraggled, but their discipline was excellent.

For the first time the captain left the bridge. A slender Arab in his thirties, he ordered Edward aboard his gunboat.

"Never! This is my ship and I stay with her. How dare you force us in here!" Edward, too, was in a seething rage. "It's against all international law, do you hear! We were in international waters. I'll charge you all with hijacking and see you all in jail."

Regardless of my newfound anger, I had a sneaking feeling that, in his place, I would have been a marvel of obsequious reconciliation. Not Edward. He stood his ground and earned far more respect. Not only that, but his anger brought the whole proceeding to a halt. Things were no longer going according to the rules. Oh yes, there were rules. We learned later that hijacking was an integral part of the naval training program for the People's Democratic Republic of Yemen. The only difference was that they usually used innocent North Yemen dhows for their practice. Not less than one night a month their gunboat went out on an "exercise," the object of which was to attack and capture some small coastal craft. They then held crew and craft captive until the game palled, after which they let the dhow go free and they themselves went out in search of further prey. That night, unknown to us, we were the further prey.

Into the lull created by Edward's fury there came a towering figure dressed in a red kaffiyeh (turban) and a brightly tassled futah or sarong. Beaming at us, the giant announced that he was the island's chief. His interpreter went further, proudly explaining that, because the man spoke Spanish, he was known as "Español." It was thus we learned that the "uninhabited" island of Perim was far from uninhabited. Not only did it have a chief, but a school as well, to say nothing of a large Soviet naval base. Edward's jokes about steaks might have been pushing it, but Russian caviar was almost certainly available on Perim—for the upper classes only, of course. Abruptly, all friendly contact ceased and the men at the rail made way for a thin-lipped man from the shore dressed in a red shirt and Soviet-style trousers.

The man eyed us with cold hostility. Through the interpreter he ordered us to be interrogated.

"Do come below," purred Edward, baring his teeth in a welcoming grimace. We lifted the hatch. Hot, dieselly air shot out into the night. Squashing our interrogators close together on the main settee, we watched with mounting pleasure as beads of sweat hatched out up on their foreheads and dribbled like spittle down their jaws. First they interrogated us separately. Nationality, age, and name, all were carefully recorded and the statements signed. Lola caused a terrible ruckus because she hadn't enough names. Arabs have three names: their own and then, depending on their gender, their mother's and grandmother's or father's and grandfather's. Lola had only two. What fiendish plot was this? In the end the impasse was broken when Lola dreamed up a third name off the top of her head. The fact that this new name was not on her passport did not bother them at all. In their experience, passports were only for highly privileged citizens, those few who were allowed to leave the Worker's Paradise. Our interrogators knew nothing of passports. What they wanted to see were our birth certificates. We could not produce a single one. Even more suspicious! What proof had they that we had been born at all?

"And why did you not stop?"

"We did."

"Why did you spend all day off our coast?"

"We were tacking. There was a headwind."

"You were spying! Spying! We saw you! You sailed into every bay."

"We were tacking."

"Why did you only turn your stern light on as we approached?"

"To save light bulbs."

"Why did you try to escape?"

"We didn't."

"Why are you going to the Seychelles?"

"It is our home."

Red Shirt turned on Edward: "Did our gunboat fire at you?"

I glanced at the little captain. Rigid with apprehension, he rolled his
eyes with relief when Edward replied, "I did hear a couple of bangs but
they were not important."

Before Edward had finished Red Shirt whipped around on me, his
eyes narrowed to slits of cunning. "Why did you stop your ship if you
were doing nothing wrong?"

Whether it was the heat, or the strain of the past two days, or the
idiot's petty aggression I do not know, but something snapped. I lost my
temper.

"What the bloody hell would you do if a boat with no lights came at
you in the dark and a pack of lunatics started firing at you from a rolling
ship? We stopped because we were frightened we'd be killed!"

The interpreter's eyes twinkled. He had been on the gunboat and he
knew as well as I did that they had fired on us. I don't know what he
said to Red Shirt. To us he said, "Okay, okay, don't worry! You go to
sleep now. Take your rest. Don't worry. In the morning you can go."
With that they bolted for the hatch and the cool night air. Red Shirt left
last and, as he passed, he grabbed my hand. Staring into my eyes with
open hatred, he deliberately crushed my fingers in a vicious grip. Much
more of that behavior and the hatred would be mutual.

Fearful still of thieves, we slept on deck. Close by, the gunboat's
crew were also bedding down. Several said a final prayer to Allah before
they curled up on the gunship's hard steel deck with nothing but a thin
mat under them and a thin futah to protect their bodies from the desert
cold.

Shortly after 1 A.M., fingers dug deep into my shoulder and a hand
shook me awake. For a moment I thought I was still stuck in my
nightmare, Red Shirt's evil face pushed close to mine. But then, from
beside him, the interpreter called, "Come! You must go with us. Higher
Authority want to interrogate you. Up now!" It was the first of many
times that we heard Higher Authority mentioned in that way, pronounced with capital letters and the same awe that others offer to the
name of God. In so-called Communist countries, where the leaders had
proclaimed a "Government of the Proletariat" and then usurped that
government to themselves, Higher Authority took on both the power
and the awesomeness of a medieval God. Because each new bunch of
Higher Authorities invented their own interpretation of The Word, no

ordinary mortal, studying *Das Kapital,* could discover why this was banned and this permitted or what he should do about it. For him the "Will of the People" was as mysterious and incomprehensible as that of God. His solution was to do nothing unusual, take no initiative, make no decision without first checking with Higher Authority—passing the buck. And who could blame him. History, his bones, and the bones of his ancestors had taught him to keep his head tucked well below the parapet.

When the South Yemenis captured us, old-style communism reigned paramount behind the Iron Curtain. Edward's remonstrances were brushed aside. We had to move from *Johanne*—at once. Higher Authority had spoken. There was nothing more to say.

Hastily putting together a few essentials—contact lenses, tampons, pain-killers, diary, and pen—I stuffed the lot into a small string evening bag. Edward pocketed a flashlight and, walking in single file, we followed armed men to a waiting Land Rover. Along the shore the village stood dark and deserted. There were no street lamps or streets. Cairns of stones marked the place where the flinty track led out of town.

We drove, bumping through the darkness, in total silence, the air between us turning musty with our fear. What did they want with us at one in the morning? Where could they be taking us on this island shrouded like the dead? Outside, the moon showed a landscape barren and flat except for one small hill. The Land Rover braked, and the driver backed up to the base of that small hill and stopped. There was not a soul in sight.

The men with the guns got out. So, this was it. Here, against this flint-dry hill. No trial. No grave. Each one of us knew a sickening surge of fear. Our families would think us lost at sea. Katy . . .

A moment later the driver and his followers climbed back into the car and we drove off in a different direction. They had lost their way in the dark.

After that, things could only look up. The full moon was almost at its zenith when the driver stopped again, this time beside a half-built bungalow. All around it men lay swaddled in sarongs like corpses. Tiptoeing past, we entered the house. A kerosene lamp burned on a low table. Beside it sat our interpreter, Aziz, inviting us, as always, to take our rest.

"You like some coffee? You must not worry. Soon Higher Authority come. Then you can leave. Must not worry." My fondness for Aziz grew by the minute. Five foam mattresses plus pillows and blankets had been laid out on the floor.

"You want sleep? Go sleep. I wake you when Higher Authority

come." Four of the mattresses had been placed so as to make a single, continuous bed. Without thinking, Lola and I chose the outside berths. Aziz blew out the lamp and, totally exhausted, I fell fast asleep. I woke to a smothered curse from Lola. A man was fumbling with her trousers. It took me several seconds to remember the torch. Edward turned it on in time to catch a stranger ramming his open palm into Jean Louis's protesting face. One flash of the light and Lola's lecher fled. No longer able to sleep, I lay alert and watchful as, half an hour later, another shadow, crouching low under the moonlit window, advanced into the room. The next think I knew, a hand was groping up my leg. Damn this for a lark! Silently drawing back my foot, I took careful aim and kicked out with all my might. That was the last time either of us had trouble from the men of Perim.

It seemed but minutes later that they were at it again, shaking us awake. Apparently Higher Authority had sent orders for us to be moved elsewhere, before dawn. No matter about Higher Authority, I had an urgent need to go elsewhere right away. I asked Aziz for a lavatory. He pointed to the back of a ruined house a hundred yards down the road and told me, yet again, to take my rest, I did and felt enormously relieved. It's amazing what an empty bladder can do for one's morale. I was suddenly on top of the world, ready to face anything this improbable bunch of disorganized humanity could spring on us. Though "spring" was far too active a word for Perim. Dawn broke and the sun rose and we were still waiting for transport. If we really had been spies we were getting a far better look at their secret base than if they'd left us to sail on to the Seychelles unmolested.

Urged once more into the back of a Land Rover, they took us on a coccyx-crunching journey down unpaved tracks toward the harbor. On either side, rough stone houses tottered on the brink of collapse. This part of Perim had been a British military base when Aden was a British colony (in 1967 Aden became part of the People's Democratic Republic of Yemen). Now not a roof remained. Eventually the Land Rover pulled up outside a two-room cement bunkhouse, a building that was to be our prison until we left.

It could have been worse. None of the windows had panes but two had shutters. The roof was without tiles but the main door was still there, hanging drunk and deformed from a single hinge. Apart from some scraps of plywood on the roof, the only concession to habitation was the same set of five outsize mattresses now stacked against one wall. This time there were no pillows; we were going down in the world. A second, equally naked room led off the first, and out through the far archway was a walled but roofless area where the kitchen had once stood. Here too was the latrine. Above a smooth, sloping concrete gutter, an arched concrete tunnel had been built with a circular hole cut in its top. Over the hole sat a black plastic lavatory seat. After use, water was supposed to be sluiced through the tunnel, down the gutter, and into a hole outside. But there was no running water and the outside gutter had filled with sand long ago. After one day of use the stench was all-pervasive.

To the end Edward and I disagreed about how best to fight our jailers. He accepted nothing, fought every move, was uncooperative to the last. For my part, once I was certain we would not be shot at dawn, I couldn't decide whether to treat the whole bizarre interlude as grand adventure or high farce. But then I wasn't worrying about the wind. Edward stood, craning his neck out of a side window, eyes fixed on a distant patch of Gulf. Flat calm. We were missing the last, vital hours before the change. Right then we should have been racing for the Indian Ocean under power. (One more day of calms and captivity and poor Edward's frustration erupted in a fiery rash around his waist.)

After the initial inspection of our jail, we dragged a couple of mattresses to the floor and, sitting cross-legged upon them, faced the door and waited. Slowly the sun rose in the sky. Slowly we grew hungrier and hungrier and hotter and hotter. Sweat, trickling down my neck, stirred a memory. Fishing inside my evening bag I brought out a packet of Christian Dior face fresheners and passed them around. In a moment the ludicrous contrast between Christian Dior and our prison hut had us all laughing and set Jean Louis, with his gentle wit, to poking deeper in my bag. "Come on, Clare!" he chided. "What about breakfast? I know you've got it tucked in there somewhere."

Taking the hint, Aziz inquired what we would care to eat. We didn't think twice. We ordered eggs and bread—oh, and perhaps a little fresh fruit would be nice too. We came from a society where even the poorest can afford eggs and a little fruit. Aziz came from a society where hospitality required that he ransack the island in an attempt to satisfy his importunate guests' demands. Our punishment for such thoughtlessness was to have to wait until well into the afternoon before we broke our fast. We had been seventeen hours without food. But our Arab hosts had done their best. Admittedly there were only three minute eggs when we had asked for four. But then, as they explained, there were only three eggs in the village. The watermelon, too, had the air of a much prized and pampered fruit. Hunger barely touched, we were surprised and delighted to be offered stew to follow. The guards' only surprise was at our delight. They were condemned to eat that same canned, Bulgarian stew every single day that they remained on Perim.

Some were posted to the island for years at a time. Sitting on the mattresses we were served by a barefoot servant. On the floor between us, he placed one large platter of unleavened bread, or hobs, and another of stew.

Aziz led the way. No unhygienic knives and forks here. In accordance with Oriental custom, he used only his right hand to tear off a bit of the wafer-thin hobs. This he deftly wrapped around a gob of liquid stew before carrying the whole parcel neatly to his mouth. Our efforts were not nearly so neat but then we were only beginners. As we finished our meal the servant poured hot water over our fingers and hot green tea into our floral cups. Sipping delicately, Aziz lounged back upon his mattress and, as the heat of the afternoon pressed down upon our brains, he attempted to satisfy his curiosity.

Jean Louis and Lola worried him. During their interrogation, they had called themselves teachers. And yet they were not teaching. To Aziz this was criminal. How could they, after their expensive training, ignore the needs of their people and go sailing the world for pleasure? We tried to explain that, at that time in France, there were more trained teachers than jobs for them to fill. But that was going to far. No country could have unemployed teachers.

Next Aziz turned his attention to Jean Louis's person. "We Yemeni people, we do not like your face. Why you always look frightened?" This assault sent poor Jean Louis even further into retreat. I weighed in, in his defense. "I bet you'd look frightened too if we put you in jail."

"Yes, but you are not frightened. You always smiling."

"Ah, but I'm half mad!" and I laughed and tapped my temple. In fact, unknown to Aziz, something was getting me down. Out of respect for Muslim culture, Lola and I had covered ourselves from neck to ankles in long-sleeved shirts and trousers. With temperatures in the nineties, we boiled. But it was not the actual heat that got me down, or the confinement, or the guards, or even the latrine and the ghastly clouds of clinging flies. What I really could not stand was the stink of my own stale sweat. It got so that I could hardly bring myself to breathe. In desperation I begged for soap and water. Aziz warned us that Perim had no wells, that every drop of water came from a desalination plant. Troops were allowed to wash their clothes but once a week. Aha! We'd got them at last! We would use as much of their precious water as we possibly could. Maybe then Higher Authority would set us free.

When a pail of water did arrive we took turns to wash. I used one sleeve of my blouse as a washrag and the rest as a towel before I rinsed the whole thing out and put it back on, cool and wet. With our bodies vaguely cleansed, we set to work on the sheets. They were disgusting, stiff and gray with filth—and the filth wasn't even ours. Aziz almost wept to see us squander all that water on mere sheets.

While the rest of us played at petty sabotage, Edward concentrated all his energies on getting out. Talking in French—to foil Aziz's official job as snoop—we sifted through our jailers' weaknesses and came to a conclusion. What we needed was our own Higher Authority. One so high that he would frighten their Higher Authority into setting us free. This task of intimidation from on high fell upon my genial father. Unbeknownst to him, he was endowed with a wholly imaginary occupation. Turning to Aziz, Edward demanded that he send for the chief. Half an hour later a smiling Español arrived, and we rounded on him.

"We demand to see our ambassadors immediately!"

"We've had enough, you hear! You must set us free or we will report you to the United Nations!"

"My father works for the United Nations. He'll see your country punished for this!"

Put on the spot, Español wriggled through a whole series of placating lies ending up with the declaration that bad weather was the trouble. It had prevented Higher Authority's message from reaching us. We would have to wait. We refused. We made a colossal fuss and Español left. According to Aziz, he had gone to get the chief—the *real* chief, you understand. Apparently Español was not the chief at all! By then I was ready to throttle Aziz with my bare hands.

About an hour later the chief Chief arrived. With his black mustache and thin, pinched face he looked like many other Yemenis. A serious man, Aziz said he was headmaster of Perim's school. The new chief informed us that a message had just been sent off—by boat. This strategically important Soviet base appeared to suffer from a serious communications problem. From the Chief's courteous demeanor, it was clear that he had been warned of my father's position. (By the time we'd finished, I think they feared he was the U.N. Secretary General himself.) Taking advantage of such fear, Edward demanded to go back on board *Johanne.* If she was not pumped out she would sink and they would be to blame. Permission was granted on three conditions: we could go only between eight and eleven at night, we must always move in pairs, and we must converse only in English. It was good to know that our speaking together in French annoyed them. It was meant to. Emotionally exhausted, yet feeling that some progress had been made, we subsided back into the torpor, flies, and smells of our unsavory jail.

Along with much else, our jail lacked electricity, so as soon as darkness fell the guards carried our bedding out onto the sand. It was a fabulous night. Ruined houses cast black shadows on the moon-white sand. From our feet the desert sloped away to where the still, inky waters of the straits lapped softly at the shore. Three miles beyond, ships plowed faint furrows east and west. We tracked those ships with longing, exiled eyes. To them we were invisible beings, nonexistent. Did we then no longer exist? A light breeze ruffled the grains of sand and I shivered in the desert night.

Promptly at eight we were driven down to *Johanne* to find the gunboat captain in a pitiful state. The lines holding one of *Johanne*'s old fenders had chafed through and the fender had disappeared. The captain implored Edward not to accuse him of its theft.

"Of course I won't," said Edward to Aziz, "but why is he so worried? What is the punishment for theft?"

"On the mainland they chop your hand off—so! But here . . ." Aziz drew a dramatic finger right across his throat.

We pumped *Johanne* dry. Then, just as we were gathering up fruit and towels and cooler clothes, Red Shirt appeared. Higher Authority had spoken. They must search *Johanne*—at once. A search was the one thing I still feared. One glimpse of Edward's flintlocks and, with their obsession with spies, we'd be done for. As to the semi-automatic shotgun—Mama mia!

The search began in the saloon. There, to one side, were three or four charts—detailed maps of enemy coastlines no less. They would start with those. Or, to be accurate, Aziz would. He had first to copy down the title of each chart in English and then laboriously transcribe it into Arabic. I had to bury my nose in a book to hide my grin. Patience. That's all that was required. Then, when those few charts were listed I'd fling back the settee cushions—and offer them a further 200 to record. To my great disappointment their patience ran out before even the first charts were tabulated. After that they browsed through our possessions like goats nosing through a garbage bin in search of tidbits. What they eventually found were photo albums dotted with pictures of naked female flesh: elbows, knees, even the odd erotic shoulder flaunted for all to see. With those albums to hand, further search in the saloon was deemed unnecessary.

Meanwhile, in the aft cabin, Mustafa, our second English-speaking guard, was being particularly trying, though only because he was so spectacularly dim. Convinced we were spies, he imagined that every cornice and doorknob held a hidden camera. There was no doubt about it, fate had been exceedingly kind. Imagine if John and Lana had been on board and Mustafa or Red Shirt had found their store of underwater film equipment. No lawyer on earth could have persuaded them then

that we were not saboteurs. And still Mustafa did not find Edward's
gun case. Twice he kicked it with his clumsy army boots but he never
once looked down.

Back in the saloon, fed up with them pawing my photos and still
eager to prove our innocence, I dragged out books that mentioned Edward's name and found an article he had written for the American
Magazine *Boating.* The captain was so tickled with that article that he
asked if he could keep the magazine. So it was on a friendly note that
the search ended and we were driven back to our bed beneath the stars.

The next day Aziz became quite agitated about Edward. "I see Mr.
Allcard is very tired. He is old. I am worried about him. You must
speak to the Chief. You must get angry. Then maybe you can leave."
After some discussion we agreed. Aziz looked most relieved. He must
have been as fed up with sweltering in that smelly hole as we were.

Jean Louis had spent some time among the Arabs. He knew that
hospitality played a central role in their culture. Speaking in French, he
suggested that next time a plate of Bulgarian stew arrived we pick it up
and fling it out the door. A dramatic rejection of their hospitality, it
would emphasize our anger at being held in prison. I suspect it was also
intended to serve a more private purpose. After months as a vegetarian,
that stew was playing havoc with Jean Louis's guts.

Sadly this rebellion was foiled too. Red Shirt arrived before the
stew. For a moment we were totally confused. What was Red Shirt
doing here? We had sent for the Chief, the headmaster with the check
shirt and small black mustache. Slowly the penny dropped. Red Shirt,
too, had a small black mustache. He, too, had a thin, pinched face. Red
Shirt, the man who first interrogated us on board *Johanne,* was also the
headmaster. Red Shirt was the Chief. So Red Shirt, that sly, vicious,
sharp-faced rat, was the sole cause of all our troubles. We attacked him
on all four fronts. Even Jean Louis threw insults at him and stood firm
when Red Shirt tried to push him to the floor. A great orgy of fury
followed.

"You've no right to keep us here!"

"You're just a pack of cowards, attacking unarmed boats in the
dead of night."

"Yemen wants to belong to the United Nations, huh? My father will
see that you and your government are thrown out of the U.N. for this.
The U.N. is for civilized countries, not governments that behave like
pirates!"

"All you can do is lie! You drank in lies with your mother's milk.
Even now you haven't contacted our ambassadors, have you? Have you!
If you don't release us very soon you'll be in big trouble."

By then Red Shirt had also had enough. Shaking with anger and fear and loss of face, he yelled back, "Any more trouble from you and I lock you all in solitary confinement!" Then he stormed out.

Aziz was almost as white and shaking as we were. But his shaking was from sheer terror. "What you doing! You must never get angry with Chief like that!"

"My God, Aziz, it was you who told us to!"

When lunch eventually arrived (we ate only twice each day), it turned out to be fish and rice, not tasteless stew. Funny how, on seeing that fresh fried fish, we realized all at once that we had made enough demonstrations for one day. One shouldn't overdo these things. After which we tucked in with gusto and, by the time Aziz had offered round some spicy sauce from his side of the plate, peace between us had been restored.

They say every cloud has a silver lining; if so, then for me Aziz was the lining to that dreary stay on Perim. During the British occupation of Aden, he had been educated by English monks—"At school we must worship this stone lady called Mary. Now I pray to God." Claims of "O"-level passes in math, science, and Arabic notwithstanding, Aziz knew very little beyond his own immediate experience of life. But he told us how those pupils who got 90–100 percent in their final school exams were allowed to go to Cairo to train as doctors. Lower exam results entitled one to become an engineer, and lower still a teacher. Once you were trained, Higher Authority told you where to work.

"And how does one become Higher Authority?" we asked.

Aziz looked confused. "This I do not know. I think you have to work very, very hard. Our president, he is from the small people. He fought in the hills against the British." At times Aziz talked of grand voyages he would make, to Cairo and Djibouti. At other times he begged to sail with us. Otherwise, he said, he would never, ever escape from his country. When we stormed against our illegal imprisonment, Aziz would nod and whisper, "I know. For us it is the same. We too cannot leave." Sixty miles away, on the mainland, our jailer had a wife and young son but he feared it might be another two years before he was allowed home to visit them. Higher Authority wouldn't even let him go to Aden to get the cracked lens of his glasses fixed. But Aziz was not always downcast. I remember one time when some of his soldier friends dropped by to visit us. They were full of scorn for their Soviet masters. "Do you know," said one, giggling, "they say we have to call each other 'Brother'!" and they all fell about laughing. Communism would never be more than a withered graft on the virile culture of the Yemeni people.

Aziz watched Lola and me with something of the same hypnotic fascination others reserve for horror movies or snakes. Liberated females, we were what communism promised to bring to Yemen and Aziz was quite clearly shocked. In his culture it brought shame on a woman even to sit in the same room with a man. Outside Aden marriages were still arranged by the parents. "The girl is brought to the boy's house for him to see if there is good 'contact.' If she is nice and her skin isn't too black or too white, if her color is just right, see, like mine"—and he held out his arm—"then they get married." He told us with pride that his own young wife never went outside his parents' house and that a boy was employed to do the shopping. I hoped, rather forlornly, that this was yet another of Aziz's flights of fancy.

It had taken us a while to realize that truth, as an invariable and nonnegotiable concept, was unknown to our Yemeni friends. Truth to them was like light: depending on the needs of the moment, truth could be split to reflect events in many different colors. Later we discussed bride prices. Lola, it turned out, was a most valuable commodity. At least ten camels, Aziz reckoned, and, at £50 to £100 per camel, well—! I, being so much older (in his eyes), was worth a lot less but, on the other hand, he added kindly, as such I could go to Mecca, provided I became a Muslim first.

Worried about Edward's health and that nasty rash around his waist, I offered him a bowl of prunes transported specially from the boat. "Where's the spoon?" Edward demanded fretfully. "Oh, won't fingers do?" I had completely forgotten about spoons. Around midmorning Español joined us, followed by his entourage. He might not be the island's political chief but he was undoubtedly the popular leader of his people. He came to tell us that instructions from Higher Authority would arrive by ship that very afternoon. Later we must move *Johanne* so the ship could dock. Message delivered, our visitors settled themselves cross-legged on the mattresses and began to question us. Clearly they had been sent to find out what tale we planned to tell the outside world. As my father's position, growing more exalted by the day, was the main cause of their anxiety, most of their questions were addressed to me.

"What do you think of our political chief?" Red Shirt was absent and the question was delivered with a slightly embarrassed smile.

"Ah. Well now. That all depends on his shirt. When he wears a red shirt he is pompous and unpleasant." And I pulled a long face and stuck out my chest. They chuckled. "When he wears his check shirt and is headmaster, then he's okay." Español, himself the owner of an exceptionally tolerant heart, cut in upon their laughter. He explained that

Red Shirt did not mean to be harsh. It was his nature. Really he was a very good man.

One of the younger soldiers then chirped up. "And what do you think of Español?"

"Oh, we all *love* him!" And I grinned mischievously at them. The young men slapped their leader on the back and beamed, happy to find their own opinion endorsed. Español smiled sheepishly and stayed silent.

Eventually our guests took their leave and lunch arrived. No doubt about it, things were looking up. There, on the floor, was a positive banquet: not only fresh-caught fish crisply fried and laid on a bed of spicy rice but, for the first time, spoons appeared. There was even a dash of milk in the tea. Surely they must have heard we were to be set free.

The meal over, we were driven in broad daylight down to the dock to move *Johanne*. With no attempt to hide anything, they walked us straight through the gunboat's bridge. Edward, gazing around, noticed a chess set. "Do you play chess?" he asked, and the captain nodded. "We must have a game," Edward said, and the captain smiled. Slipping *Johanne*'s mooring lines, we motored off alone and unguarded to anchor *Johanne* in the middle of the bay. All that previous creeping about at dead of night had been completely pointless. Back ashore, our jail overflowed with visitors when, in mid-afternoon, a large Soviet warship docked, crammed full of troops. They brought with them permission from Higher Authority. We could leave that night at the witching hour of eight.

Our last supper began in a festive mood. Everyone we had met over the past few days was there. The captain brought his chess set and he and Edward played two games of chess. The rest of us, using Aziz and Mustafa as interpreters, chatted and relaxed. Only when Red Shirt arrived and sat himself deliberately beside me did we realize the full importance of the meal. This was to be the buttering-up session before we told the world, and the U.N., of our experiences. From a relaxed and friendly gathering, the meeting deteriorated into a wholly repugnant session of "public self-criticism." First Mustafa and Aziz had to stand in front of everyone and say how deeply sorry they were for all they had done to us. This ordeal was made bearable only because, to them, it quite clearly meant nothing at all. Self-criticism was just another of those silly games their masters made them play. But then Red Shirt began. A worried and frightened man, his self-criticism was in deadly earnest. I felt sick to the stomach as he sat there debasing himself where two days before he had done his best to terrorize us. He apologized abjectly for threatening us with solitary confinement. Then he went on

to exonerate his country with a long spiel that featured the People's
Democratic Republic of Yemen at every breath. (If you're ever in doubt
as to whether a country is democratic or not, see if "Democratic" ap-
pears in the country's name. If it does, then it isn't.) While Red Shirt
was still abject, I seized the opportunity to remind him that other
yachts might also tack in the international waters off his coast. They,
too, would be innocent passersby and not spies.

Half an hour of his bootlicking and, for the first time since the whole
crazy hijacking began, my head was pounding like a tom-tom. But Red
Shirt had not finished—there was one more critical question to ask.
Drawing a deep breath, he turned his anxious eyes to mine. "And
please, you won't tell your father, will you? Or make trouble at the
U.N.?" For one ghastly moment I thought I was going to giggle. To
avoid Edward's eye, I lowered my gaze modestly to my crossed feet and
gave grave utterance. "As a dutiful daughter I will have to tell my
father. But maybe, this once, he won't make trouble at the U.N." Re-
venge may not be ethical, but nonetheless I felt triumphant. I'd sworn
we'd make them sorry and we had.

And so the curtain rose on the final act. Our guards came forward to
present Edward with small sacks of tea and sugar; to Lola and me they
gave pink and blue ballpoint pens from China—presents which, when
measured against their value to the givers, were among the most precious we have received. By now the curious phenomenon known as the
Swedish hostage syndrome was in full swing. We were genuinely sorry
to leave our kidnappers: not Red Shirt perhaps, but the others. The
captain already had his *Boating* magazine. To Español we gave a large
bottle of scotch, guessing that his bonhomie would soon overcome any
religious scruples. For Aziz, our special jailer, I made up a special
parcel: a pack of playing cards for himself, an Irish linen tray cloth for
his wife, and a toy village, a set of jacks, and a packet of jelly babies for
his small son. My last gesture was to put the lot in a Harrods carrier
bag. Does that plastic bag still hang in some mud-walled house in
Southern Yemen? It was given in the spirit of a promise. A promise to
Aziz that one day his people, too, would be free to prosper.

Outside, the moon was already on the wane. For the last time we
piled into the truck and drove down to the water's edge. Not to the
dock, for there we would see the Soviet ship, but to a distant beach. As
we stood waiting for the sambuk to ferry us out to *Johanne,* Aziz turned
and, in a flood of words, pleaded with Edward to take him with us.
"Ask the Chief! Please ask the Chief if I can come!" Dear Aziz, he lived
in a world filled with confused half-truths and fantasies. Did he not
realize that such a request would have marked him forever as a poten-

tial traitor, might even have sent him to jail? Gently Edward turned him down but promised instead to send him a postcard from Seychelles. Even there the paranoia of communism came between us. Aziz's eyes darkened with fear. "No, no, you must not do that! They will say I am a spy. There is a law in this country. We must never receive letters from abroad." Never despise the ordinary people of Communist countries but despise the men and women who use the name of communism to hold captive their own people.

Escorted by the sambuk to the open waters of the Gulf, we waved and waved until the darkness swallowed up their boat. We'd known Aziz and Español for just three days.

21. Final Haul to the Garden of Eden

~~~~~~~~

OUT IN THE GULF Edward's worst fears were realized: the past three days of calms had turned to easterlies. Four hundred and seventy frustrating miles of headwinds stretched between us and the Indian Ocean. We did everything to entice the old girl to windward. Planning to work the land and sea breezes, we tacked her this way and that near the South Yemen coast, but the breezes never came. Perim Island remained firmly in view. We made a single, long tack right across the Gulf toward Somalia and a second long tack back to Yemen. Perim Island was still in sight. In twenty-five hours we had gained two miles. Edward groaned. "Let's sell *Johanne* and buy a Swan 65!"—which only goes to show to what depths of depression he had sunk. Adding to his misery, the rash he had sprouted in jail had turned to septic sores and required several days of soap and sunshine before they cleared up. Then *Johanne* sprang a leak.

Under power, Edward made for the lee of Ras Imran, a headland on the Yemen coast ten miles west of Aden. As we edged in toward the shallows, Lola noticed a hamlet, its sandy-colored houses camouflaged by Yemen's sandy soil. We dared not anchor. Instead we hove-to and, while Jean Louis, Lola, and I kept an anxious watch for marauding gunboats, Edward dived over the side to look for the leak. It wasn't easy. The easterly swell, working around the headland, sent *Johanne* into a rolling hornpipe. With difficulty Edward traced the leak to a seam aft, under the turn of the bilge. He would have to hold his breath (we still had no scuba gear of our own), dive down, turn himself upside down, and then try to caulk upward, during which time *Johanne* rolled from side to side and progressed slowly forward as well. At least the water was warm. At 80°F Edward reported that it was like working in a large bath.

Leak fixed, Edward clambered back on board. A few twists on the rigging screws set up *Johanne*'s rigging. Maybe with her shrouds and forestays tauter, she'd point a wee bit better to windward. Nothing, however, could counteract our worst headache: a foul current kept killing any progress we might otherwise have made.

Ashore, craggy sand-blown hills conjured visions of desperate bandits and curly-horned mountain goats. I was not surprised to read in that doom-laden tome, the Admiralty pilot, that this coast was "inhabited by tribes of aggressive habits." Shortly afterward events were to prove the book right. As we took a tack toward the coast, Jean Louis pointed to a sailing dhow running close inshore. Like a white-winged bird she was, flying west, riven by a huge lateen foresail. According to an old Arab saying, "No one but madmen or Christians sail to windward." Comparing our speeds, I conceded them the point. We, the Christian infidels, were close-hauled, bashing against a Force 5 wind, and making no progress at all. Even as we stood admiring the dhow's grace and speed, her crew spied us. In seconds those "tribes of aggressive habits" had their great sail down. In seconds more they had altered course and were powering out to intercept us. Discretion being the greater part of valor, we tacked and, letting *Johanne* run free, headed her back toward Somalia as fast as she would go. The dhow followed. We loaded the guns. For once the choppy waters of the Gulf played in our favor. Astern of us the dhow's much lighter hull pitched and bucked and wallowed abominably. I know because I never took my eyes off her. I was convinced they were getting closer; Edward was equally convinced that they were not and flatly refused to start the engine. Before we reached the Seychelles we would need every drop of fuel we had—and anyway, it was so much more fun to beat the scoundrels using sail alone. For their part, the dhow's crew did not abandon the chase until well after dark. Then, abruptly, they turned around and headed back to shore.

Slowly, slowly *Johanne* edged forward. Cap Elephante on the Somali coast was identified and passed, though we saw none of the trade in sponges, pearls, and incense promised by the pilot book. Finally, three weeks exactly after leaving Perim, Ras Asir, the most easterly point of Africa, was bearing west—and a big disappointment it was, too. But then we saw Ras Scenaghef, ten miles to the south. Climbing 3,041 feet straight into the air, Scenaghef was a headland of which any continent might be proud. And bobbing in the water at its feet, as if to pay homage, was an extraordinary variety of wildlife. Here, where the Indian Ocean hurls itself against the continental mass of Africa, great whirlpools, ringed by foot-high banks of foam, lapped at *Johanne*'s hull. Tide rips and calms succeeded one another, churning the water and dredging up rich secrets from the deep. Hundreds of white-faced storm petrels and wedge-tailed shearwaters sat and gossiped on the water, every now and then dripping their beaks to fish for some tasty morsel that had caught their ever-watchful eye. Mother Carey's chicks scampered over the sea's surface like frantic farmyard hens attempting to take flight. At our approach a whole flock of red-footed boobies took to the air while around *Johanne* some fifty small, red-shelled crabs busied themselves, nibbling clean her weedy waterline. Hoping to catch a fish, I threaded a slither of salami onto a hook and dangled it in the water. Immediately fluorescent-blue "blobs," half an inch in diameter, sidled up to investigate the lure. Whether they were minute fish or colorful plankton I could not decide.

Then the dorados arrived, a whole school of them, their multicolored scales glittering like sequins in the sun. Scattering ground bait on the water, Edward enticed them to him and then he struck. In a flash he had the first dorado hauled aboard. A shimmer of greens and golds, silver, purple, and blue, I wanted to take its photo.

"Oh no!" cried our vegetarian Lola, "let's catch ten, then take a picture." And so we caught ten. To begin with Jean Louis stood well back, protesting that he had never killed anything in his life. But what with Edward pulling in fish one a minute, and Lola and me standing guard with deck brooms to stop the catch from slipping back through the scupperboards into the sea, Jean Louis had, perforce, to play the executioner. By the time the tenth was landed he was swinging our wooden cosh at those fish with enough verve to relieve the pent-up frustrations of a whole lifetime of brotherly love.

Dorado dry superbly. Gutting and filleting them so as to remove the backbone but leave the two fillets still attached to the tail, we rubbed their flesh with salt and put them in the sun to dry. Two days later, Edward tied a broom handle in the rigging and slung the fish over it, tails up. Stored like that, we could cut off a fillet whenever one was wanted for soaking and cooking. In theory anyway. In practice few fillets reached the pot. Lola, usually so abstemious, developed a passion for dry, salted dorado. Each time she passed the line of upturned tails she peeled off a scrap more flesh, then chewed on it, salt and all.

As with farming, so with sailing: every year's weather is abnormal. According to the pilot charts for October, our part of the Indian Ocean should have had winds mostly from the north or northwest, rarely, if ever, from the south or southwest. As the Seychelles Islands lie approximately 1,000 miles due south of Ras Asir, the rest of the trip should have been downhill all the way. Why, we had only to average 100 miles a day and we'd be there in ten days flat. Alas, we chose the wrong

October. For twenty-one solid days the wind blew from the south or southwest—from the Seychelles—and it drove *Johanne* straight into the arms of a sixty-mile-a-day, easterly current. Even with some shrewd use of the motor, we had quickly passed the longitude of the Seychelles and were being dragged and blown toward the Maldives and India.

October 28th should, by rights, have been a wretched day. It was our seventieth day out from Zea Marina and thirty-first from Perim. We had only 140 miles of fuel left, 532 miles to go to reach the Seychelles, and we were being forced farther from them by the hour. Yet morale aboard *Johanne* was excellent, due in no small part to Jean Louis and Lola. Although Jean Louis's hypersensitivity sometimes drove us scatty—the mildest, most tactfully worded suggestion threw him into an agony of self-justification—and though their disinclination ever to volunteer help sometimes irritated, I can think of no crew who would have accepted *Johanne*'s abysmal progress better. Besides that, the weather was glorious. Calm seas and clear horizons made ideal conditions for navigation classes. Jean Louis, highly intelligent, proved to be one of Edward's most apt pupils and Lola wasn't far behind, despite her handicap. Taking a sight with a sextant is like taking a photograph with a camera; you have to shut one eye and look through a "viewfinder" with the other. Lola was incapable of shutting one eye. In the end she covered it with a scarf. Soon Edward had all three of us making graphs, calculating dead reckonings, and plotting position lines that worked out nearer and nearer to his own. One noon Jean Louis came aft, his soft brown eyes laughing. "Well?" he asked Edward. "How many miles do you calculate we lost this time?" You couldn't ask for a more relaxed attitude than that.

For the umpteenth time I thanked Providence for removing Tony and Paul. For one thing we'd probably have run out of food and, for another, none of *Johanne*'s present crew was bored. Lola kept busy stitching clothes for herself and Jean Louis. She also sifted through the remaining flour, clearing it of weevils. Jean Louis hardened up the deck caulking over their bunks and painstakingly copied an intricate star map from a Spanish encyclopedia. After that we all went star crazy. With a Rude star chart to guide us, we soon had most of the major constellations, such as Gemini, Taurus, and Orion, under our belts. There followed the individual stars: Belatrix, Betelgeuse, and Rigel in Orion; Pollux in Gemini; Sirius in Canis Major; and Deneb in Cygnus; to name but a few. Yet for me, none could compare with Scorpio, that fantastic cluster of stars, including Antares, that spill, all fluent curves, across the sky.

When neither staring at stars nor steering *Johanne,* I was struggling

with the practical difficulties of writing afloat. Not many would-be au-
thors can have written their first book sitting, hot and naked, in a ship's
bunk, a rusty typewriter balanced on their knees, its keys jamming each
time the ship rolled.

Edward, too, was writing: composing his official report on how the
navy of the People's Democratic Republic of Yemen had, in international waters, hijacked the British yacht *Johanne Regina* and her crew.
He took considerable pains over that document, determined that the
Yemen government should be forced to realize that piracy was no longer acceptable and hoping, at the same time, to protect other yachtsmen
from similar unpleasant experiences. He could have spared the ink.
Some days after delivering the document to the British High Commission in Seychelles we were asked to return for an interview.

"You must understand, Britain is extremely lucky to have a High
Commission in Aden. We do not want to do anything that would jeop-
ardize our relationship or upset the Yemen government." (My word,
Chamberlain would have been proud of that man.) "After all," he continued, "they didn't steal anything from you, did they?" No, they didn't
steal anything—apart from our freedom and our peace of mind, though
now it was rarely, and only when I was asleep, that I experienced again
the suffocating fear that had gripped us by that small hill on Perim. The
official was quite right. They did not steal anything.

The water barely rippled as *Johanne* slipped silently through the
night-blackened sea. Alone on watch, I first sensed rather than saw the
dolphins—ghostly sighs rising from around *Johanne*'s stern. Lashing
the helm, I went to peer over the side, and found the sea ablaze with
phosphorescence—dolphin phosphorescence more brilliant than any
fireworks display. In a pack they charged *Johanne*'s stern, flashing
great streamers of white light, knifing through the water in dazzling
formation, waiting, like daredevil stunt pilots, till the last possible moment before peeling away in two equal groups. Their physical bodies
were almost invisible in the darkness yet each stirred up such a glitter of
otherwordly light that I saw each individual swathed in stardust. Again
and again they surged toward *Johanne*. Again and again they dived to
trail their sparkling ribbons through the sea. Then they left. My private
dance of lights was over.

The next morning, finding an effort to dry some tuna had failed, I
dropped the hunk of rotten flesh overboard. In an instant a fin appeared. Large jaws opened and the hunk of flesh vanished. We were
being followed, which was a bore as *Johanne*'s hull was in dire need of a
cleaning and the conditions, flat calm, were otherwise ideal. Carefully

loading the Colt with black powder and a lead ball, Edward took aim at the shark's head and fired. The shark vanished.

An hour later, armed only with a scraper, Edward slipped into the water to rake off *Johanne*'s garden of goose barnacles. On deck we divided up into shark watches. When Edward, and then I, had had enough, Jean Louis took over in the water and Lola stood watch. Suddenly she gave an almighty shriek: *"Requin!* Shark!" Jean Louis was on the wrong side of *Johanne,* where there was no boarding tire. I sped over with one and he was up it and on board before I even had time to make it fast.

October 31st, Edward's sixty-third birthday, called for a special celebration supper. Sweet-and-sour pork laid on a bed of rice was accompanied by finely sliced vegetables stir-fried in soy sauce and mixed with pineapple and brown sugar. A chocolate mousse decorated with nuts and cream followed. Not bad, seventy-five days out of Zea Marina.

Day after day that fiendish wind blew from the Seychelles. Day after day the current pushed us east, past the Seychelles and toward the Chagos Archipelago. Edward had given up any attempt at a direct approach and was concentrating all his efforts on getting south in order to meet up with the southeast trades.

Before leaving Zea Marina we had filled up with 450 gallons of fresh water. Twelve weeks later what remained echoed hollowly against the sides of *Johanne*'s metal tanks. Then, in the nick of time, there came a downpour. Dark rain squalls marched hand in hand across the sky and drinking water crashed down in torrents. I'd never seen such rain. Amid the warm, pungent smell of hot, wet decks, *Johanne*'s crew darted hither and thither like maddened bees, protecting bunks and books with oilcloth, slinging awnings low over the foredeck to catch the rain, and fishing out buckets and baths and saucepans to retain the precious stuff. As soon as the water tasted salt-free, we positioned Katy's old baby bath below the largest gouts running off the main, then bailed the bath out by the bucketful and carted the water below to the tanks. We couldn't keep up. The bath overflowed. We put a hose into the bath and siphoned water below and still the bath overflowed. In that one deluge we caught 150 gallons of fresh drinking water and had enough left over to scrub ourselves and our hair squeaky clean and launder a great mountain of dirty sheets and towels as well.

Those rain squalls brought with them one further benefit: for the first time in thirteen days we gained toward Mahé—eight miles. At that rate it would take us only another ninety days and we'd be there. One of the sillier obsessions of long-distance sailors is that of taking a single day's run and interpolating from that one, totally unrepresentative day how long the remaining voyage will take. If, instead of eight miles, we had done a fairly average hundred, we would have been saying we'd be there in a week. But right then even an eight-mile gain gave us reason to rejoice. It meant we had found the equatorial current. Soon it was dragging us south at forty miles per day while, above us, the southeast trades gradually gathered strength.

Ahead a line squall was lifting toward *Johanne*. Alone on deck, I lashed the helm and nipped forward to tighten in the headsails, then the main and mizzen. As I pulled in on *Johanne*'s sheets I hummed a little hum under my breath. I was feeling wonderfully, marvelously happy. Quite apart from being on the move at long last, I had also discovered, rather belatedly, that adjusting sails was not simply a matter of pulling and easing sheets, that it involved both skill and challenge, that there was a deep satisfaction to be found in balancing a boat's sails so exactly that one coaxed every last erg of energy out of her. As the squall hit, I swung the helm to catch the coming blast. *Johanne* tore through the water, close-hauled, her sails taut as drumheads. Then the squall passed and the wind freed us. I went forward again and eased the sheets a fraction. That night, to the accompaniment of more squalls and thunder and torrential rain, I saw my first Saint Elmo's fire, a weird, ghostly light atop our radio antennae.

The trades, once established, sent *Johanne* galloping over the ocean toward the Seychelles, albeit from the wrong direction. On November 16th *Johanne* was at long last a couple of miles closer to Seychelles than she had been on October 24th, twenty-three days before. She had been driven in an enormous arc. Anyone seeing us arrive would assume we had sailed in from Australia, not Europe.

At 11:15 A.M. on November 21st Edward shouted out: "LAND HO!"

Directly ahead of us, cut in half by *Johanne*'s forestay, was the tip of Mahé Island. Fifty-seven days had passed since we last stood on terra firma. The trip, which we had hoped would take fifty days from Zea Marina, had taken ninety-three. Yet, as the island of Mahé rose slowly out of the sea, her Morne Seychellois stretching 2,969 feet into the air, I felt an odd reluctance to approach the shore, to reconnect with the hassles of the outside world.

The ocean's rhythm had worked into my soul. Night and daytime watches, dressing before dawn to steer through the sun's rising, the peace of sitting alone at night, a speck under a firmament of stars, it had all become an integral part of our reality. But there was elation, too, at seeing those green-clad island mountains once again; elation that, in a few more days, I would have Katy back and that, together, we would sail over to La Digue, an island one mile by three by a thousand feet high. There we would walk the white sands of our very own beach, visit the whispering palms of our diminutive plantation, and, best of all, see again the palm-thatched hut, the Ants' Nest, that I loved and, along with *Johanne,* called our home. Praslin, La Digue's larger, next-door neighbor, might have been hailed by General Gordon as the original Garden of Eden, but to us La Digue was better still. Edward, after sailing the world over, had chosen La Digue to be his home. Maybe, at last, we would settle down.

Going below to dig out passports, ship's papers, and all the other paraphernalia demanded by bureaucracy, I switched on my radio. A new sound, Radio Seychelles, blared forth. The new president, Albert René, had a proclamation and a pledge to make. First he wished to welcome the great Soviet fleet to his country. Second he promised that, within five months, he would have transformed the Seychelles into a socialist state.

Maybe our gypsy life wasn't over after all.

Glossary of Nautical Terms

(as they apply to *Johanne Regina*)

ABEAM   At right angles to the length of the boat.

AFT   Toward the back or stern of the boat.

ALOFT   Up in the rigging.

AMIDSHIPS   In the middle of the ship.

ANTI-FOULING   Highly poisonous paint used to prevent weed, barnacles, and shipworms from taking up residence on a boat's bottom and making it "foul."

ASTERN   To go backward, as in "going astern." Also, behind the boat: "Astern lay a fantastic blaze of phosphorescence."

ATHWARTSHIPS   From side to side across the ship.

AUTOMATIC PILOT   An electrical device for keeping a boat on course.

BACK   (1) A verb used to describe the wind changing direction counterclockwise (in the Northern Hemisphere); e.g., when the wind goes from north to west, it has backed. (2) To push a sail against the wind so as to slow or stop the boat or help her tack.

BALLAST   Additional weight, usually of iron or lead, placed either in the keel (ballast keel) or low down inside a single-hulled boat to improve its stability and stop it from falling over at sea.

BARE POLES   Masts without sails on them.

BATTEN DOWN   To close hatches tight, sometimes with battens so that heavy seas cannot drive in.

BEAM   (1) The greatest width of a boat. (2) The athwartships members on which the deck is laid. The ends of these beams are referred to in wind directions: "forward of the beam" means the wind is blowing from a direction in the right angle between amidships and the bow. A sea which hits a boat on the side hits her beam-on. Finally, when a boat is heeled far over on her side, she is said to be "on her beam ends."

BEAM SHELF   A heavy, fore-and-aft piece of wood to which the ends of the beams are fastened.

BEAR AWAY   To alter course farther from the wind or another object.

BEAT   To gain against the wind by sailing zigzag toward it; to tack.

BEAUFORT SCALE   International scale assessing wind strength from Force 0 (flat calm) to Force 12 (hurricane).

BELAYING PIN   A short, upright rod of wood fitted through a board or rail for making halyards and sheets fast. Also useful as a small club for repelling boarders.

BELOW   Inside the boat. "One moment, I'll call him, he's down below."

BEND   (1) To fit a sail in place on a boat. So it is congratulations, not sympathy, that are wanted when the mate says "I've bent the mainsail." (2) A knot that joins two ropes together.

BILGE   The round bit of hull, low down under the floorboards, where bilge water, leaked gas, and dead rats collect.

BLOCK   A pulley.

BOLLARD   A circular, upright metal fitting for making lines fast. Large versions are often found on jetties and docks.

BOOM   A spar along the foot of the sail.

BOTTOM   (1) The hull below the waterline. (2) The seabed: "a sandy bottom."

BOW   The front end of a vessel.

BOWLINE   A slightly complicated knot that forms a loop and is often used for tying up dinghies or yachts.

BOWSPRIT   The spar that sticks out in front of *Johanne*'s stem.

BROACHED   Refers to a boat being swirled around so that she lies sideways on to the waves.

BULKHEAD   The nautical term for an interior wall in a boat.

BULLDOG CLIP   A small, Ü-shaped rod of metal that has been threaded at both ends. A second piece of metal, placed over both the ends and then tightened down with two nuts, allows the bulldog clip to squeeze two pieces of wire tightly together.

BULWARK CAPPING   A narrow, horizontal plank nailed to the top of the vertical bulwarks. On *Johanne* it makes an excellent seat all around the boat.

BULWARKS   Extension of topsides above the deck.

BUNK   A bed on a boat.

BUNK BOARD   A single plank of wood, attached to the side of a bunk, to stop its occupant from rolling out at sea.

CAREEN   To lay a floating boat down on her side in the water so as to get at her bottom.

CAULKING   Cotton or oakum used for filling the seams between *Johanne*'s planks.

CEILING   The inside planking that lines some hulls.

CHAIN PLATES   Strong metal strips, bolted to the hull, to which rigging screws and shrouds are attached.

CLEAT   A metal, wooden, or plastic fitting to which one makes lines fast.

CLEW   The aft, lower corner of a sail.

CLINKER BUILT   A way of building a wooden boat where one plank overlaps the one below. The more common form of construction, that found on *Johanne,* is "carvel" where each plank is directly above the next giving the hull a smooth finish.

CLOSE-HAULED   Having the boat sail as close into the direction of the wind as is possible.

COVERING BOARD   The outer plank on the deck. Often wider and thicker than other deck planks, it covers the top edge of the frames and hull planking.

CRADLE   A special wooden or metal frame used to keep a boat upright when it is pulled ashore.

DAVITS   Pieces of wood projecting over the water for lifting things. Stern davits lift dinghies; anchor davits lift anchors.

DEAD RECKONING   An informed estimate of one's position at sea.

DEAD WOOD   Solid chunks of wood found inside the bow and stern of *Johanne* to give her added strength.

DECKHEAD   Underside of the deck which, when viewed from below, forms what in a house would be called the ceiling.

DINGHY   A small boat carried on a yacht and used for ferrying people and supplies between the yacht and the shore.

DOWNHAUL   A rope for hauling or pulling down a sail or spar.

DRAFT   The depth of hull below the waterline.

DRAGGING   To be avoided. The slipping of an anchor along the top of the seabed when, by rights, it should have dug well in.

EBB TIDE   Falling tide, ebbing away from the land.

ECHO SOUNDER   An electrical gadget for measuring the depth of water under the boat.

FAIR LEAD   A fitting that allows lines to slide easily without chafe.

FASHION BOARDS   Short lengths of wood slotted one above the other to close off a companionway below. Depending on the weather, one or more boards can be removed to let in light and air.

FENDERS   Normally balloon- or sausage-shaped objects made of strong flexible material, often rubber, used to protect the ship's side when against docks or other boats. On *Johanne* we use old car and tractor tires.

FEND OFF   (1) To stop boats from touching when alongside each other or the dock. (2) The cry of a desperate skipper to his hapless crew when the yacht is about to collide with an immovable object, such as a granite quay.

FID   In this case, a solid, metal rod.

FLOOD TIDE   Rising tide, flooding in toward the land.

FLUKE   The flat, pointed bit on a traditional, fisherman's anchor that digs into the seabed.

FOOT   The bottom edge of a sail.

FORECABIN   The cabin found just behind the fo'c'sle.

FORECASTLE, or FO'C'SLE   Forwardmost accommodation.

FOREDECK   Deck at forward end of boat.

FOREGUY   A length of line attached to the end of the boom and then made fast forward to stop the sail accidentally jibing.

FORESTAY   A permanent piece of wire rigging that goes from near the top of the mast to the stem of the boat.

FORWARD   Toward the front end of the boat.

FRAMES   Ribs that rise up from the keel to give the boat its shape or framework.

FREEBOARD   The distance from the water to the deck of a vessel.

GAFF   The spar along the upper edge of a quadrilateral gaff-sail.

GAFF-SAIL   A quadrilateral rather than triangular fore-and-aft sail often found on traditional work boats.

GAITER   A piece of canvas sewn around the screw part of a rigging screw to protect it from salty air and water.

GALLEY   A ship's kitchen.

GALLOWS   A raised rest to keep the boom horizontal when the sail is lowered.

GASKETS   Long lengths of canvas or line used to tie up sails when they are lowered.

HALYARD   Line or wire for hoisting and lowering sails.

HATCH   The hole which leads down to the inside of a boat.

HATCH COVERS   Heavy, flat, wooden covers used to close *Johanne*'s hatches.

HAWSE PIPE   A large metal pipe that passes through the bulwarks or hull of a ship to lead warps or anchor chain outboard without causing chafe.

HEAD   Marine lavatory.

HEAD OF SAIL   The top corner of a triangular sail and the top edge of a gaff-sail.

HEADSAILS   All sails forward of the foremast.

HEAVE TO   To slow a vessel down by making one sail work against another. (*See* BACK.)

HEEL   A verb used to describe what happens when a boat leans over to one side, usually due to the pressure of wind on sails.

HELM   The wheel.

HITCHES   Knots used to make a line fast to something else.

HOLD   The main inside of a ship where the cargo is stowed.

HOUNDS   Pieces of wood high up on the mast which hold the rigging wire in place.

HULL   The main body of the boat.

HURRICANE LAMP   An oil lamp with a glass shield designed to stay alight in a hurricane.

INBOARD   Toward the center of the boat.

JIB   The triangular headsail which is set farthest forward on a vessel.

JIBE   To change the side of the sail on which the wind presses while the ship is running downwind. This is done by first pulling the mainsail in to near amidships and then maneuvering the stern of the boat toward the direction of the wind until the wind strikes on the opposite side of the sail which can then be let out on the new jibe. An accidental jibe can be dangerous as the boom crashes right across the boat from far out on one side to far out on the other, but a controlled jibe is a normal maneuver to be undertaken with care.

JURY-RIG   Improvised rig normally used only after damage.

KEEL   The lowest part or backbone of the hull running fore-and-aft.

KEEL SHOE   A protective length of wood nailed to the bottom of *Johanne*'s keel.

KEELSON   A strengthening member, the keelson is a heavy piece of wood that runs along the bottom of the inside of *Johanne*'s hull.

KETCH   A two-masted vessel with the taller mainmast forward and the shorter mizzenmast aft. *Johanne* is a ketch.

KNOT   A measurement of speed equal to one nautical mile per hour. It is not a distance; therefore one does not say "five knots per hour," but "We were doing five knots."

LEE SHORE   The coast onto which the wind is blowing. Good captains try to avoid close contact with lee shores.

LEEWARD (LOO'RD)   Downwind; one tries not to be to leeward of dragging yachts, bad fish, and town drains.

LOG   An instrument for measuring the distance a boat covers through the water.

LOGBOOK, or THE LOG   An hour-by-hour account of weather conditions, boat's position, speed, etc., while at sea.

MAINMAST   The tallest mast on a yacht.

MAINSAIL   The principal sail.

MAKE FAST   To secure a line to something solid such as a cleat, bollard, or belaying pin.

MARLIN SPIKE   A solid, steel rod, tapering to a point, this tool is used for many jobs on a boat such as prizing open knots or separating strands of rigging wire.

MASTHEAD   The top of the mast (as opposed to the FOOT). A masthead light is traditionally white and attached to the top of the mast.

MAST STEP   A slot in the keelson into which the foot of *Johanne*'s mast is stepped.

MIZZENMAST   The shorter, aft mast of a ketch.

MONOHULL   A vessel with only one hull—i.e., the vast majority of boats.

NAVIGATION LIGHTS   Lights used on a vessel that is under way at night: red to port; green to starboard; white at masthead and stern.

OAKUM   Matted fibers, usually of lightly tarred hemp, which are rolled into hanks and then hammered between plank seams to keep them water-tight. Oakum is mainly used on traditional craft.

O.B.   Nautical slang, short for "overboard."

OGGIN   Nautical slang for the sea, as in "He fell in the oggin."

OUTBOARD   (1) Toward the outer edge of a boat or even outside the hull. (2) A small engine, usually attached to a dinghy and taking the place of oars.

PAINTER   The line on a dinghy for making it fast (tying it up).

PAYING   Tar, putty, rubber compound, or marine glue used to cover the caulking and protect it from the elements.

PAY OFF   To turn the ship's bow away from the wind.

PEAK   The highest point of a gaff-sail (the peak halyard hoists the outer, or peak, end of the gaff).

POLEMAST   A tall mast consisting of a single spar rather than a mast plus topmast.

POOP   The raised piece of deck, about fifteen feet long, found at the aft end of *Johanne.*

POOPED   A most unpleasant experience when a wave comes right over the stern and, more often than not, right down the helmsman's neck.

PORT SIDE   The left side of a vessel looking forward.

PORT TACK   To sail with the wind coming over the port side, forward of the beam—i.e., the sails are on the starboard side.

PREVENTER   A piece of line looped through an eye at the end of the boom and then made fast to a ring bolt on the deck; it prevents the boom and sail jerking about too much.

QUARTER   Between astern and abeam (a quarter of the way from the stern to the bow). A ship appearing on the port quarter would be about forty-five degrees abaft the port beam.

RATLINES   Pieces of line or wood fixed across the shrouds like a ladder to enable people to climb aloft.

REEVE   A verb meaning to thread and often used about running rigging. "He rove the mainsheet through the block."

RIG   The individual system of masts, booms, and standing rigging used on a yacht. *Johanne* is a gaff-rigged ketch.

RIGGING   (1) Immovable wires holding the masts in place, known as standing rigging. (2) Lines or wires which move as they hoist or control sails— i.e., sheets and halyards—called running rigging.

RIGGING SCREWS   Metal fittings with screws at both ends usually used to join shrouds to chain plates so that tension can be adjusted. Sometimes called "bottle screws" or "turnbuckles" in the States.

ROLLER REEFING   A mechanical device for reducing *Johanne*'s mainsail by wrapping the sail around itself on the main boom.

RUNNING   Sailing with the wind well aft of the beam. *Running by the lee* is a tricky feat of running with the wind so far aft that it is actually slightly on the wrong side of the stern and could cause an accidental jibe. Used only in emergencies.

SAILMAKER'S PALM   A sailmaker's "thimble," this is a leather tool that fits over the thumb across the palm and buckles at the back of the hand. It holds an indented metal disk over the ball of the thumb which is then used to force large sail needles through thick cloth.

SCHOONER   Fore-and-aft rigged vessel usually having two masts with the mainmast aft.

SEXTANT   An instrument for measuring the angle between stars or planets and the horizon. Used by sailors in conjunction with navigation tables and a chronometer to find out where they are. Most often used for shooting the sun.

SHEER   The graceful, up-and-down curve of a vessel that runs from bow to stern; sadly missing in many modern yachts.

SHEET   The line attached to the lower, aft corner of a sail or boom to control it—e.g., mainsheet, jib sheet.

SHEEVE   The roller inside a block, or pulley, that allows lines to turn freely.

SHIP   (1) To take on board, as in "We shipped a heavy sea." (2) To put oars back inside a rowboat after rowing, as in "She shipped the oars as she came alongside the yacht."

SHROUDS   Fixed wires which go from high up on the mast down to the rigging screws on either side of the boat and so hold the mast firmly in position.

SIGHT   Measuring the angle between horizon and a heavenly body using a SEXTANT. Known as "taking a sight."

SLIPWAY   A special hard slope of land running down to the water and used for slipping boats in and out of the water.

SLOOP   A one-masted vessel which has only one sail forward of the mast.

SOLE   The deck or floor in the interior of a yacht—e.g., the cabin sole.

SPAR   A long piece of rounded wood used for masts, booms, gaffs, etc.

SPRING TIDE   Large range of tide coming twice each month two days after full and new moon.

STANCHIONS   Upright wooden posts on the outer deck edge used to support the bulwarks and stop people from falling O.B.

STARBOARD   The right-hand side of a vessel when one looks forward.

STARBOARD TACK   Sailing with the wind coming over the starboard side, forward of the beam. (If it is aft of the beam, then you are on the starboard jibe.) The sails will be to port.

STAY   A permanent wire which supports the mast in a fore-and-aft direction.

STAYSAIL   A triangular sail set immediately forward of the mast and usually clipped to a stay.

STEM   The farthest forward part of the hull forming the bow.

STERN   The aft end of a vessel.

STERN POST   The farthest aft part of the hull through which the propeller shaft passes.

TACK   To bring the wind on the other side of sails by passing the vessel's bow through the eye of the wind.

TAIL   To hold on tightly to a sheet or halyard and take up the slack as others haul in on it.

THIMBLE   A tear-shaped metal or plastic fitting which allows a line to pass through it without chafe.

THROAT   The place where the gaff joins the mast. Throat halyards hoist the mast end of the gaff.

TOPSIDES   The outside of the hull between the WATERLINE and the deck.

TRANSOM   The flat piece of planking across *Johanne*'s stern.

TRIMARAN   A yacht with three hulls.

VEER   A verb describing when the wind changes direction clockwise (in the Northern Hemisphere)—e.g., east to south.

WARP   To maneuver a vessel using only mooring lines.

WARPS   Heavy lines for towing or mooring.

WATERLINE   (1) The invisible line around a boat's hull where water ends and air begins. (2) The place where the topside paint meets anti-fouling. Alas, the two are seldom the same.

WINCH   A mechanical device, giving mechanical advantage, for hauling in sheets and halyards by turning a handle.

WINDLASS   A winch for pulling up the anchor.

WINDWARD   Toward the wind.

YAWL BOAT   A small boat or dinghy that is kept slung on davits over the stern of a boat.